International Political Economy Series

General Editor: Timothy M. Shaw, Professor and Director, Institute of International Relations, The University of the West Indies, Trinidad & Tobago

Titles include:

Lucian M. Ashworth and David Long (*editors*)
NEW PERSPECTIVES ON INTERNATIONAL FUNCTIONALISM

Jeff Atkinson and Martin Scurrah
GLOBALIZING SOCIAL JUSTICE
The Role of Non-Governmental Organizations in Bringing about Social Change

André Broome
THE CURRENCY OF POWER
The IMF and Monetary Reform in Central Asia

Robert W. Cox (*editor*)
THE NEW REALISM
Perspectives on Multilateralism and World Order

Frederick Deyo (*editor*)
GLOBAL CAPITAL, LOCAL LABOUR

Stephen Gill (*editor*)
GLOBALIZATION, DEMOCRATIZATION AND MULTILATERALISM

Björn Hettne, András Inotai and Osvaldo Sunkel (*editors*)
GLOBALISM AND THE NEW REGIONALISM

Christopher C. Meyerson
DOMESTIC POLITICS AND INTERNATIONAL RELATIONS IN US–JAPAN TRADE POLICYMAKING
The GATT Uruguay Round Agriculture Negotiations

Isidro Morales
POST-NAFTA NORTH AMERICA

Volker Rittberger and Martin Nettesheim (*editor*)
AUTHORITY IN THE GLOBAL POLITICAL ECONOMY

Justin Robertson (*editor*)
POWER AND POLITICS AFTER FINANCIAL CRISES
Rethinking Foreign Opportunism in Emerging Markets

Michael G. Schechter (*editor*)
FUTURE MULTILATERALISM
The Political and Social Framework

INNOVATION IN MULTILATERALISM

Ben Thirkell-White
THE IMF AND THE POLITICS OF FINANCIAL GLOBALIZATION
From the Asian Crisis to a New International Financial Architecture?

Thomas G. Weiss (*editor*)
BEYOND UN SUBCONTRACTING
Task Sharing with Regional Security Arrangements and Service-Providing NGOs

Robert Wolfe
FARM WARS

International Political Economy Series
Series Standing Order ISBN 978–0–333–71708–0 hardcover
Series Standing Order ISBN 978–0–333–71110–1 paperback
(*outside North America only*)

You can receive future titles in this series as they are published by placing a standing order. Please contact your bookseller or, in case of difficulty, write to us at the address below with your name and address, the title of the series and one of the ISBNs quoted above.

Customer Services Department, Macmillan Distribution Ltd, Houndmills, Basingstoke, Hampshire RG21 6XS, England

The Currency of Power

The IMF and Monetary Reform in Central Asia

André Broome
Lecturer in International Political Economy
University of Birmingham

palgrave
macmillan

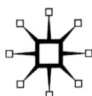

First published 2010 by
PALGRAVE MACMILLAN

Palgrave Macmillan in the UK is an imprint of Macmillan Publishers Limited, registered in England, company number 785998, of Houndmills, Basingstoke, Hampshire RG21 6XS.

Palgrave Macmillan in the US is a division of St Martin's Press LLC, 175 Fifth Avenue, New York, NY 10010.

Palgrave Macmillan is the global academic imprint of the above companies and has companies and representatives throughout the world.

Palgrave® and Macmillan® are registered trademarks in the United States, the United Kingdom, Europe and other countries

ISBN 978–0–230–24005–6 hardback

This book is printed on paper suitable for recycling and made from fully managed and sustained forest sources. Logging, pulping and manufacturing processes are expected to conform to the environmental regulations of the country of origin.

A catalogue record for this book is available from the British Library.

A catalogue record for this book is available from the Library of Congress.

10   9   8   7   6   5   4   3   2   1
19   18   17   16   15   14   13   12   11   10

Printed and bound in Great Britain by
CPI Antony Rowe, Chippenham and Eastbourne

For Alexandra

Contents

List of Tables

List of Illustrations

Map

Figures

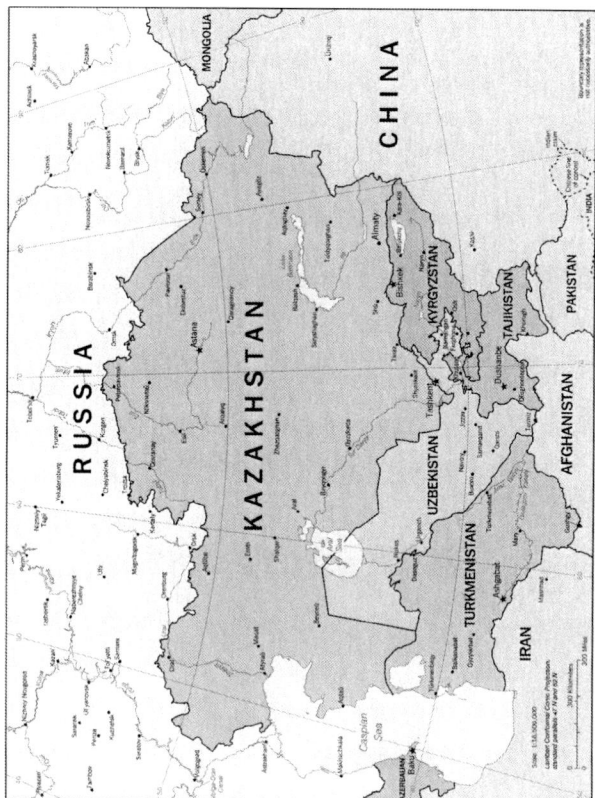

Map 1.1   The Former Soviet Republics of Central Asia
Source: University of Texas Libraries.

List of Abbreviations

BIS	Bank for International Settlements
CBR	Central Bank of Russia
CBU	Central Bank of Uzbekistan
EBRD	European Bank for Reconstruction and Development
FDI	Foreign Direct Investment
FSU	Former Soviet Union
GDP	Gross Domestic Product
HIPC	Heavily-Indebted Poor Country
IEO	Independent Evaluation Office
IFIs	International Financial Institutions
IMF	International Monetary Fund
IPE	International Political Economy
MER	Multiple Exchange Rates
NBK	National Bank of Kazakhstan
NBKR	National Bank of the Kyrgyz Republic
NBU	National Bank of Uzbekistan
ODA	Official Development Assistance
OECD	Organization for Economic Cooperation and Development
SBA	Stand-By Arrangement
STF	Systemic Transformation Facility
USSR	Union of Soviet Socialist Republics
WWII	World War Two

Preface

As with most books, this one was only possible because of the assistance and support of a wide range of people. My thanks go, first, to John Ravenhill and Leonard Seabrooke. As my doctoral supervisors at the Australian National University (ANU), I am immensely grateful for their consistent professional and personal encouragement, their patience, and their readiness to help me navigate the various intellectual twists and turns that I have traveled in the course of this project. My grateful thanks also go to those who have provided me with written feedback and long talks over aspects of the book throughout its development. I thank in particular Daniel Biro, Sarah Graham, Barry Hindess, Joel Quirk, Taylor Speed, Shogo Suzuki, Shannon Tow, Ryan Walter, and Annie Williams. My gratitude goes to all the staff and students from the Department of International Relations in the Research School of Pacific and Asian Studies, for providing a friendly and intellectually stimulating environment during my years at the ANU. A special note of thanks goes to the participants at the Warwick Manuscript Development workshop in May 2009, and especially to Ben Clift for helping push me to clarify the main contribution of the book. I am also grateful to my colleagues in the Department of Political Science and International Studies at the University of Birmingham, in particular David Bailey, Mark Beeson, Ted Newman, and Emily Pia for their friendship, advice, and encouragement.

The research for this book was made possible by financial support from the Department of International Relations at the ANU, the Department of Political Science and International Studies at the University of Birmingham, as well as the generosity of an old friend, Gary Baker, for which I am very grateful. The research for this book has included three visits to the International Monetary Fund headquarters in Washington DC in August 2005, March 2006, and April 2008. My grateful thanks go to all the current and former Fund staff in Washington who contributed their time for interviews, as well as to Christoph Rosenberg from the Fund's regional office in Warsaw for granting me an extensive interview during my visit to Poland in September 2005. My gratitude goes especially to Madonna Gaudette, Clare Huang, Premela Isaacs, and Jean Marcoyeux for their research assistance during my visits to the International Monetary Fund Archives. I am also grateful to the individuals from other international organizations, non-governmental organizations, and the private sector that gave their time for interviews and offered candid advice on the research during my visits to Kazakhstan, Uzbekistan, and the Kyrgyz Republic during September to December 2005.

In addition to those already mentioned, my grateful thanks go to both old and new friends who have helped to make social life enjoyable and who have been an important source of intellectual support while I was writing this book. In particular, this list includes Seth Bateman, Chris Beer, Mike Boyle, Julie Broome, Anna Carnerup, Nick Henry, Jamie Hull, Arthur Muhlen-Schulte, Shruti Navathe, Eleni Tsingou, and Antje Vetterlein. My deepest gratitude goes also to my sister Adele, my father David, and my mother Wendy, who have been a constant source of support. In particular, my special thanks go to my mother for her constant encouragement throughout and for her generosity with financial assistance to help cover fieldwork costs, especially when I found myself down and out in Uzbekistan in October 2005.

This book is dedicated to Alexandra Homolar-Riechmann, whose laughter, love, and fierce intellect were indispensable to its completion. *Ich liebe dich mit meinem ganzem Herzen.*

André Broome
Birmingham, United Kingdom.

Introduction

States will aggressively defend their right to make national economic policy choices as a fundamental sovereign prerogative. This is especially so with respect to monetary change, the effects of which impinge upon the material interests of a country's political and business elites as well as the everyday lives – and the social and economic fortunes – of the broader population. This book examines how the International Monetary Fund (IMF, or the Fund) shapes monetary change in conditions of extreme economic uncertainty. Monetary system change can alter the pattern of economic incentives within a society, reconfigure a country's trade and financial relationships with other states, and generate a redistribution of wealth between different social groups, all of which provides a powerful motivation for governments to retain tight control over the process of enacting major monetary policy reforms at the national level.

Achieving structural economic change, however, often requires governments to seek external support, in particular when they attempt to introduce monetary policy reforms in the middle of an economic crisis where predictions of the outcomes of major policy changes are clouded by a high degree of uncertainty. When governments seek the IMF's help to design and implement structural reforms, this can give the organization enormous influence over the dynamics of institutional change within national economies, especially in situations where states lack sufficient financial resources of their own to bear the steep costs that systemic transformation entails. At the same time, the IMF's intervention brings with it a high political cost for governments. For this reason alone, achieving a decisive influence over domestic institutional change remains a complex challenge for the IMF, one that hinges on how effectively the organization can engage in the politics of economic ideas and intellectual persuasion.

Two decades after the fall of the Berlin Wall in 1989 and the subsequent collapse of communism in East and Central Europe and the former Soviet Union, the postcommunist 'transition' to a market-based economy remains the archetype for studying the political economy of the IMF's influence over structural economic change in its member states (see, for example, Pop-Eleches, 2009). However, in contrast to the IMF's involvement with the process of economic reform in many of the postcommunist economies of East and Central Europe and Russia, the IMF's influence can be expected to be most clearly demonstrated in the case of the post-Soviet 'frontier economies' of Central Asia. These states had poor credit reputations in the international financial community throughout the 1990s, and therefore struggled to attract inward investment and to raise capital on their own after the demise of the Soviet Union in 1991. Prior to 1992 the Central Asian republics also had no previous experience of independent statehood and were tightly integrated during the Soviet era as a single economic unit, which makes them particularly useful cases for studying the impact that the IMF has had in 'new' states that lack a track record of previous interactions with external actors, and where new monetary policy frameworks have to be developed from scratch. This book suggests that the key to unlocking the black box of the IMF's involvement in institutional change is examining how the organization 'sees' its member states' economies, which informs the design of its advice for national policy reforms as well as the conditions under which states are able to access IMF loans.

In its 65-year history, the IMF has become one of the most controversial and well-known institutions within the contemporary architecture of global economic governance (see Willett, 2001), and yet the IMF remains one of the most commonly misunderstood international organizations. In particular, there is a basic inconsistency between how the global role and influence of the IMF is commonly discussed in the International Political Economy (IPE) literature and the organization's actual track record. On the one hand, the IMF is assumed to be a uniquely powerful international organization – at least with respect to its borrowing member states – because it can apply material incentives to achieve compliance with its policy reform preferences, while a country's access to additional sources of external finance may hinge on maintaining cooperation with the IMF (Stone, 2008; Gould, 2003; Killick, 1997). On the other hand, despite being able to pull on these levers of material power, IMF-sponsored structural reform programs often fail to meet their targets, either in terms of policy reform benchmarks, expected economic performance, or both (Bird, 2002a; Bird and Willett, 2004; Woods, 2006). Focusing on understanding the sources of the IMF's influence in the political economy of the postcommunist 'transition' in post-Soviet Central Asia provides an important platform for resolving this tension in the existing literature on the impact of the IMF on national policy change. As this book illustrates, the IMF is not able to simply impose policy reforms on unwilling governments. Rather, this study shows how weak states can resist global pressures, and how the behavior of weak actors within those states matters for understanding national processes of economic transformation.

Since the 1980s the effectiveness and the broader political and social impact of the IMF's activities have become a central concern among IPE scholars who work on the evolution of the contemporary architecture of global economic governance, prompted by the IMF's problematic legacy in shaping structural adjustment programs during the Latin American debt crisis and subsequent financial crises in emerging market economies during the 1990s (cf. Best, 2005; Momani, 2005a, 2007; Moschella, 2009; Pop-Eleches, 2009; Woods, 2006; Vetterlein, 2006; Vreeland, 2003a). Research in this field has tended to divide between three distinct areas of focus: (1) the IMF's impact on economic development in borrower countries; (2) the use of the IMF as a foreign policy tool by its major power creditors such as the United States; and (3) the sources of change and continuity within the organization itself. Within this three-fold division of analytical inquiry, the most common theoretical divide has centered on the differences between a rationalist approach – inspired by game theory and principal-agent theory – and a constructivist approach that attempts to understand the importance of ideas, norms, and organizational culture in shaping the actions of international organizations (see Nielson et al., 2006; cf. Hawkins et al., 2006; Barnett and Finnemore, 2004).

At a broader level, the IMF has been an important object of study in its own right as one of the chief proponents of globalization. Indeed, if globalization is defined narrowly as the international integration of national markets for trade in goods, services, and capital then the IMF's interactions with borrowers and the policy conditions it attaches to loans makes the organization a powerful 'globalizer' (Woods, 2006). This vein of research on the IMF and international integration tends to split between scholars whose primary focus is tracing and understanding international processes of policy transfer and norm diffusion (Chwieroth, 2007a, 2007b; Simmons, 2000), and those who are interested in investigating the sources of ideological hegemony in the world economy and understanding the shift between distinct international economic orders in the post-World War Two (WWII) era (Best, 2003; Babb, 2003; Hall, 2003).

The complex issues examined in this book are important for each of these debates, but will be of most interest to those interested in understanding how the IMF acts as a diffuser of global economic policy norms. If the IMF's influence over monetary change is to be found in any national context, it should be clearly observed in the three frontier economies of post-Soviet Central Asia examined here, because these states sought substantial loans, policy advice, and technical assistance from the IMF during the 1990s, and commenced the 'transition' to a market economy from similar institutional starting points. The IMF's attempt to integrate the former Soviet republics of Central Asia into the world economy is also an important case of the limits of formal policy reforms and institutional change in practice, which shows the necessity of studying informal processes of change and how everyday economic actions can frustrate formal policy changes. In Central Asia, the IMF was not able to drive through neoliberal reforms that transformed the Central Asian economies into paragons of market-based capitalism, despite their high level of dependence on the IMF for external support. Instead, people's everyday economic behavior contributed to hastening the end of the ruble zone monetary union in the early 1990s, while Central Asian governments often paid lip service to adopting the IMF's policy preferences at the same time as undermining them in practice.

The account of the IMF's interactions with the frontier economies of Central Asia presented in this book aims to strengthen our empirical understanding of how global economic policy norms are extended to regimes at the margins of the contemporary society of states. The book has two major focal points. First and foremost, the IMF spends a great deal of its time to acquire and transmit comparative policy knowledge among national economies. While the foundation of the IMF's influence over national governments that draw on its resources is conventionally understood as stemming primarily from its lending capacity and loan policy conditionality, this study gives particular attention to how Fund staff engage in the politics of ideas with national policymakers to influence formal processes of policy reform and institutional design. This is important in order to comprehensively understand the pattern of the IMF's interactions with its borrowers, and how the IMF's influence over structural economic reforms is achieved in practice. Rather than access to IMF loans being tightly controlled by the organization's dominant member states through their influence on the IMF's Executive Board, this study of the IMF's interactions with Central Asian economies shows how Fund staff play a primary role in determining whether – and under what conditions – member states are able to borrow from the IMF.

The second major focus is the IMF's role as a *reputational intermediary* for its borrowing member states. Drawing on its own institutional reputation for enforcing strict policy conditions, the IMF can potentially help states to signal their policy credibility to broader domestic and international audiences. Through these reputational tactics, the IMF seeks to improve the sovereign creditworthiness of borrowers as a destination for private investment and official development assistance (ODA). This increases the importance for national policymakers of cooperating with the IMF in order to achieve broader political and economic objectives, which amplifies the organization's influence over the everyday process of institutional change.

The IMF and macroeconomic stability in fragile economies

One of the primary roles of the IMF is to help shore up macroeconomic stability in fragile economies. Central to this process is the organization's ability to exert external influence over a state's economic policy settings and – in the medium term – to foster institutional change to enable countries to improve their macroeconomic performance. In performing this controversial role, the IMF constitutes one of the most important sources of policy diffusion among national economies, which has attracted heated criticism from across the political spectrum. Despite the surge of criticism directed against the IMF in recent years, however, the organization has never been likely to win a popularity contest among international organizations since it opened its doors in the aftermath of the Second World War. Over the last two decades in particular, the IMF has attracted greater political controversy due to its support for neoliberal monetary reforms that reconfigure the state's role in managing economic outcomes. Specifically, the IMF has promoted monetary policy changes that are intended to constrain political influence over the allocation of credit and financial resources within national economies, such as legally establishing central bank 'independence' from the government and liberalizing access to foreign exchange. While the IMF argues that creating a market-based monetary system will help to achieve greater macroeconomic stability over the long term, these reforms often run into a wall of political resistance. In particular, for the Central Asian economies that are examined in this book the regulation of money was intimately connected to regime stability, postcommunist state-building, and the extraction of economic rents after the breakdown of the Soviet Union.

It is common for scholars who study the IMF's influence on national policy change to investigate how closely the policy conditions detailed in IMF loan packages are reflected in a borrower's economic reforms during the life span of a short-term loan agreement. In many cases, however, a long-term analysis that qualitatively traces the IMF's relationship with a particular state over time can provide a more comprehensive picture of the political economy of policy diffusion, which is an inherently dynamic and ongoing process. In addition, in order to assess the IMF's influence over national policy change it is important to examine the local context in a particular country, and the probable level of difficulty associated with different types of economic reforms. For instance, studies that attempt to measure the influence of the IMF by creating aggregate indices of policy compliance risk treating reforms across different policy areas as functionally equivalent (Vreeland, 2006: 363). The problem with this approach is that the IMF is likely to find some policy areas easier to reform than others are. As a consequence, its influence over domestic policy change may either be exaggerated (in the case of reforms in less-demanding policy areas) or understated (in the case of difficult policy areas where the IMF may only achieve change through incremental steps). Quantitative research on the total number of reforms that a country enacts over time that match the IMF's policy preferences, or limiting analysis to a short period of IMF engagement, is therefore insufficient to comprehend how – or how much – policy diffusion takes place.

In contrast to the existing rationalist literature on the IMF, the relationship between the IMF and its borrowing member states should not be conceived simply as a strategic game over policy conditionality, with actor A (the IMF) trying to establish the short-term material incentives that will cause actor B (the national government) to comply. Rather, what matters more for understanding the IMF's influence over both the scope and the durability of policy change with respect to borrowing states is examining how external material incentives are repeatedly used to establish a pattern of interaction between Fund staff and national officials – a *policy reform corridor* – which creates recurring opportunities for domestic actors to be persuaded to re-conceptualize their interests. This involves studying how the IMF has attempted to incrementally cultivate new policy frameworks among key actors in an economy through normative persuasion over a medium- or long-term time horizon, which can gradually generate the ideational conditions for achieving – and, more importantly, sustaining – the implementation of global economic norms at the national level.

This broader understanding of the sources of the IMF's influence *vis-à-vis* its borrowing member states suggests that the following four points are important for comprehending how the organization has attempted to diffuse global monetary norms to the frontier economies of Central Asia. First, persuasion, in this sense, is less about encouraging actors to reform their behavior in order to achieve social recognition, as a response to social cues, or to avoid public shaming, and is more about exploiting the use of positive material inducements to reconstruct how actors perceive their interests. Second, the process of achieving normative change is not a straightforward matter of exchanging material rewards for nominal shifts in a government's policy stance. Third, the attempt to diffuse global economic norms to frontier economies is unlikely to follow a unilinear trajectory whereby a new norm is introduced, becomes familiar, and is subsequently internalized by the recipient somewhere down the track. Rather, diffusing global normative standards to frontier economies is likely to be a much more irregular process, whereby any policy gains that are achieved might quickly be eroded by backward steps, or what the IMF terms 'policy slippage'. Finally, seeking to achieve reforms in monetary behavior by frontier economies can be expected to be particularly difficult because changes in monetary policy and exchange rate arrangements have important distributional consequences, which are likely to be most salient in countries that previously maintained intensive exchange controls such as the former Soviet republics.

The IMF's long-term policy preferences are characterized throughout this book as 'IMF-friendly' reforms – those that the IMF seeks to persuade its member states to adopt through policy dialogue and ongoing negotiation. The IMF's policy advice is not necessarily the same in different countries or over time in the same country, as the organization may see a number of policy alternatives as equally satisfactory. For these reasons I use the term IMF-friendly policies to describe the IMF's common reform preferences across countries, rather than adopt the more hackneyed label of the 'Washington consensus' or 'neoliberalism' (cf. the chapters in Macdonald and Ruckert, 2009).

An investigation of the sources of the IMF's influence over national policy change suggests two main lines of inquiry. The first line of inquiry involves assessing whether the IMF exerts a significant influence over the evolution of states' economic policies. States have historically defended their right to pursue economic policies both as a normative principle and as a means to build up material power, especially in the area of monetary policy. Many IPE scholars might therefore expect to find a negative answer here or to find that the IMF's advice only counts at the margin, with the IMF simply firming up support for a policy change already being considered by national officials. Where it seems that the IMF has exerted a significant influence on national economic policy, the second line of inquiry involves exploring how it has been able to do so. The existing evidence from quantitative research on the effectiveness of formal loan conditionality is mixed at best, which suggests that the IMF's influence cannot be assessed simply through quantitative measurements of a state's compliance with loan program targets.

Both lines of inquiry involve the search for answers to intensely political questions. They cannot be comprehended if we only ask technical questions about how good the IMF's advice is at achieving the intended material outcomes because it is not possible in practice to draw a neat distinction between the IMF's economic activities and the politicking of its member states. Economics is not a value-neutral science, no matter how much the IMF may insist that it is. Therefore, this book focuses primarily on whether the IMF was able to exercise significant influence over monetary reform in post-Soviet Central Asia, and how this was achieved.

Within the existing IPE literature on the IMF, scholars commonly seek to answer these questions by focusing on: (1) the external factors that influence the IMF's capacity to do its job; (2) the domestic factors that inform whether or not a government is serious about adopting the IMF's reform preferences; and (3) the compliance mechanisms employed by the IMF. In the first group of conventional explanations of the IMF's influence, it is common for rationalist scholars of the IMF to turn to external factors that are beyond the organization's control and can inhibit its influence over domestic policy change. The most obvious constraint here is political interference in the IMF's operations by its major shareholders through their dominance on the IMF's Executive Board, which must approve all IMF loans. In this scenario, the formal decisionmaking process within the IMF – as well as the opportunity for major shareholders to exert informal pressure – shapes the IMF's influence when loan decisions are politicized and explicitly reflect the strategic interests of its powerful member states rather than the needs of the country in question. In rationalist scholarship, the capacity for the IMF to exert an independent influence on domestic policy change is therefore constrained from the start if its major share-holders push for soft loan conditions for allies (Thacker, 1999), veto loans for foes (Boughton, 2001: 1031), or promote policy conditions that serve the private interests of their commercial banks (Gould, 2003). Where political interference by the IMF's major shareholders is absent, however, it is expected that the IMF's threats to enforce its loan conditions by withholding financing generate greater incentives for borrowing countries to enact IMF-friendly reforms (Stone, 2002, 2004, 2008).

The second group of explanations concentrate on the circumstances within a country that determine the effectiveness of the IMF's actions. Most important here is whether or not a government is serious about enacting IMF-friendly policy reforms (Bird, 1996: 494, Bird and Willett, 2004), which is now defined by the IMF itself as the degree of 'country ownership' for a reform program. Here the IMF's capacity to influence domestic policy change depends on whether the IMF can find 'sympathetic interlocutors' in a country's policymaking community who are willing to listen to the IMF's advice and pilot reforms through the political process (Woods, 2006: 72–3). For these sympathetic elites, IMF conditionality is not simply a straitjacket imposed as a penalty for poor policy performance, but can offer politicians and bureaucrats a power-ful political tool to force policy change (Vreeland, 2003b: 339).

The third group of conventional explanations of the IMF's influence focus on the organization itself, in particular the formal mechanisms it employs to achieve compliance on the part of borrowing states (see Dijkstra, 2002; Killick, 1997). The IMF's capacity to influence domestic policy change is considered to be greatest when the IMF insists on the achievement of explicit policy actions before a loan program begins ('prior actions'), and when loan programs entail quantified perfor-mance criteria that provide the IMF with a clear snapshot of the degree of state compliance (Bird, 1996: 483). In addition, program completion is thought to depend upon whether the net benefits of ongoing com-pliance (additional external finance) outweigh the costs that govern-ments face from a loss of sovereignty over economic policy, which may increase over the life cycle of a loan program (Bird, 2002b: 841–2). The IMF's impact is therefore expected to be most decisive when: (a) clear quantitative goals are set, including the conditions states must imple-ment before a loan is disbursed; and (b) the marginal material benefits for states of maintaining compliance with the IMF continue to outweigh compliance costs. In contrast to these conventional explanations of the IMF's influence, this book examines how the IMF engages in the politics of ideas at the national level in borrowing states, with a particular focus on the role played by Fund staff in persuading national policymakers to adopt IMF-friendly reforms.

Seeing like the IMF on institutional change

An important source of power for the IMF lies in its capacity to build reputational authority to shape how other actors view a particular policy problem and how they determine appropriate political solutions, which rests on the organization's intellectual resources. This is a point that is often highlighted in constructivist scholarship on international organizations (Barnett and Finnemore, 1999, 2004), and yet this insight is seldom applied to studying the impact of the IMF's involvement with borrowing member states. An essential dimension of the postcommunist 'transition' in the former Soviet Union was the effort to adapt societies to new forms of governance and control based on a fundamentally different form of technical knowledge. This highlights the importance of the informal context in which change takes place, because the introduction of new formal schemes of order always depends on changing informal processes in order for these to be effective in motivating new forms of everyday behaviour (Scott, 1998: 310). 'Seeing like the IMF' increases our understanding of how the IMF seeks to use its intellectual resources to achieve domestic policy change, the conditions that enable its influence, and how the organization attempts to turn these to its advantage to sustain IMF-friendly institutional change. By exploring how the IMF sees its member states' economies, we can therefore increase our understanding of how the organization seeks to remake their institutional frameworks over time.

Rather than concentrate on quantitative analysis of program completion rates, which can both overstate and understate the IMF's influence over the design and implementation of institutional reforms, the focus of this study is on exploring the nuances of how the IMF sought to change monetary ideas and practices in post-Soviet Central Asia over multiple years. I trace the footsteps down what I call through the 'policy reform corridor' (explained in Chapter 1) by drawing upon archived policy documents, Executive Board debates, and interviews with current and former IMF staff. Drawing on qualitative content analysis of IMF archival documents and background interviews with staff, the IMF's 'success' is assessed by examining the gradual implementation of IMF-friendly monetary reforms. In contrast to measuring specific program completion rates, this helps to build a more comprehensive understanding of the IMF's influence over the medium term. I concentrate in particular on examining the IMF's efforts to achieve central bank independence and current account convertibility in Central Asia. Encouraging policymakers to enact these reforms posed a major challenge for the IMF because it involved persuading political elites to seize new ways to pursue their interests. Both central bank independence and currency convertibility had significant implications for the capacity of political elites to maintain their newfound monetary policy autonomy, gained with the demise of the Soviet Union and the subsequent collapse of the Russian-dominated ruble zone.

With any attempt to build new formal institutions designed to achieve fundamentally different social and economic goals, the legacy of the past weighs heavily on the dynamics of national policy change (see Campbell and Pedersen, 1996). Following a systemic shock, actors do not construct new institutions in a social vacuum but are constrained by the legacy of previous institutional frameworks, as well as shared understandings about how the economy works and how it *ought* to work. Historical legacies were especially significant in Central Asia, where the political transition from the Soviet Union to national independence, concomitant with the need to construct a new national economic system, was carried out by decisionmakers who were accustomed to the rules and incentive structure of the old regime. At the same time, systemic shocks such as the political disintegration of the Soviet Union and the dismantling of the inter-republican monetary relationships that had characterized the Soviet system can also open up a window of opportunity for rapid institutional change. What domestic actors choose to do with this window of opportunity is shaped by their existing understandings of their interests, but their interests are also mutable because of the acute uncertainty they face.

On the one hand, the severe economic uncertainty generated by a monetary crisis can inhibit the IMF's ability to achieve a decisive influence over policy reforms. As the political interactions between the IMF and Central Asian governments show, when states face a major economic crisis how policymakers respond is informed by how they interpret their options – not simply by the list of options that are available. This informs whether they seek good relations with the IMF in order to achieve other economic and political objectives, such as accessing additional sources of external finance, or whether they choose to keep the IMF at arm's-length. On the other hand, national policymakers facing an economic crisis require systematic knowledge that can help them to navigate economic uncertainty. For example, Central Asian policymakers in the early 1990s were unfamiliar with how market-based mechanisms work, which made it difficult for political leaders to ascertain in advance who would benefit and who would lose from economic reforms. In such circumstances, the ambiguity of information generates individual-level confusion, which may prompt decisionmakers to turn to the IMF's intellectual resources to provide a policy roadmap that might lessen their cognitive uncertainty. Where this is the case, domestic reform is mediated by the IMF's attempts to change ideas and practices, with the IMF drawing on its intellectual resources in order to shape both the direction and the content of institutional reforms.

This book examines the nature of the IMF's influence over institutional change in the Kyrgyz Republic, Kazakhstan, and Uzbekistan, which each gained their independence with the demise of the Soviet Union in 1991. These countries were selected because they share several important characteristics that make them an ideal testing ground for investigating the sources of variation in the IMF's impact on national policy change over time. They each represent frontier economies in which the IMF might be expected to exercise a strong influence over the course of institutional change, due to each facing major economic shocks caused by the breakdown of the Soviet system and having few alternative sources of external financing available. Moreover, when they became independent states in 1991, each had little experience with macroeconomic policymaking and were accustomed to having monetary policy handed down from Moscow. Policymakers were therefore in need of the IMF's advice on how to construct new monetary systems and how to proceed with the transition to a market-based economy.

Furthermore, the Kyrgyz Republic, Kazakhstan, and Uzbekistan each gained political independence and joined the IMF at the same time, and each inherited similar institutional frameworks. Because initial institutional conditions were the same, this provides an opportunity to study the sources of variation in IMF-friendly reform outcomes over time without assuming path dependence. All three states also established strong presidential systems following independence that were commonly characterized as authoritarian patronage-based regimes. In contrast to other postcommunist transitions, therefore, where popular social movements demanded political independence and economic reform (see Abdelal, 2001), the scope and speed of economic change in Central Asia was largely determined by ruling elites (Luong, 2002: 104–5; Akiner, 2004: 119). In each case, political leaders committed themselves to the goal of enacting market-based economic reforms following the collapse of the Soviet Union. In all three countries, the IMF also had to deal with a high level of economic uncertainty. This impeded the organization's capacity to formulate appropriate reform programs, as well as making it difficult for the IMF to persuade national policymakers to adopt reforms when the outcomes were indeterminate and political leaders were preoccupied with the need to ensure regime survival.

Plan of the book

The central argument put forward in this book is that the IMF's interactions with its borrowing member states are not always strictly controlled by its dominant members through their influence on the Executive Board. Instead, 'seeing like the IMF' helps to show how Fund staff play a crucial role in developing and strengthening the organization's relationship with national policymakers. Their judgments on national policymakers' future intentions therefore weigh heavily on IMF loan decisions and the organization's flexibility with applying loan policy conditions, which both increases Fund staff discretion and provides repeated openings for staff to persuade national policymakers to adopt – and to maintain – IMF-friendly reforms.

Chapter 1 builds upon existing theories of institutional change to map out how the IMF influences the process of domestic institution-building and policy reform. The chapter concentrates in particular on the symbolic role the IMF can play in cases where actors undertake institutional change in conditions of acute uncertainty. In contrast to standard accounts of the organization, it is argued that the IMF should be understood as a reputational intermediary that can potentially act with a high degree of independence from its major power shareholders, but which must attract support from other important actors in the international financial community to boost its efforts to effect domestic institutional change. The chapter also examines how the IMF's dual roles as an intellectual actor and as a source of external credit intersect. This provides an overview of the toolkit that the IMF draws on to persuade its member states to adopt its long-term preferences for institutional change, concentrating in particular on how the IMF seeks to use its reputational authority in order to persuade policymakers to adopt a common intellectual framework for understanding national economic problems over time.

Chapter 2 provides some historical background to the systemic transformation that followed the collapse of communism in the former

Soviet Union through briefly examining the development of the contemporary international monetary order in the post-WWII era. It also examines the construction of the IMF's monetary reform template for postcommunist economies, which the IMF designed in order to facilitate the expansion of the international monetary order in the aftermath of the Cold War. The chapter focuses in particular on exploring the development of two fundamental global monetary norms that the IMF now seeks to persuade member states to adopt – currency convertibility and central bank independence – and the political contests that these normative shifts entail.

Chapter 3 explores the demise of the ruble zone monetary union during the early 1990s, which lead to the establishment of 15 new national monetary systems in the former Soviet republics. This chapter illustrates how informal practices led to demonetization and the growth of barter economies that undermined the IMF's attempts to establish monetary stability in the region. In particular, it emphasizes the social dimension of existing monetary practices and the monetary policy challenges that accompanied the breakdown of the Soviet economy and the chaotic shift towards market-based monetary policies. The chapter examines the political struggles that characterized the IMF's efforts to achieve monetary cooperation in the former Soviet Union, and shows how the everyday politics of money in the former Soviet republics inhibited the ability of post-Soviet policymakers to make the ruble zone work despite their professed commitment to a multilateral solution. The chapter also traces the internal debates within the organization to show how the IMF's policy preferences evolved over the period from 1991 to 1993. It argues that the IMF's freedom of action was constrained by how both the IMF Executive Board and Fund staff interpreted the limits to the organization's authority with regard to the political choice of whether governments should introduce new national currencies.

Chapters 4 and 5 examine the evolution of the IMF's efforts to build new national monetary systems based on market mechanisms in Central Asia during the 1990s, how the organization sought to shape national policy change in each case, and the conditions that enabled it do so. In contrast to other cases where national officials used the IMF's support to force through policy change (see Woods, 2006: Ch. 4), the frontier economies of Central Asia do not fit a story where policy elites sought to use the IMF to drive domestic policy change because they were committed to IMF-friendly reform ideas *per se*. In addition, unlike other cases of postcommunist reform such as Russia, the IMF was able to make credible threats to suspend financing in Central Asia without major shareholder interference to soften loan conditions. In all three cases examined here the IMF also made widespread use of 'prior actions' for loans and set clear quantitative performance targets for loan programs. Yet despite appearing to fit conventional expectations of the IMF's impact, these explanations cannot fully account for variation in the IMF's influence over institutional change in Central Asian economies during the first decade of the postcommunist transition.

Chapter 4 examines the development of the IMF's policy dialogue with the Kyrgyz Republic, Kazakhstan, and Uzbekistan after they joined the IMF, and focuses on how quickly the IMF was able to put an initial loan agreement in place. The chapter shows how Fund staff only supported countries' loan applications when they believed that national policymakers intended to cooperate with them to devise IMF-friendly monetary reforms. In these cases, discretion lay with how Fund staff interpreted each government's intentions, rather than the implied voting weight of major shareholders on the Executive Board. Despite their urgent need for policy advice and external financing, the chapter demonstrates that all three countries presented difficult cases for the IMF. Central Asian policymakers were not attuned to internalizing new policy norms from external actors like the IMF, and exhibited different degrees of resistance to the IMF's attempts to change how they perceived their interests. This chapter illustrates the slow progress the organization made in its early efforts to influence the process of institutional change in each country, where the IMF sought to change the financial behavior of the government, the central bank, commercial banks, and state-owned firms by restructuring the formal institutional relationships between them and constructing a market-based monetary system for determining the allocation of credit.

After this discussion of the early stages of the IMF's involvement in Central Asia, Chapter 5 is devoted to analyzing the scope of the IMF's influence over monetary reform in the Kyrgyz Republic, Kazakhstan, and Uzbekistan over time. In particular, it concentrates on examining how the IMF was able to influence each state, and explaining why the scope of its influence varied across the three countries during the 1990s. The chapter demonstrates that by increasing compliance with the new formal rules of the game, the IMF sought to bring about a permanent change in actors' financial behavior, disregarding the informal political and economic order in these societies. This discussion shows that the IMF's concentration on achieving formal institutional change also generated new informal outcomes as actors sought to mediate domestic uncertainty, which shaped the overall results of the IMF's efforts to persuade policymakers to sustain a market-based policy orientation in each country.

The conclusion recapitulates the findings and the main argument of the book, and reflects on the implications for the field of International Political Economy of understanding the IMF as a reputational intermediary, rather than as a neoliberal 'policy enforcer'. It contends that seeing the IMF primarily as a reputational intermediary for its borrowers can help to improve our understanding of the organization by orienting the focus of analysis from member state control of the IMF to the sources of the organization's autonomy as an intellectual agent of change. This dynamic process varies across cases and over time. The concluding chapter also argues that examining the importance of the informal context in which economic reform takes place can contribute to the wider literature on institutional change and policy diffusion in International Political Economy by helping to improve our understanding of how institutions are reformed without seeing outcomes as resulting from path dependent formal rules. The conclusion suggests that what is more important than the path dependence of inherited institutions when states are confronted with a systemic crisis is how political leaders interpret the options that are available to them – especially if these same leaders remain in power over an extended period of time, as they did in each of the Central Asian economies examined in this book. While formal changes to a government's policy settings may produce evidence of IMF influence in the short term, this study shows that the diffusion of new economic policies is likely to result in reform failure over time in the absence of broader ideational changes.

1
Institutional Change and the IMF

How does the International Monetary Fund shape the reform of domestic institutions in an uncertain environment? As an organization, the IMF concentrates on achieving changes in formal economic institutions within its member states, but these reforms can easily be frustrated when uncertainty increases the salience of informal rules and processes within a society. This chapter examines the role that the IMF has sought to play in states that embark on structural changes in an environment of acute domestic uncertainty. The conventional wisdom in much of the International Political Economy literature suggests that the IMF's interactions with borrowing member states are largely driven by its major shareholders, and in particular the United States (Thacker, 1999; Momani, 2004; Oatley and Yackee, 2004). However, while scholars have brought to light numerous instances where major powers such as the US have influenced the development of loan programs with borrowing states, Fund staff retain considerable discretion over the performance of everyday operations. This chapter argues that the IMF should be understood as a semi-autonomous agent that can often act with a high degree of independence from its member state principals, but which aims to attract support from other important actors in the global political economy to boost its efforts to achieve domestic institutional change.

Everyday practices and institutional change

Achieving institutional change depends upon not only designing and introducing the formal architecture of new institutions, but also upon implementing reforms through changes in officials' day-to-day practices. In addition, formal institutional changes can potentially be undone by the everyday economic behavior of the wider population. Institutions are commonly defined as the 'rules of the game' in a particular society (North, 1990). They exert a systematic influence over how people are likely to perform a given social activity and shape the definition of political goals by providing the tools that people use to make sense of the world (March and Olsen, 1989: 39–40). Specifically, institutions are formal and informal rules and processes that guide how people interact by constraining and enabling certain forms of behavior (Helmke and Levitsky, 2004: 727). Formal institutions are officially sanctioned rules, such as constitutional structures or legislation, while informal institutions are uncodified rules and unofficial structures. For investigating domestic institutional change, formal institutions are the most obvious units of analysis and the most open to observation over time. For instance, the formal institutionalized relationships among political actors in different countries may generate conditions that facilitate domestic policy change, such as a 'winner takes all' majoritarian electoral system in a unitary state. Alternatively, formal institutions might impede policy change by permitting a greater number of veto-players to influence the political process, such as a proportional electoral system in a federal state (Scharpf, 2000: 766–7). In these examples, while the informal rules of the game also influence political outcomes, it is much easier to observe how a change in the formal institutional architecture alters actors' behavior.

When international organizations like the IMF seek to reform states' economic institutions, they do so by concentrating primarily on tracking and providing advice on formal institutional change. In this respect, a large part of the IMF's work is concerned with 'institutional engineering', based on the assumption that formal institutions are not simply epiphenomenal but can influence actors' behavior and political and economic outcomes independent of the informal order in a given society. Understanding the IMF's impact on national economies involves examining how the IMF tries to change formal institutions, while acknowledging that formal changes generate uncertainty that actors seek to mediate through informal processes. Assessing the IMF's influence (or lack thereof) therefore entails investigating the informal context of institutional change, because this helps to 'bridge the gap between official regulations and everyday practices' (Tsai, 2006: 119).

Informal institutions are not merely the residual effects of cultural traditions or simply informal patterns of behavior. Nor are they only created and utilized by private or 'civil society' actors for they can also be integral to the functioning of formal state institutions, although they are not automatically implied by the existence of weak formal institutions. Rather, informal institutions are *'socially shared rules, usually unwritten, that are created, communicated, and enforced outside of officially sanctioned channels'* (Helmke and Levitsky, 2004: 727, emphasis in original). Informal institutions interact with formal structures and procedures in a complex range of ways. They cannot be distinguished simply as dichotomous variables that either effect or block the functioning of formal institutions, but often exert a crucial influence over formal institutional outcomes.

In the new states to emerge from the former Soviet Union and the countries of East and Central Europe, the formal rules of the game changed rapidly during the 1990s. In the process, societies experienced varying degrees of 'deinstitutionalization' and 'reinstitutionalization' (Soulsby and Clark, 1996: 476). In this uncertain environment, implicit social norms and informal networks sometimes became crucial determinants of political change as local actors responded to uncertainty and the institutional gaps produced by weak formal rules (Wedel, 2003: 429). The importance of informal processes in postcommunist economies had a major impact upon the IMF's ability to influence institutional change. For example, the gap between formal institutions and everyday practices often made it difficult for the staff of the IMF to understand using their usual analytical techniques how local systems actually worked (Way, 2002: 581), while a lack of knowledge about the key features of centrally planned economies contributed to inaccurate predictions and expectations regarding the short-term outcomes of formal institutional reforms (Winiecki, 1995). These issues were especially pertinent in the frontier economies of Central Asia, where external actors promoting formal institutional change had to contend with informal systems of governance based on pre-Soviet social cleavages mobilized around 'clan' identities, which became increasingly salient when formal institutions were weakened or disestablished after the collapse of the Soviet Union (Collins, 2004, 2006). The following section compares two of the main branches of institutional theory – related to both formal and informal institutional change – and discusses how they can help to shed light on the IMF's relationship with frontier economies.

The political economy of institutional change

From a rationalist perspective, elite actors are motivated to build institutions in an attempt to increase economic efficiency by reducing the transaction costs of doing business in a particular environment, thereby maximizing material gains (Campbell, 1997: 18–20; Grafstein, 1988: 579). A rationalist approach to institutional change suggests that both formal rules and informal constraints are essential for guiding 'the way the game is played' in a particular society, although most research still tends to focus on explaining change in formal institutions (North, 1999: 495; cf. Blyth, 2003: 696). Institutions, from this perspective, are the result of iterated games. Rationalist scholars assume that most of the time actors in the political and economic marketplace will exhibit calculating, self-interested behavior, and will seek to build or to reform institutions to maximize their expected utility gains according to their existing set of individual preferences (Ben-Ner and Putterman, 1999: 17–22; Knight, 1995). The development of game theory in particular has provided an important theoretical stimulus for rationalist scholarship. Here institutions are conceived as equilibrium points, which are produced from the strategic interaction of the relevant players in a specific game (each with their own self-enforcing beliefs, preferences, and resources) and their responses to the exogenous circumstances they face (Calvert, 1995). As such, institutional change is motivated by an exogenous shock that alters the parameters of the game.

Rationalist institutionalism can contribute to an understanding of the IMF's influence on the process of institutional change in the frontier economies of post-Soviet Central Asia in two main ways. First, it points to an explanation for why formal institutional change was either difficult to achieve or why it was slow to result in a substantive alteration in economic practices, a phenomenon common across the three Central Asian economies examined here. Because the Central Asian republics operated with a comparative absence of economic legality and effective formal institutions, the policy challenge was not simply a matter of replacing the existing formal Soviet institutions with formal market institutions. Rather, postcommunist institutional change involved establishing economic legality and effective formal institutions in an environment where people were accustomed to conducting business according to informal mechanisms, and where economic activity was governed by the use of discretionary bureaucratic power rather than universal rules (Litwack, 1991). A rationalist approach can therefore provide part of an explanation for the persistence and the expanded role of informal behavioral norms in postcommunist economies.

Second, with its emphasis on game theory and strategic bargaining, a rationalist approach suggests that the variation in institutional outcomes across Central Asia can be explained by examining variables such as the parameters of the 'institutional game' in each country, the relevant actors' institutional preferences, and the bargaining resources available to them (Knight, 1995: 117–18). Game theoretic studies of postcommunism expect to see institutional actors who have already internalized the new rules of the game slugging it out against those who cling to the old rules. From this perspective, the outcomes of institutional games will be decided by the group, reformists or conservatives, which have the greater power resources available to them and are able to prevail. Game theorists therefore assume that institutional change is determined at different points in time by the speed with which actors move up this learning curve to adapt to their new environment (Kyriazis and Zouboulakis, 2005: 112).

Whereas rationalist institutionalists assume that human behavior in the political and economic marketplace is mostly self-regarding and that individuals enter this environment already endowed with a fixed set of interests, constructivists emphasize the intersubjectivity of beliefs, identities, and interests, and focus on understanding how these are socially produced. The key assumption common to both 'conventional' and 'critical' strands of constructivism in contemporary International Relations theory is that understanding the intersubjective bases of everyday social reality is essential for understanding political processes, practices, and outcomes. Constructivist approaches differ most from rationalist approaches because of the specific role they assign to ideational factors in the process of institutional change. That is, constructivists understand ideas as constitutive of political practices and political power (Adler, 1997; Finnemore and Sikkink, 1998; Hopf, 1998; Laffey and Weldes, 1997; Ruggie, 1998). Ideas, therefore, have autonomy from formal institutions, and can have an independent causal impact on institutional change. For constructivists, ideas are also considered to be an essential ingredient in the social production of both: (1) who an actor thinks he or she is within a particular context (their identity); and (2) what he or she is inclined to seek to gain through the performance of their social role (their interests).

From the vantage point of nearly two decades after the collapse of the Soviet Union, it is clear that understanding the role of ideas is crucial if we wish to understand the politics of institutional change and continuity in the frontier economies of post-Soviet Central Asia. While new laws for a market economy were sometimes written 'overnight' based on an institutional blueprint supplied by an external actor, the diffusion of similar formal rules did not result in them being implemented in the same way as intended (Broome, 2006; Campbell, 2004: 77–9; Way, 2002). Instead, the intersubjective understandings that informed decisionmaking processes in Central Asia following independence proved to be more resilient to the diffusion of new intellectual frameworks than many scholars had expected in the early 1990s, similar to reform experiences in Russia and the European centrally planned economies (Zweynert, 2006; Appel, 2000; Soulsby and Clark, 1996; Seleny, 1999). When new ideas did gain traction in postcommunist economies, this was often because international organizations acted as facilitators of change by supplying crucial intellectual and financial support (Appel, 2004; Cooley, 2000, 2003).

In addition to highlighting the importance of ideas in the process of institutional design, a constructivist approach also provides a set of conceptual tools with which to explore how ideas played a key role in shaping variation in institutional reform outcomes across the frontier economies of post-Soviet Central Asia. In this regard, constructivism prioritizes an inductive approach to understanding how actors' interpretations of their circumstances informed political and economic change, with actors' interests understood as tightly linked with intersubjective ideas about appropriate forms of behavior and the appropriate role of state institutions. This has an analytical advantage over rationalist theory because it avoids the analytical deficiency of assuming that actors' interpretations of their changing circumstances were distorted by a bounded rationality (Goldstein and Keohane, 1993), which would be stripped away to allow self-interest to guide decisionmaking as economic reforms became naturalized. Despite these shortcomings, however, explaining individuals' strategic actions to maximize their material interests remains important for understanding institutional outcomes. If the ontological debates between rationalist and constructivist perspectives are put to one side (Nielson, et al., 2006: 115), combining both approaches can potentially provide a more comprehensive understanding of the process of institutional change than either rationalist or constructivist perspectives can achieve on their own.

While conventional strands of rationalist and constructivist perspectives have often tended to engage in paradigm competition, with proponents seeking to 'out-explain' each other to prove whether ideas or interests matter more for understanding institutional change, recent scholarship has suggested the need to surmount a strict ontological distinction between the two approaches (Seabrooke, 2007a: 408; Broome, 2009). There has already been significant cross-fertilization or 'bridge-building' between these different perspectives as scholars have attempted to integrate the analytical strengths of a 'soft' rationalist approach with those of a constructivist perspective, to illuminate the contingent and context-specific bases of collective ideas and social action (see Nielson et al., 2006; Luong, 2002; Seabrooke, 2006; Sinclair, 2005). This book is located squarely in this camp, and utilizes the analytical strengths of both rationalist and constructivist approaches to gain greater understanding of the IMF's influence on institutional change in the postcommunist economies of Central Asia.

Economic uncertainty and policy credibility

The preceding theoretical discussion is important for understanding how an international organization such as the IMF tries to mediate domestic uncertainty to achieve institutional change. The conventional wisdom in much of the political science literature suggests that structural crises such as the demise of the Soviet Union open up crucial windows of opportunity that can allow actors to achieve radical institutional change at a rapid pace (Krasner, 1984; Keeler, 1993; cf. Cortell and Peterson, 1999). But the job of international organizations like the IMF that seek to achieve domestic institutional change based on exogenous ideas may in some cases be much more difficult in a crisis than during a period of institutional stasis or incremental institutional adaptation. The persuasive force of the IMF's arguments for change might very well have greater resonance when a major shock to the system serves to discredit existing institutional structures and intellectual frameworks, which potentially allows the IMF to construct a shared understanding of a crisis by defining the problem, diagnosing the causes of the problem, and prescribing an appropriate solution. However, the IMF can often find its analytical capacity to assess day-to-day developments in a particular economy severely impaired in conditions of acute uncertainty. This increases the likelihood that policy mistakes will be made, and institutional reforms will be prescribed that cannot feasibly be implemented or which lead to unintended consequences.

New institutional structures, including those based on external blueprints, 'do not come with an instruction sheet' (Blyth, 2003). When political and economic uncertainty lead to systemic monetary instability, and when monetary instability prompts economic actors to engage in individual strategic behavior that further worsens a country's macroeconomic conditions, the IMF can find itself facing a vicious circle that perpetuates uncertainty and undermines the impact of formal regulatory mechanisms on everyday behavior. When formal institutions must compete with unofficial rules of the game that generate different outcomes – such as a system of personalized credit allocation when officials are trying to construct an impersonal system where financial resources are distributed through market mechanisms – the IMF is likely to struggle to achieve substantive institutional change. This problem was especially salient in the early period of postcommunist transformations, where both elite and non-elite actors needed time to learn how new institutional rules based on 'identity-blind' market mechanisms were meant to work. In such circumstances, the IMF faced a steep challenge in its efforts to achieve behavioral change, despite having increased scope to introduce formal reforms.

In the environment of acute uncertainty that characterized the demise of Soviet central planning mechanisms, the IMF saw the achievement of monetary stability as a fundamental criterion for post-Soviet economic transformation. In theory, the early achievement of monetary stability would help states to send a signal of 'policy credibility' to domestic and international audiences about the authorities' commitment to a market-oriented reform program. It was hoped that strengthening governments' policy credibility would add further momentum to structural reform efforts by coordinating the price expectations of domestic actors, facilitating official development assistance from major donor states, and improving the ability of transition economies to attract foreign direct investment (FDI).

To help establish the credibility of their plans for institutional change, post-Soviet states were expected to form a close working relationship with the IMF to enhance the chances of successful monetary stabilization by tapping into the IMF's pool of comparative knowledge on monetary reform, and to help ameliorate policy ambiguity. As Stone (2002: 11) observes, 'a sound investment climate is a state of mind that has to be painstakingly constructed'. In states that have a history of macroeconomic instability, or like the former Soviet republics have limited institutional capacity to manage an effective monetary framework, the policy conditions attached to IMF loan programs potentially 'creates a focal point for investors to coordinate their expectations' (Stone, 2002: 11). The perceived problem for states is that in an environment of acute uncertainty 'the lack of policy predictability may create doubts about the sustainability of the reform process and affect the degree of credibility of an otherwise consistent and viable program' (Agénor, 1993: 6). Achieving policy credibility is especially problematic if there are widespread expectations that policy-makers' rhetorical commitments to implement painful economic reforms will prove to be politically unfeasible. By maintaining a cooperative policy relationship with the IMF, it was expected that the former Soviet centrally planned economies might borrow credibility from the IMF's institutional reputation for being excessively conservative about extend-ing its public 'stamp of approval' for a government's policy program (Cottarelli and Giannini, 1998: 14).

For newly independent states, even IMF membership itself could potentially speak volumes to international audiences about a govern-ment's policy orientation, because of the explicit obligations member-ship implies. For instance, demonstrating a willingness to conform to international monetary standards such as current account convert-ibility, which is one of the obligations of IMF membership, might help to enhance the credibility of a government's rhetorical policy com-mitments in the eyes of market actors (Simmons, 2000). Although the IMF is often seen as a hard-nosed enforcer of policy prescriptions that are derived from economic theory with scant regard for the messy world of economic practice, the emphasis on establishing and main-taining policy credibility with international and domestic audiences indicates a recognition within the IMF that actors' intersubjective understandings help shape reform outcomes. This is especially impor-tant in an environment of policy ambiguity and monetary instability such as the conditions that characterized the early period of post-Soviet independence. In circumstances where it is difficult for most external observers to assess local economic conditions and a govern-ment's policy intentions for themselves, the public pronouncements and lending decisions of an economically conservative international organization such as the IMF potentially carry great weight.

The reputational authority of the IMF

The authority of the IMF's assessment of the policy environment in a particular economy rests not so much on the quality of its knowledge of local conditions, the depth and accuracy of which may be impossible for independent observers to evaluate at the time, but rather on its *institutional reputation* in the eyes of key international audiences (Sharman, 2006: 135–8). Conceived in this way, an actor's reputation is not an asset or a property that is owned by an international organ-ization and is directly under its control, but instead refers to the more common sense definition of reputation as how others intersubjectively view an actor (Sharman, 2007: 26). In this case, the IMF's reputation in the eyes of bilateral and multilateral donors and international investors underpinned the causal impact of its judgments on a government's reform program and a country's economic prospects (see Broome, 2008).

Nevertheless, the credibility of an international organization's institutional reputation for technical expertise among international audiences can outstrip the quality of its knowledge of local policy conditions (Sharman, 2006: 137). When an international organization has a reputation for producing high quality statistics and economic surveillance among national policymakers, private market actors, the media, and other multilateral forums, its assessments may be consequential for these actors even in instances where the evidence on which they are based is thin (on the 'scientific' authority of IMF assessments, see Barnett and Finnemore, 2004: 67–8). In the post-Soviet context, the analytical capacity of the IMF to understand local conditions was significantly impeded by the interface between formal and informal institutions. Woodruff (2000) has shown how monetary reforms in Russia came awry because of the attenuated reach of formal institutions in post-Soviet society, with actors' behavior instead regulated by other principles rooted in social norms. In post-Soviet Central Asia, this is aptly illustrated by the practice of managers remunerating workers through 'payments in kind' rather than simply sacking staff when a firm could no longer afford to pay their cash wages (Broome, 2006). A further example of the importance of Soviet-era regulative norms is the priority that some Russian banks continued to attach to providing easy credit to their industrial clients rather than prioritizing the objective of maximizing profit (Tompson, 1997: 1171).

These examples of the weak regulatory link between formal institutions and informal practices help to highlight the reputational problem facing the international donor community in post-Soviet states in the early 1990s. In these difficult circumstances, bilateral donors and other multilateral lenders looked to the IMF to provide the ODA equivalent of a creditworthiness assessment on the newly independent states, and made the extension of financial support dependent on an IMF reform program being in place with the expectation that this would help to ensure that their money was well spent. While the 'screening function' of international organizations is often an important part of their work and can provide them with a crucial source of influence (Marchesi and Thomas, 1999: 112–13; Thompson, 2006: 232–3), the IMF is only accustomed to monitoring and providing advice on changes in states' formal institutional structures and *de jure* policy settings. It lacks analytical experience with exploring how informal institutions and practices may complement, accommodate, compete with, or substitute for the formal rules of the game (Helmke and Levitsky, 2004: 727–9). In a context where the salience of informal institutions is high, the IMF's institutional reputation might be sufficient to activate other sources of financial support when the IMF signs off on a government's reform program, but the IMF's lack of local knowledge will make the job of economic transformation extremely difficult. Setbacks, policy failures, and unintended consequences are highly likely if the IMF promotes poorly conceived institutional changes that fail to take into account the informal rules and processes that shape people's everyday economic behavior.

Rather than simply being a technocratic agency, the significance of the IMF's activities for international audiences implies that the IMF also plays an important symbolic role. This role can be seen as providing the function of a 'reputational intermediary' that helps states to improve their creditworthiness by communicating essential information to market participants and providing a symbolic assurance about a government's policy intentions. In this respect a rationalist approach only takes us so far in terms of its explanatory value. As Sinclair (2005: 52–4) points out in the case of credit rating agencies, the status and consequentiality of symbolic actions depends on 'what people believe about them and act on accordingly, even if those beliefs are demonstrably false'. While it is difficult to uncover observable effects that are wholly independent of other causal variables, this symbolic interchange is pertinent to the IMF's activities as well.

The IMF has frequently been criticized for espousing one-size-fits-all institutional blueprints based on a neoliberal ideological straitjacket. While the IMF's proclivity to push for generic policy reforms in its member states is often exaggerated (see Broome and Seabrooke, 2007; Kang, 2007; Stone, 2008), in areas where the IMF does exhibit a high degree of consistency – such as urging governments to get inflation rates and budget deficits down – the search for ideological drivers of the IMF's advice risks obscuring a more pragmatic motivation. The concept of reputation can potentially explain why an actor like the IMF might behave in similar ways in very different situations. By promoting a narrow set of isomorphic policies that the Fund staff believe allow states more autonomy in other policy areas in the post-Bretton Woods era of globalized capital markets, the IMF is also trying to protect the value of its institutional reputation. More specifically, the symbolic impact of the IMF's assessment of a state's policy settings may depend upon its reputation for promoting conservative macroeconomic policies. The constraining effects of the IMF's institutional reputation can be seen in both a positive and a negative light. On the one hand, the IMF's focus on enhancing the credibility of a government's policy settings in the eyes of private actors can be criticized as transforming the IMF into 'a proxy disciplinarian for the market' (Best, 2005: 133). On the other hand, the IMF's reputation for policy conservatism can potentially have a positive effect by helping developing country governments to sell their policies to the international donor community, to credit rating agencies, and to international investors (Lohmann, 2003: 108).

The IMF's efforts to maintain its institutional reputation include its public pronouncements on a state's policy settings as well as its material actions such as the approval of loan agreements, which can send a powerful symbolic signal to international audiences about the credibility of a government's policy intentions. But in order to resonate with a wider international audience the IMF's use of rhetorical action must take advantage of the shared values and norms of the international community, and especially those of the international financial community. Existing evidence in International Political Economy scholarship suggests that contemporary financial market actors prefer governments to have low inflation and small budget deficits (Mosley, 2001: 766). It should therefore come as no surprise that the IMF and other international financial institutions (IFIs) have promoted conservative policies such as the restriction of public expenditure and an independent central bank that focuses on achieving low inflation as a way to signal a state's creditworthiness to private actors. In addition, the Paris Club group of official creditors and other bilateral and multilateral lenders are keen to assure themselves that recipient governments will not fritter away the potential benefits of debt relief or development loans by racking up large budget deficits or pursuing policies that stimulate high inflation. This is backed up by evidence from a survey conducted by Fund staff of 32 major bilateral and multilateral donors, which found that an overwhelming 97 per cent of donors stated that they used the IMF's 'information/signals' to inform decisions on extending aid for low-income countries (IMF, 2005).

Figure 1.1 depicts how the IMF's reputational authority potentially allows governments to send positive signals to numerous actors in both international and domestic audiences. The list of actors repre-

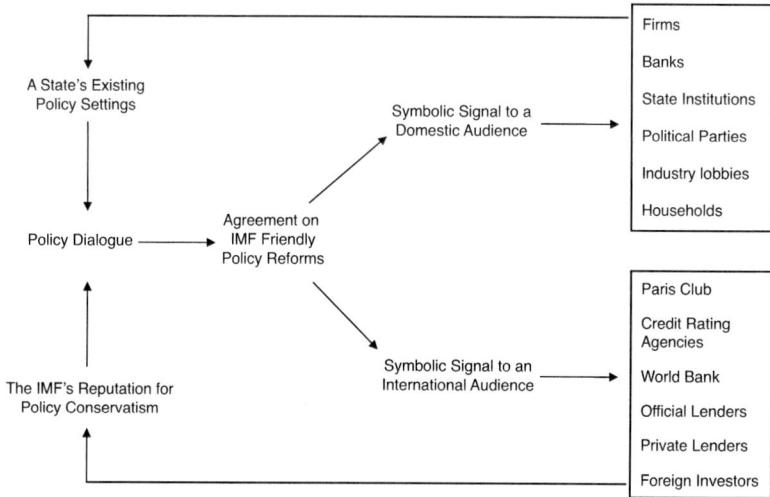

Figure 1.1   The Formation of IMF-Friendly Policy Reforms and Reputational Constraints

sented in both audiences is by no means exhaustive, but helps to illustrate the range of different actors at the international level and the domestic level whose behavior might be influenced by the quality of a state's relationship with the IMF. Figure 1.1 also shows a circuit of policy reform formation whereby the expectations of international audiences create incentives for the IMF to act in a way that remains consistent with its reputation in order to garner international support for its loan programs in strategic games over policy efficacy with national officials. That is, while the IMF's reputation provides it with an important institutional resource, it also places constraints on its scope for action because key actors in the global political economy may sanction deviant behavior that does not correspond with their expectations by withholding international support, such as additional external financing for a state under an IMF loan program.

Strategic games over policy efficacy

Whether the IMF's policy advice and loan programs actually exert an independent causal effect on inflation rates and budget deficits in the countries it deals with is important, but this is not the main point here (cf. Vreeland, 2003a: 158–9; Bird, 2002a: 809–10). What may matter more is whether the various actors involved believe that the IMF's intervention will help to ensure a greater degree of domestic certainty and will mitigate policy risk. Even more important is whether they act on this belief by extending loans, rescheduling debt, raising a country's credit rating, and increasing capital flows (or at least not withdrawing capital). Because actors may make these decisions before the economic outcomes of an IMF-sponsored reform program are apparent, they rely on an expectation that the IMF will act in accordance with its institutional reputation. Furthermore, the IMF itself believes that its involvement with a country's policy settings will be consequential for international audiences. As the UK executive director at the IMF, David Peretz, argued in an Executive Board debate over a staff report that assessed Russia's economic challenges in 1993, a full loan program with the IMF 'is the best way to unlock further financial flows – not only official flows but also, and perhaps more important, flows of finance and inward investment from the private sector' (IMF, 1993a). At both the Executive Board level and among the Fund staff, the assumption that the IMF's actions are consequential for a host of other public and private actors is built into its decisionmaking process and the formulation of its advice on institutional change. But this causal chain runs both ways, and although the symbolic importance of the IMF's actions for a range of other actors might amplify its influence many times over, it also operates as a potential constraint on its behavior.

While the IMF has scope to use its own initiative, the success of its actions will often rely upon its initiatives receiving the support of other powerful actors in the world economy. Moreover, the IMF's influence over institutional change in target states – and the scope of its independence from major shareholders – varies over time and depending on the context in which it seeks to act. Because the IMF's own financial resources have dwindled relative to global trade and capital flows, the involvement of both private and official 'supplementary financiers' has become essential to the success of the IMF's lending programs (Gould, 2003). The notion that the IMF is neither wholly autonomous nor dependent on its leading member states but is a semi-autonomous agent reinforces the need to 'bridge the rationalist-constructivist divide' in the field of International Political Economy in order to develop a comprehensive understanding of the influence and the behavior of international organizations as actors in their own right. Doing so is not a straightforward matter of asking 'who is in the driving seat?' steering the IMF's behavior, but also involves probing the domestic political conditions in which the IMF is able to 'get the car to start' in the first place.

The focus here is not simply on the IMF-member state relationship conceived as a strategic game over policy conditionality, with actor A (the IMF) trying to establish the material incentives that will cause actor B (the member state) to comply by offering policy concessions. This book explores how the IMF has attempted to gradually cultivate new intellectual frameworks among key state actors in postcommunist economies, which might generate the ideational conditions for achieving and sustaining IMF-friendly institutional change. This process centers on the politics of ideas, and involves a series of repeated strategic games over policy efficacy, with the IMF attempting to diffuse new policy norms to national officials through the provision of material incentives coupled with intellectual persuasion.

Changing the prevailing economic ideas in a country is a crucial part of the IMF's role. While formal changes to a state's policy settings may produce evidence of reform success in the short term, this can easily result in reform failure over time in the absence of broader ideational changes. As James (1996: 133) observes in his comprehensive history of the IMF and its member states, 'The likelihood of a long-term success is greatest when a common framework for analysis is established'. While James sees potential for the IMF to play a major part in the formation of a state's economic policies through the provision of material support for policy shifts, he views the IMF as having an even greater impact as a ready source of ideas and information. We can think of this distinction as the difference between a headline change in *policy* – which might easily be reversed – and a gradual change in *policy orientation*, which can be expected to have a more enduring effect.

Using Stern and Ferreira's (1997) characterization of the World Bank, we can understand the IMF's role in this regard as that of an *intellectual actor*, which seeks to persuade national officials into a common way of thinking about economic policy. This is compatible with Oran Young's (1991: 288) notion of intellectual leadership. While Young (1991: 298) suggests that only individuals can be 'intellectual leaders', this book argues that the IMF also relies on the power of ideas to shape how national officials think about economic challenges and how they understand the range of policy alternatives that they might adopt to respond to them. The transmission of ideas from the IMF can be bolstered when the IMF lessens the potential transition costs of adopting its advice for a switch in economic strategy by extending loans, similar to Young's (1991: 289) concept of 'structural leadership' when an actor is able to convert material resources into bargaining leverage. But external advice is unlikely to have an enduring impact if it is *imposed* through loan conditionality or other short-term material incentives. The IMF's policy advice is more likely to result in substantive long-term change when the IMF can develop a common approach with member states to understanding their economic problems and the design of policy solutions. This might be achieved by matching its advice with domestic perceptions of how to reason through uncertainty, which can potentially give the IMF's arguments greater legitimating force (Broome and Seabrooke, 2007: 578–9). The IMF has recently developed its own version of this argument (IMF, 2001a; Best, 2007), where member states are expected to be more likely to achieve performance criteria under IMF loans if the relevant actors within a country feel that they 'own' the reform program. While 'country ownership' might be enhanced by greater input from national officials in the design of loan programs, it also depends upon the IMF being able to persuade policymakers to adopt a common framework for analysis. This can be difficult for the IMF to achieve in the short life cycle of a single loan arrangement. As Young (1991: 298) suggests, intellectual leadership tends to be more time-consuming compared with other forms of influence, because 'new ideas generally have to triumph over the entrenched mindsets or worldviews held by policymakers'. Therefore, to establish whether the IMF is able to generate a gradual change in a state's policy orientation requires an analysis of the IMF's relationship with policymakers over time.

Moving beyond criticisms of the Washington consensus

Working under strict operational guidelines determined by the IMF management, the staff are the primary conduit for the IMF's relations with its member states – a fact which brings to the fore the intellectual frameworks and the organizational norms that the staff depend upon to perform their duties. Whether it is the United States, Sudan, Australia, or Uzbekistan, for the Fund staff a country is 'an object that is looked at in a particular way' (Harper, 1998: 183). This cognitive impulse was built into the IMF's mandate when it was established and has since been reinforced by the cultivation of the IMF's organizational identity as a bastion of objective technical economic expertise. The staff are not expected to view member states as cultural, religious, or military entities, but as *economic* entities that are to be comprehended through an analysis of their economic policies and institutions, and by tracing the causal relationship between these formal rules of the game and standardized indicators of economic performance to recommend how this might be improved. The intellectual frameworks used by the IMF to catalogue a pre-defined set of circumstances in their member states therefore constitutes an institutional discourse that can potentially become 'a creative part of the reality it purports to understand' (Keeley, 1990: 91), by rendering a country's economy legible according to criteria produced by the IMF's own analytical practices. Simply put, the methods through which the IMF tries to establish what is going on in the economic affairs of a particular country necessarily shapes the picture that emerges. When translated into policy advice that a state may act upon, this can have a practical impact on a country's economy by defining something as a problem, diagnosing the causes, and prescribing new forms of regulation as the solution.

To be clear, the contention here is that the IMF's intellectual frameworks provide a cognitive impulse that influences *how* a country's economy is looked at by the staff. The intention is not to portray the IMF's activities as simply expressing the ideological interests of a transnational social class, hegemonic state interests, or as generic outcomes that are determined by the prevailing ideational conditions among the major international financial institutions. This view is hard to sustain given their substantial organizational differences. The common tendency of IPE scholars during the past decade and a half to treat the idea of a consensus between the IMF and the World Bank as given ignores inconvenient empirical evidence that should constantly call into question such expedient charactizations (see Kang, 2007). Too often, IPE scholars have readily accepted as axiomatic the notion that the IMF goes about its business seeking to coercively impose a standard set of neoliberal 'Washington consensus' policies in each case. Such an approach risks exaggerating the IMF's potential to exercise direct influence over national policymakers, and misunderstanding how the IMF works by excluding analysis of its organizational culture and internal policy debates. Actions within the physical corridors and meeting rooms of the IMF inform what I call the *policy reform corridor* just as much, if not more, than decisions taken in the executive boardroom.

Furthermore, sweeping criticisms of the IMF and the World Bank for promoting 'Washington consensus' policies risk treating the putative consensus as an independent variable that explains political outcomes, rather than seeing this as a political outcome itself that needs to be specified and explained. This can create a blind spot that prevents scholars from examining actions of the IMF or the World Bank that do not fit comfortably within a 'Washington consensus' framework. Among other things, this might diminish our capacity to explain change within the organizations. In short, taking the notion of the 'Washington consensus' as an axiomatic explanatory variable risks ignoring the importance of everyday contests over ideas between and within the organizations, as well as between the IFIs and their member states – and thus presents a static view of what might actually be a dynamic and changing terrain. At issue is not whether the IMF and the World Bank generally promote policies that could be accurately characterized as 'economic liberalism'. Rather, the point is that within this broad field of apparent theoretical consensus are crucial debates over policy alternatives that can have significantly different political and economic outcomes (see Crouch, 2007: 262), debates that play out in diverse ways at different times and in different contexts.

Seeing like the IMF

Rather than engaging in the binary debate between critics who see the IMF inappropriately pushing one-size-fits-all 'Washington consensus' policies and defenders who argue that the IMF has been made a political scapegoat for the inconsistent policy choices of national elites, we should instead aim to provide a more nuanced and context-sensitive analysis of how the IMF operates. Borrowing from James C. Scott's work on the policy actions that flow from how states 'see' their societies (1998: 3), how the Fund staff in turn 'see' their member states impinges upon the scope and content of their advice for economic policy reform and institutional change. These effects may be part-and-parcel of the contemporary activities of international organizations, but they are not manifested in uniform ways. Studying how they play out can therefore provide us with an additional 'piece of the puzzle' in seeking to understand the role that the IMF performs in the global political economy. How, then, do the Fund staff's intellectual frameworks and organizational norms work in practice in their policy dialogue with member states?

The most obvious instances of policy dialogue between the IMF and member states are staff missions to national capitals (and in some cases to other major metropolitan centers) to meet with public servants, politicians, and, increasingly, a variety of domestic interest groups. Contemporary staff missions to member states involve both the area department desk officer and division chief who are responsible for the country, in conjunction with staff from relevant functional departments (Harper, 1998: 108). Ideally, this process combines the institutional memory and country-specific knowledge that is 'stored' in the area departments (supplemented by the IMF's resident represent-ative in a country, where they exist) with the more generic technical expertise of the functional departments.

When abstract interpretive frameworks are used to understand a particular country this will crowd out local knowledge (Woods, 2006: 54–5). Because each country has its own specific economic circum-stances, the lack of local knowledge can undermine whatever advantages the use of general policy blueprints or cognitive maps for economic reforms may have for the operational efficiency of the IMF. In parti-cular, this rarefied approach may decrease the domestic legitimacy of reforms and consequently diminish the likelihood of desired policy changes being achieved and then sustained over time. Moreover, the apparent efficiency benefit gained from standardized solutions might instead produce new problems for a country where policies are not tai-lored to fit local circumstances, and could result in the failure of formal policy shifts to be translated into behavioral changes in practice. While scholars have suggested that IMF programs need to become more customized and context-sensitive to increase their legitimacy in the eyes of member states (Seabrooke, 2007b; Beeson and Broome, 2008; cf. Best, 2007), such arguments presume that the Fund staff and national officials do in fact disagree. What may be more important in terms of understanding the IMF's influence is to examine the areas where policymakers such as ministry of finance and central bank officials are able to reach agreement on policy reforms with the IMF.

How valid are the widespread criticisms that Fund staff adhere to a homogenous intellectual framework? Research conducted through content-analysis of internal IMF documents and interviews with staff has suggested that individuals recruited to the IMF quickly become socialized into a technocratic and intellectually homogenous approach to economic policy, based on a narrow set of intersubjective under-standings about how national economies work and how they *should* work (Momani, 2005a: 155–6, 2005b: 169–70). Moreover, the formal organizational structure of the IMF provides bureaucratic incentives that encourage intellectual conformity, because individual staff mem-bers face less risk to their careers when something goes wrong if they are operating within a uniform intellectual template (Woods, 2006: 63). Intersubjective agreement among Fund staff on how to com-prehend and define economic problems – and what policy actions to recommend to states as appropriate solutions – also allows them to represent IMF surveillance and advice as the objective application of universal rules for sound economic management (Barnett and

Finnemore, 2004: 68–9). While the input from area departments means that this might not quite represent the 'cookie cutter' approach to policy design that some critics of the IFIs have alleged (Xu, 2005: 660; Boone and Henry, 2004: 357), framing staff advice in terms of the diffusion of universally valid economic policy 'best practice' has numerous benefits for the IMF.

Framing their policy advice as 'world's best practice' enables Fund staff to identify common economic problems across different national economies, and to link a diagnosis of the causes of a problem with a generic prescription for policy solutions. There is a clear efficiency advantage for the IMF in being able to deploy generic policy solutions rapidly in a crisis, rather than assuming that each economy is fundamentally different and designing more time-consuming reforms from scratch. Another possible advantage is that advocating similar policy advice may help the IMF to seem fair and even-handed in its relations with member states. Official 'uniformity of treatment' by the staff for all its member states is one of the primary ways that the IMF claims procedural legitimacy for its activities (Cottarelli, 2005: 19). But even if this was achieved in practice, which evidence from the IMF's early and more recent history suggests is not the case (Best, 2005: 101; Momani, 2004: 895–8), *equal* treatment is not always synonymous with *fair* treatment from the perspective of the IMF's member states.

The claim that states receive 'uniformity of treatment' has become harder to sustain with the post-1970s emergence of developed countries as persistent IMF creditors, subject in most cases only to annual or biennial policy surveillance by Fund staff (see Momani, 2006; Broome and Seabrooke, 2007; Lombardi and Woods, 2008). Developing country borrowers that are subject to intensive surveillance and an expansive range of policy conditions therefore undergo a qualitatively different experience in their policy dialogue with Fund staff (with some states continuing to be subject to a higher level of surveillance once loans are completed through 'post-programme monitoring'). This creates *de facto* differential treatment for states depending on whether they fall into the borrower or creditor categories.

How the IMF sees its member states is also influenced by its strong emphasis on constructing objectivity via internal discipline. As Figure 1.2 shows, several other departments review the work of area departments to ensure that their policy dialogue with member states takes place within the framework of a 'single corporate line' presented by the IMF. Before a mission takes place, the mission chief submits draft terms of reference to the relevant functional departments for review, incorporates their feedback, then submits the revised document to the area department director who passes it on to be cleared by the management. The IMF's negotiating position in its policy dialogue with member states is therefore the result of both a clear hierarchical chain of command and a set of internal review procedures that 'are designed to ensure cabinet-like solidarity after decisions are made' (Clark, 1996: 178). Following a mission, the draft of a staff report goes through a similar process, mapped out in Figure 1.3, which is sent to the Executive Board for discussion only after it is again cleared by the management. As Harper (1998: 129) has observed in a detailed study of the IMF's internal operations, back-to-office reports that are drafted once a mission team returns to Washington are important because they allow the IMF to 'talk *about* itself' reflexively (which can involve making excuses for negative outcomes, self-criticism, and self-congratulation) and because they enable the staff to 'talk to themselves in the future' by building institutional memory. Figure 1.4 maps out the hierarchical process through which the IMF generates its stock of 'country knowledge', beginning with the country desks that store the detail of the IMF's local information. The higher levels involved in the process – up to and including the Executive Board – retain greater scope of knowledge across countries.

Staff reports are intended to clearly lay out a state's current policies and to put them in a brief historical context, while each report also involves making a value judgment on those policies and often includes an evaluation of the authorities' *motivations* for specific policy actions

Mission Chief/Desk Officer Prepare Draft Terms of Reference ⟶ Area Department Director ⟶ Cleared by IMF Management

↓ ↑

Reviewed by Functional Departments   IMF Mission Terms of Reference

Figure 1.2   Generating an IMF Mission's Negotiating Position

Mission Chief/Desk Officer Prepare Draft Terms of Reference ⟶ Area Department Director ⟶ Cleared by IMF Management

↓ ↑

Reviewed by Functional Departments   Executive Board Discussion

Figure 1.3   Generating Back-to-Office Staff Reports

IMF Executive Board

IMF Management

Functional Departments

Area Department Director

Area Department Division Chief

Resident Representative
(Where Applicable)

Member State
Information

Country Desk
Institutional Memory

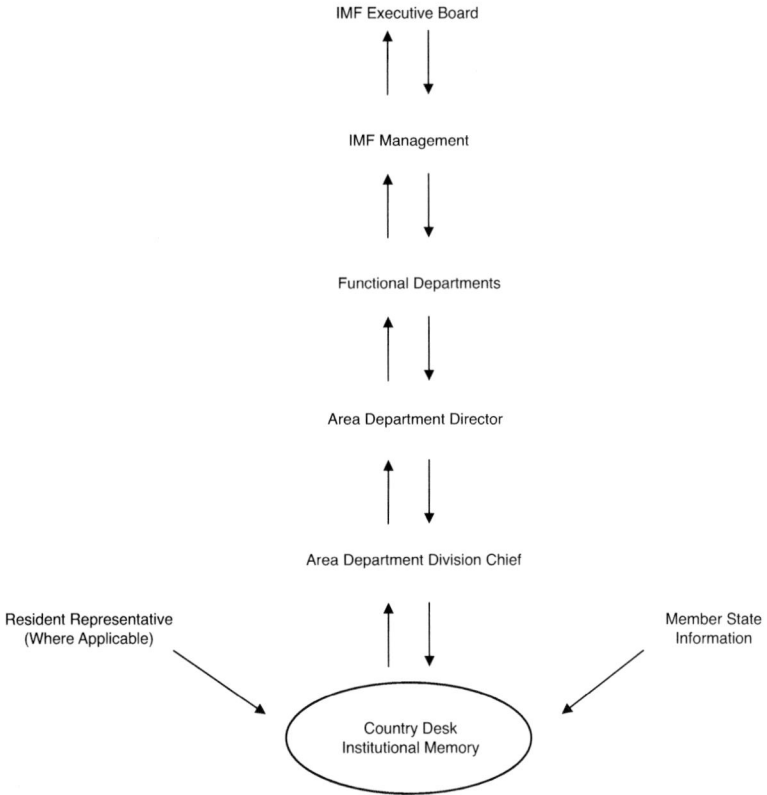

Figure 1.4   Generating IMF Country Knowledge

and their level of cooperation with Fund staff. This leaves a lot of room
for controversy over IMF country documents, especially those stemming from a staff mission. The IMF has sought to neutralize potential
disputes over staff country reports by balancing the need to produce
country-specific knowledge with its rigorous internal review process. In
the words of one former executive director, 'the IMF tends to view its
outputs as unique rather than as standardized products' but the
processes by which these outputs are produced are highly standardized
(Clark, 1996: 177). This means that by the time a country report
reaches the Executive Board for discussion, the IMF's internal review
processes should enable the staff from the area and functional departments as well as the IMF management to stand by the document as an
'objective' assessment of a country's current policy settings (Harper,

1998: 233). It can then be presented as an authoritative appraisal that communicates to executive directors how the IMF sees a state's economy, with a wider base of support than if it only represented the assessment of the mission chief and his or her staff.

IMF loan conditionality

Conventional wisdom suggests that the capacity of the IMF to exercise influence over its member states' comes primarily from its ability to enforce conditions attached to loans to extract policy concessions, at least in the case of states that seek to borrow from the organization. The IMF began extending loans to member states in exchange for specific commitments to implement policy changes and to achieve economic performance goals following the establishment of stand-by arrangements (SBA) in 1952. Each stand-by arrangement usually lasts for a period of 12 to 18 months, with loan conditions increasing as states draw on higher credit tranches. In addition to stand-by arrangements, IMF loan facilities have proliferated since the 1960s. While conditionality was not attached to the organization's early loans and was applied unevenly during the 1950s and 1960s, it was formalized as standard practice following a 1968 review of lending policies with the first amendment to the IMF's Articles of Agreement, which came into effect in 1969 (Boughton, 2001: 558). As new loan windows have been established, IMF conditionality has varied for the different lending facilities. Early compensatory financing facility loans and temporary lending windows such as the oil facility involved low conditionality compared with the high conditionality of upper credit tranche stand-by arrangements, the extended fund facility, and concessionary loans under the enhanced structural adjustment facility or poverty reduction and growth facility (Bird, 2003: 231–2). In addition, the IMF's flagship response to the onset of the global credit crunch in 2008, the Flexible Credit Line, involves an experimental shift from *ex post* conditionality to *ex ante* conditionality for states judged by the IMF to have a sound policy track record (Broome, 2010a). Differences in lending conditions have reflected the IMF's assessment of whether economic problems were temporary and resulted from external factors beyond a state's control, such as a brief decline in exports and crises such as the oil shocks of the 1970s, or whether they were structural problems that resulted from major deficiencies in a state's economic policies and its institutional arrangements.

As the Fund staff and numerous outside observers have pointed out, conditionality can provide a strategic political advantage for national actors in certain circumstances. For instance, borrowers with poor credit reputations may use the suggestion that the IMF has insisted upon particular policy changes to send a signal to investors that their policy commitments are credible (Dhonte, 1997; cf. Bird, 2002a: 802), or to signal to political opponents and the wider public that they have had no choice but to accept the IMF's policy reforms (Vreeland, 2003a: 13). In addition, ministry of finance or central bank officials might use the IMF's advice to strengthen their arguments for particular policy reforms in bureaucratic contests with other state agencies (Broome and Seabrooke, 2007: 578).

As discussed above, states may draw on the credibility of the IMF's institutional reputation for demanding tough conditionality and macro-economic restraint as a way to signal to international and domestic audiences that they have chosen to 'tie their hands' (cf. Fearon, 1997). While the IMF's conservative institutional reputation can potentially provide states with an important means of ameliorating domestic economic uncertainty and policy ambiguity, if this is taken too far it may lead to severe unintended consequences that impede the process of institutional change. On the one hand, a 'scapegoat' strategy risks provoking widespread civil unrest or 'IMF riots'. This has occurred on a number of occasions (see Vreeland, 2003a: 6; Bienen and Gersovitz, 1985: 730), but what may matter more is whether elites perceive that economic liberalization will increase the risk of political instability (Bienen, 1990: 715–16, 723, 727; Nelson, 1984: 987, 999). On the other hand, blaming the IMF might help to increase domestic acceptance of politically unpopular policy reforms if people perceive the changes to be inevitable.

Underlying much of the early criticism of loan conditionality from journalists, academics, and social activists was a largely unchallenged assumption that the IMF can successfully *impose* its policy conditions on states. The IMF has often been viewed as a neoliberal 'policy enforcer', which performs the role of a global economic policeman and uses coercion to ensure compliance with the international rules of the game (for an overview of the various criticisms of the IMF, see Willett, 2001). However, recent evidence suggests that IMF conditionality is in fact a blunt instrument that is poorly suited to achieving the introduction and the long-term maintenance of IMF-friendly policies. While loan programs are commonly associated with negative outcomes for a country's economic growth rates and its pattern of income distribution

(Vreeland, 2002; Garuda, 2000) most are not successfully completed, which is often a result of low levels of compliance that prompt program interruptions (Joyce, 2006: 342; Bird, 2002a). Rather than conditionality simply being an ineffective tool to ensure compliance, this suggests that conditionality only functions well when it goes hand-in-hand with an effective process of intellectual persuasion, which can potentially alter how national actors perceive their policy preferences. In addition, quantitative targets might help the IMF to realize a greater degree of policy change than would have been possible in the absence of loan conditionality, even if targets are not fully achieved on schedule.

IMF technical assistance

As well as loan programs, the IMF now engages in a wide range of training activities and other forms of support that come under the rubric of 'technical assistance', amounting to around 300 years of staff time annually at a cost of US$80 million (IEO, 2005: 8). These activities tend to receive much less attention and to be far less controversial than IMF loans as they are not perceived to entail the same degree of external coercion usually associated with conditionality. As the term implies, the IMF does not consider technical assistance to constitute a political process so much as a value-neutral 'scientific' one, which aims to bring about the transfer of knowledge among the IMF's member states based on what works elsewhere. In this sense, the IMF sees its technical assistance role as similar to that of an external service-provider, with the aim of providing specialized support to governments that wish to enhance the technical expertise of domestic bureaucracies through accessing the IMF's pool of comparative knowledge about policy reforms and institutional innovations elsewhere. Through staff missions, the placement of resident experts, the preparation of diagnostic reports, and the provision of training courses, seminars, and workshops, the IMF provides technical assistance to member states with the aim of strengthening both their policymaking capacity (i.e., human skills, the institutional structure of the state, and governance procedures) and the quality of policy design in specific issue areas.

In its capacity as a provider of technical assistance the IMF resembles less an agent of 'coercive' transfer of ideas and information and acts more as an agent of 'voluntary' transfer and persuasion (Dolowitz and Marsh, 2000: 11). Unlike loan agreements, for instance, the IMF does not usually link technical assistance to policy conditions and provides this support at no charge (IMF, 2003a). Governments therefore tend to actively seek technical assistance from the IMF rather than being driven into its arms by the need for emergency credit in a balance of payments crisis. Technical assistance may be a more attractive option for states than IMF loan programs that involve a higher participation threshold because they diminish decisionmakers' policy autonomy. Yet IMF technical assistance still involves an element of constraint, as Fund staff do not present country officials with a wide menu of policy options from which to choose so much as the diffusion of what the IMF sees as 'world's best practice'.

While the IMF's technical assistance has been criticized for resembling a colonial-era 'missionary' project (Stiglitz, 2002: 13), it also has the potential to be a positive source of support to help with the functional requirements of institution-building, especially if the IMF helps states to develop roadmaps to achieve goals that countries set themselves. However, the practice of technical assistance more often involves the IMF as a 'tutor' attempting to transmit the right ideas to its member state 'pupils' (Jacoby, 2001), which constrains the capacity for IMF technical assistance to usefully inform domestic policy experimentation. But because of the lack of explicit coercion involved in technical assistance, national officials retain more agency to utilize the IMF's advice to pursue domestic priorities than they might under a loan program. With the IMF's technical assistance including features such as scrutiny of domestic legislation and institutional practices against a template of 'world's best practice' constructed by its functional departments, this can potentially provide a more efficient means of socializing officials into the IMF's way of thinking about economic management and economic problems because it goes on behind the scenes and attracts much less attention than formal loan agreements. In addition, because acceptance of technical assistance recommendations from the IMF tends to be less controversial for states compared with loan conditionality, there may be greater scope for officials to achieve institutional change gradually based on IMF advice than through the headline-grabbing policy reforms that tend to be associated with loan programs.

The IMF's activities in this area nonetheless remain geared towards altering a state's economic policy orientation. For instance, IMF technical assistance can potentially foster institutional conditions that set the foundations for reform implementation in future loan programs. This can be achieved through the provision of economic training – priming officials to be more receptive to particular ideas by making them more familiar with how they work – or encouraging institutional changes that are essential for loan policy conditions to be effective, such as altering the statistical techniques that are used to measure economic indicators or overseeing the development of new legislation to establish central bank independence. While the IMF's provision of technical assistance to its member states free of charge utilizes only a fraction of its lending resources, it can be a crucial mechanism by which Fund staff reinforce the persuasion of states into adopting norm-conforming behavior that gradually cultivates the ideational environment necessary for a change of policy orientation.

Conclusion

Rationalist and constructivist approaches provide complementary insights for understanding the IMF's influence over the politics of institutional change in its member states. For the particular cases of postcommunist economic transformation examined in this book, these analytical perspectives suggest the following insights. Rationalist approaches suggest institutional change will be difficult for an external actor such as the IMF to achieve when the effectiveness of existing formal institutions rests on complex interactions with informal rules. These will prove resistant to change if individuals seek to maximize their own self-interest by engaging in actions that further worsen macroeconomic conditions, and undermine the regulatory impact of the formal rules of the game. A rationalist perspective also suggests the need to examine the bargaining resources that are available to elite actors as they compete amongst themselves in iterative games in order to understand variation in institutional outcomes between different countries. In addition, constructivist approaches suggest that intersubjective understandings help to inform local actors' choices as they set about implementing new formal rules promoted by the IMF, whereby the strength of existing intellectual frameworks might prompt policymakers to interpret policy challenges in unexpected ways.

While exogenous shocks to existing institutions may open a window of opportunity for actors to achieve systemic transformation, acute political and economic uncertainty can make it difficult for an external actor such as the IMF to achieve substantive institutional change. To alleviate domestic uncertainty and to help states attract external assistance to bridge financing gaps, the IMF seeks to enable policymakers to signal their policy credibility to international and domestic audiences by borrowing from its conservative reputation for demanding tough loan conditionality based on restrictive macroeconomic policies. However, the IMF's ability to be an effective reputational intermediary for states depends on its behavior corresponding with the expectations key actors in the international financial community have of it. While the IMF's institutional reputation provides an important underlying motivation for its actions – challenging those who see the organization as simply a foreign policy instrument of its leading member states or as a neoliberal policy enforcer – the IMF remains a semi-autonomous agent that relies on the support of other key actors in the global political economy.

On the one hand the IMF is subject to external pressures from its leading member states, while on the other it is engaged in a variety of activities that aim to alter the policy orientation of its borrowing members. At the same time it is an organization with its own unique internal culture, intellectual frameworks, and procedural norms. This chapter has argued that the IMF operates as an intellectual actor that seeks to persuade national officials to share a common framework for analysis, through its policy dialogue with both borrower and creditor states. The evolution of loan conditionality, technical assistance, and economic surveillance has provided the Fund staff with the main tools they now use to seek to reform member states' economic policies and institutions. While loan conditionality provides material incentives for states to implement IMF-friendly policy changes, it also affords opportunities for the IMF to transmit new economic ideas to national officials through the lengthy process of negotiation over policy conditions and through subsequent staff reviews of program compliance. Through these interactions the IMF engages in iterated strategic games over policy efficacy with national decisionmakers, which center on the politics of ideas and debates over the appropriate limits to the state's role in regulating economic activity. Depending on local circumstances, if the IMF can persuade national elites to experiment with new policies this can gradually enable the organization to influence how actors reconstruct their institutional preferences, through establishing a reform corridor that allows repeated opportunities to reinforce the persuasion of national policymakers into adopting the IMF's norms of 'good' economic management.

2
Expanding the International Monetary Order after the Cold War

One of the most important changes in the IMF's international role since the organization was created has been the gradual expansion of its activities beyond short-term balance of payments financing to encompass the diffusion of global normative standards for national economic governance. It is here that the IMF engages in repeated strategic games over policy efficacy with its member states, which center on the politics of economic ideas and – in borrowing states – the use of material incentives to create openings for intellectual persuasion. This role is carried out primarily by the Fund staff, who are the main conduit for the diffusion of economic reform ideas between the IMF and national policymakers, and whose intellectual legwork on 'best practice' economic policy norms inside the organization shapes the parameters of the IMF's advice to its member states.

During the last two decades in particular, the content of the IMF's policy advice to its members has aimed to foster a structural shift in the character of economic governance from discretionary action (where greater decisionmaking power rests with politicians) to rules-based action (where policy discretion is constrained through formal rules), which may also involve the delegation of decisionmaking authority to politically 'independent' bureaucratic actors. This shift in favor of rules-based techniques of national economic governance can be most clearly seen in macroeconomic policy, where the two core monetary norms that the IMF has sought to persuade member states to adopt include currency convertibility and central bank independence. The legal establishment of currency convertibility limits policymakers' discretion over the use of foreign exchange restrictions, while central bank independence aims to depoliticize operational decisions over interest rate changes and the growth of the money supply by shifting monetary authority from finance ministers to central bankers, and through setting explicit monetary targets for central banks to achieve. Both of these normative monetary policy standards imply an important change in the nature and use of political power with respect to economic regulation.

By the early 1990s both currency convertibility and central bank independence had become firmly established as fundamental policy standards for former centrally planned economies seeking membership in the contemporary international monetary order, the adoption of which the IMF saw as critical to the broader project of transforming the nature of state intervention in postcommunist economies and curtailing discretionary bureaucratic power. While the expansion of an international economic regime to encompass a large number of new member states is a challenging task at the best of times, it is especially difficult when this involves the inclusion of states with a legacy of economic governance based on radically different policy norms and values. This chapter examines how the expansion of the contemporary international monetary order after the Cold War to include the former centrally planned economies in East and Central Europe and the former Soviet Union placed a severe strain on the organization's intellectual and financial resources.

Despite the IMF's sustained efforts to diffuse global monetary norms to postcommunist economies as quickly as possible during the 1990s, the specific details of the IMF's policy advice were not homogenous across the region. In contrast to the common caricature of the IMF as an institution that set out to impose a one-size-fits-all blueprint for policy change upon centrally planned economies, both the Fund staff and the Executive Board acknowledged the need for different policy mixes in different cases of postcommunist reform. In addition, the IMF recognized that the chances for rapid policy changes in post-communist economies would depend upon what costs societies were willing to bear. While the IMF has been regularly criticized for doing too little to help the centrally planned economies transform their economic structures, it is clear that the organization strained to cope with the needs of so many new member states, and was forced to adopt innovative measures to try to adapt to this unprecedented challenge. This chapter helps to reveal the constraints on what the IMF could achieve in an environment of acute uncertainty with its limited resources and, in the short term at least, a lack of country-specific knowledge.

The contemporary international monetary order

With the adoption of the IMF's Articles of Agreement in 1945, member states formally accepted the principle that they should work together to prevent unfair currency competition and monetary disorder by pooling their authority to engage in permanent international monetary cooperation and consultation. As a result, the core original objective of the IMF was to maintain fixed, unitary, and non-discriminatory exchange rates in accordance with common international monetary rules (Gold, 1984: 1534, 1536). For the European and former Soviet centrally planned economies seeking to enter the capitalist international monetary order in the early 1990s, however, the monetary rules of the Bretton Woods era had been transformed by structural changes in the world economy and the policy decisions taken by states in response to these new economic challenges during the 1970s and 1980s.

The breakdown of the Bretton Woods system in the early 1970s and the emergence of 'stagflation', where capitalist economies experienced historically high inflation rates at the same time as high unemployment, precipitated a shift away from the international monetary norms of the 'embedded liberal compromise' (Ruggie, 1982; cf. Best, 2003). Until the 1970s, the postwar era had been characterized by national capital controls to allow for variation in domestic policy settings, combined with open current accounts and exchange rate coordination to provide a hospitable international environment for the expansion of world trade and economic growth. In contrast, the contemporary post-Bretton Woods international monetary order is characterized by the pursuit of low inflation and the deregulation of capital controls (Kirshner, 2003: 650–1).

The IMF's systemic role also changed in two major ways with the breakdown of the Bretton Woods system. First, the IMF became much more extensively involved with lending to developing countries, rather than being a revolving credit facility that was also used by industrialized economies when they experienced balance of payments difficulties. Second, the IMF lost its responsibility as a multilateral forum to oversee and approve adjustments in the par value of member states' exchange rates, which had established a formal constraint on states' domestic policies by committing governments to maintaining a fixed exchange rate. The IMF's role in maintaining the 'dollar standard' was superseded by a much weaker policy surveillance function that was sanctioned by an Executive Board decision on surveillance principles in 1977 and the second amendment to the IMF's Articles of Agreement that became effective in 1978. These changes have been described by Joseph Gold (1983) – a former director of the IMF's Legal Department and the chief draftsman of the first and second amendments – as a shift from 'firm' international monetary law to 'soft' law. This created a new international monetary order whereby states could choose from a range of exchange rate regimes to replace the par value exchange rates system, with the IMF expected to encourage voluntary policy coordination among its member states through regular policy surveillance and consultations.

With the ratification of the second amendment, Article IV section 3 of the IMF's Articles of Agreement now states that the IMF 'shall exercise firm surveillance over the exchange rate policies of members, and shall adopt specific principles for the guidance of all members with respect to those policies' (IMF, 2009). The reference to the IMF's new responsibility for exercising 'firm surveillance' over states' exchange rate policies was a linguistic compromise between France's preference for the language of regulation and management, and the US's preference for couching the IMF's new mandate in the softer language of oversight and surveillance (Best, 2005: 121). Their negotiating positions were underpinned by conflicting assumptions about how best to resume economic growth and international monetary stability following the breakdown of the par value exchange rates system, assumptions that were shaped by different economic circumstances as well as conflicting policy priorities. While European states sought to maintain national policy autonomy in order to sustain their existing welfare systems, key economic advisors to the US government argued in favor of liberalizing the international monetary order as a way to discipline states' fiscal and monetary policies through greater reliance on market mechanisms (Helleiner, 1994: 116; cf. the chapters in Panitch and Konings, 2008).

The international monetary order that the European and Soviet centrally planned economies sought to enter in the early 1990s had evolved through the twentieth century from a 'gold exchange standard' in the interwar years (see Simmons, 1996), to a 'dollar standard' under the Bretton Woods system, to what James (1996: 612) terms an 'information standard' in the post-Bretton Woods era. In these circumstances, the newly independent states of Central Asia were forced to be policy takers if political leaders wished to integrate their economies and financial systems with the international monetary order. Surveillance of its member states' economic policies now constitutes the central component of the IMF's global role. IMF surveillance 'is based on the principle that states are *accountable* to one another for the external implications of their internal policy decisions' (Pauly, 1997: 141). For instance, the revised Article IV obliges states to 'avoid manipulating exchange rates or the international monetary system... to gain an unfair competitive advantage over other members' (IMF, 2009). At the same time, the enforcement of states' obligations and their accountability to each other through IMF membership rests primarily upon the IMF's use of normative persuasion in the case of non-borrowers. In particular, the IMF's influence rests on its ability to appeal for all member states to conform to common standards of economic behavior in an era of financial globalization when non-conformist policy actions can potentially result in a costly response by financial markets (Best, 2003: 375–6). The IMF's contemporary surveillance of its member states' economic policies is therefore premised upon 'a continual exchange of information as a means of persuasion' (James, 1996: 274).

This clearly constitutes a much weaker source of leverage than the formal right to oversee the par value of states' exchange rates. But it stipulates a central role for the IMF as an intellectual actor that is expected to persuade its member states to accept common norms of behavior and a collective understanding of what constitutes 'good' and 'bad' economic policies. Member states are expected to take the IMF's surveillance responsibilities seriously, although they are not formally bound to accept its policy advice in practice precisely because of the greater degree of ambiguity that is inherent in the 'soft law' definition of their external economic obligations as members of the IMF following the second amendment.

Soft law is distinguishable from hard law because it refers to weaker binding obligations on states, less precise obligations, or when authority for interpreting and implementing a state's legal obligations is not delegated to an external organization but remains with states themselves (Abbott and Snidal, 2000: 421–2). In the case of the second amendment to the IMF's Articles of Agreement, the revised Article IV can be seen as: (a) weakening states' legal obligations to adjust their exchange rate policies in accordance with the IMF's recommendations; (b) creating ambiguity about the nature of their obligations with the compromise that the IMF would only exercise 'firm surveillance' over their exchange rate policies; and (c) formally relegating the responsibility to decide whether or not to act on the IMF's policy advice back to states themselves. During the 1970s, the balance of authority between the IMF and its member states over exchange rate decisions that had characterized the Bretton Woods system shifted firmly back towards exchange rate decisions becoming an internal decision for individual states, albeit with policy guidance from the IMF. While states' economic sovereignty in the contemporary international monetary order remains circumscribed by their formal acceptance of mutual obligations to each other through their membership in the IMF, the IMF's authority is exercised in a much more indirect and ambiguous fashion than it was under the Bretton Woods system, with the organization instead assuming a greater role as a diffuser of global economic policy norms.

The political economy of central bank independence

Although it is not mentioned in the IMF's Articles of Agreement, in recent years the IMF has actively sought to diffuse the principle of making central banks legally independent of the government of the day among its membership. Both inside and outside the IMF, the contemporary conventional wisdom now holds that central bank independence will help to establish a state's monetary policy credibility in the eyes of key actors in their domestic and international audiences, although statistical evidence also suggests that central bank independence can contribute to a deflationary bias in a country's domestic economy (Simmons, 1996: 436). Governments now charge their central banks with the responsibility to carry out a range of key tasks that influence the overall direction of economic policy and domestic economic outcomes, as well as shaping a state's international financial and monetary relations (Maxfield, 1994). These functions can include influencing market interest rates by controlling the supply of money to the domestic economy, managing the payments system and foreign exchange reserves, maintaining financial stability through supervision of commercial banks and by acting as a lender of last resort, determining the exchange rate, and functioning as banker to the government.

During the last two decades, monetary policy elites, private financial actors, international organizations such as the IMF, the World Bank, the Organization for Economic Cooperation and Development (OECD), and the Bank for International Settlements (BIS), as well as governments the world over have increasingly accepted the idea that central banks should be legally independent from governments (Hall, 2008; Marcussen, 2005). The concept of central bank independence from national governments comprises at least three component parts: personnel independence; financial independence; and policy independence (either in setting monetary policy goals or in choosing the instruments to achieve those goals, or both) (Eijffinger and Haan, 1996: 2–3). The degree of a central bank's personnel independence includes the legal methods by which central bank governors are appointed by their political masters, how long they serve, and the circumstances under which governments can dismiss them. Financial independence involves the nature of a central bank's budgetary autonomy from the government. Policy independence is determined by the extent and nature of a government's influence over monetary policy, whether the central bank has control over the setting of policy goals and the choice of monetary instruments, the central bank's performance incentives, and the limits on central bank financing of budget deficits (Bernhard et al., 2002: 696, 705).

As the idea of central bank independence has traveled the globe, a large number of states during the 1990s changed the legislation underpinning their central banks to grant them greater autonomy from governments (see Marcussen, 2005). The core of the argument for increasing central bank independence is that governments will seek to use monetary policy for short-term political gain at the expense of creating medium- and long-term economic problems such as high inflationary expectations. For example, monetary policy settings may be geared towards stimulating the economy in order to secure electoral support, or as a way to allocate financial resources to favored industries or specific firms. This is the crux of the 'time-inconsistency' problem: although governments want economic actors to believe that their commitment to price stability over the long term is credible, politicians often have strong short-term incentives for influencing monetary policy in ways that aggravate inflation. Proponents expect central bank independence to deliver lower levels of inflation that will benefit all members of society, which will underpin stronger and more stable macroeconomic performance that might otherwise be jeopardized by the short-term interests of politicians (for a critical appraisal of the argument that central bank independence can solve the time-inconsistency problem, see Bibow, 2004).

The logic of this argument suggests that politicians need to find a way to demonstrate to economic actors that their commitment to low inflation is credible, and that only an effective signal of credibility will alleviate people's inflationary expectations. The time-inconsistency problem rests on the assumption that central bankers and politicians such as ministers of finance have contrasting preferences, which prompt the latter to be more inflation-friendly and the former to be more inflation-averse. As Forder (2000: 168) has noted in a review of the central bank independence literature, the idea that greater central bank autonomy enhances the credibility of a state's monetary policy has become a crucial part of the argument for increasing central bank independence. Put another way, the attraction of the argument for devolving power over monetary decisions from politicians to technical experts does not rest on incontrovertible evidence that they will do a better job, but rather relies on the recognition that there is a widespread belief shared among monetary policy experts and private financial actors that they will do a better job. Proponents of central bank independence therefore assume that there is a significant symbolic advantage to be gained from taking politicians out of the equation. Indeed, critics have argued that an increasing number of governments have chosen to delegate monetary authority to central banks not to achieve the perceived material benefit of low inflation *per se*, but because of the 'legitimising and symbolic properties' that make central bank independence an attractive institutional innovation for states to adopt (McNamara, 2002: 48).

The relationship between the symbolic and the material factors driving central bank independence is especially salient in terms of the spread of central bank independence among developing and former communist countries. At a statistical level, economists have established that legal central bank independence does not generally correlate with low inflation in developing economies and postcommunist economies (Mas, 1995: 1645). While this may seem to support the argument that some countries have adopted legal central bank independence predominantly for its symbolic value or as a response to external pressure from the IMF, the evidence does not necessarily prove that this is the case, but rather suggests that other variables also intervene. For example, one study has suggested that the effectiveness of central bank independence in former communist countries may be highly dependent upon both the development of an effective legal environment, with formal rules that economic actors largely accept, and the extent of economic liberalization in general (Cukierman et al., 2002: 251). Broad compliance with the formal rules of the game is an especially important factor shaping the impact of central bank independence, because the drive for *de facto* rather than simply *de jure* central bank autonomy depends on acceptance of a form of 'economic constitutionalism' where key state institutions are split off and insulated from political decisionmaking. As Chapter 3 discusses in detail, the politics of money in post-Soviet states in the early 1990s did not represent a favorable environment in which to achieve *de facto* central bank independence, due to the breakdown of existing formal institutions as well as the salience of informal rules and practices. In a context where formal monetary rules lack legitimacy among both elites and wider society, governments may follow the IMF's advice and establish a strong form of *de jure* central bank independence that means little in practice.

The political economy of current account convertibility

Both central bank independence and current account convertibility have important consequences for the exercise of political and economic power within a particular society. Convertibility, which previously referred to the right to exchange a particular currency for gold at a given rate under the gold standard, is now commonly defined as 'the right to convert freely a national currency at the going exchange rate into any other currency' (Guitián, 1996: 22). Among other things, current account convertibility circumscribes the discretionary use of foreign exchange earnings by governments to allocate financial resources to preferred industries. Different degrees of convertibility define who is legally permitted to exchange a country's currency, and the economic purposes for which a currency is permitted to be exchanged. Full, unrestricted currency convertibility encompasses both current account convertibility and capital account convertibility. Current account convertibility permits individuals and firms within a country to access foreign exchange in order to pay for external trade transactions, including goods, services, interest payments, share dividends, and overseas travel. Capital account convertibility permits a country's residents to access foreign exchange to pay for financial assets abroad, and allows non-residents to repatriate their capital overseas (Cooper, 1999: 89–90).

Many states initially continued to use multiple currency practices in the years following the establishment of the IMF, with 36 out of the IMF's total membership of 58 states using a form of multiple exchange rates in 1955. In large part, this was because an earlier attempt to establish sterling-dollar convertibility in 1947 had ended in disaster (Best, 2005: 66–9, 84). After over a decade of preparation, European states eventually moved to accept the principle of current account convertibility between 1958 and 1961. This followed the creation of the 'Euromarkets' – 'off shore' currency markets outside the control of the IMF which emerged in 1957 as a means to buy and sell US dollars in response to national exchange restrictions (Burn, 1999: 230; James,

1996: 151; Helleiner, 1994: 71–2). Because the ideal of open current accounts was at the heart of the 'embedded liberal compromise' that comprised the Bretton Woods system of par value exchange rates, current account convertibility gradually became less controversial than capital account liberalization and today receives strong support, especially from the IMF's industrialized member states (see Figure 2.1). Although capital account liberalization remains more politically senssitive than current account convertibility, an increasing number of governments have also been willing to liberalize their capital accounts in the post-Bretton Woods era (see Chwieroth, 2007a, 2007b; Abdelal, 2007), a trend which has been reinforced and promoted by the IMF's surveillance activities and its policy dialogue with member states (Leiteritz, 2005; cf. Moschella, 2009).

Governments may see the use of current account restrictions as beneficial to support particular developmental objectives or as a response to balance of payments shortfalls, but the IMF's view has always been that such policies are counterproductive and inhibit the proper functioning of foreign exchange markets. While the second amendment to the IMF's Articles of Agreement removed the formal obligation for states to maintain a par value for their currency, it preserved the obligation under Article VIII for states to maintain an open current account as well as a unified exchange rate system. Article VIII commits members of the IMF to uphold two main rules in this regard. First, Article VIII section 2(a) stipulates that 'no member shall, without the approval of the IMF, impose restrictions on the making of payments and transfers for current international transactions'. Second, Article VIII section 3

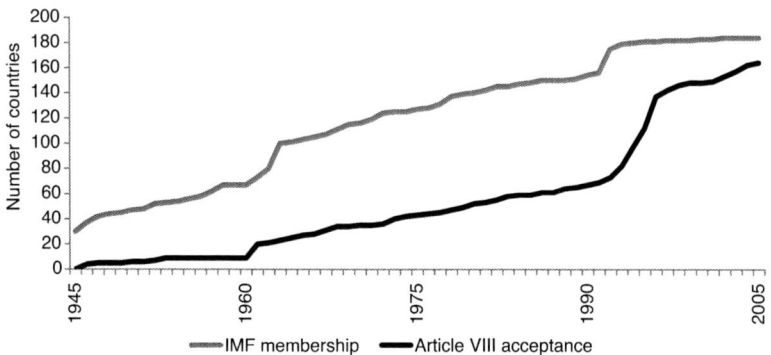

Figure 2.1   IMF Membership and Article VIII Acceptance

stipulates that no member state shall engage in 'any discriminatory currency arrangements or multiple currency practices... except as authorized under this Agreement or approved by the IMF' (IMF, 2009). Accepting 'Article VIII status' in the IMF is a voluntary choice for states, and policymakers are able to continue to maintain existing restrictions and currency practices that are in place when a country joins the IMF for an unspecified transition period. This is formally permitted under Article XIV section 2 of the Articles of Agreement, which allows each state to 'maintain and adapt to changing circumstances the restrictions on payments and transfers for current international transactions that were in effect on the date on which it became a member'. The same section nonetheless commits states to 'withdraw restrictions... as soon as they are satisfied that they will be able, in the absence of such restrictions, to settle their balance of payments' (IMF, 2009).

Despite this allowance for national discretion, the IMF actively seeks to persuade states to change their monetary behavior in order to shift them from maintaining restrictions under Article XIV towards accepting Article VIII status as quickly as possible. It is important to note, however, that a state's acceptance of Article VIII status does not necessarily mean that there are no current account restrictions in place. The Articles of Agreement explicitly give the IMF the power to approve temporary restrictions in certain circumstances, while some member states have occasionally introduced restrictions in violation of their Article VIII obligations without the IMF's approval. The IMF has sought to encourage states to accept their Article VIII obligations only when: (a) they no longer have restrictions that would require the IMF's approval under Article VIII; and (b) they are satisfied that they are unlikely to need to adopt such restrictions in the future. This reflects a desire within the IMF for the acceptance of Article VIII status to be seen as 'a public commitment on the part of the authorities to deal with balance of payments problems in future through appropriate adjustment policies (including exchange rate action) and financing rather than through recourse to restrictive exchange measures' (Galbis, 1996: 45–6). Simmons's (2000: 599) large-*n* research on when states choose to commit to the obligations of Article VIII also suggests that the ability of states to comply with the norms of current account liberalization in the future is an important factor in the decision to shift to Article VIII – states do not take the decision lightly. If the IMF encouraged states to accept their Article VIII obligations while they maintained policies that would require the IMF's approval, or when they were likely to reintroduce exchange restrictions, Article VIII status would carry less weight as a mechanism for the IMF to maintain compliance with the principle of current account convertibility, or as a signal of credibility to a state's wider international and domestic audiences.

Currency reform in postcommunist economies

Even before major market-based reforms in the former centrally planned economies were underway, external observers viewed currency reform, and in particular the establishment of currency convertibility, as an essential component of the transition to a market economy in East and Central Europe and the Soviet Union. At a conference on currency convertibility and economic liberalization in communist countries held in Vienna in January 1991, co-sponsored by the influential US-based think-tank, the Institute for International Economics and the Austrian central bank, participants emphasized the importance of establishing currency convertibility as a way of linking transition economies to the world economy (see the chapters in Williamson, 1991). One of the participants at the conference was Jacques Polak, the distinguished former executive director and staff member of the IMF who developed the organization's theoretical model for analyzing balance of payments problems, and who worked as an economist for the League of Nations in the interwar period. Polak (1991: 22) argued that currency convertibility would aid the process of transition by subjecting domestic economic producers to international competition, and by importing world market prices for goods to replace the administrative control of prices. This argument was based on the assumption that, despite the initial economic and social costs that would be involved, a rapid move towards establishing currency convertibility would force an adjustment from the distorted price structure in communist economies to the 'rational' price conditions in the world economy (Bofinger, 1991; Asselain, 1991). An additional argument in favor of the rapid establishment of currency convertibility was that it would circumscribe the potential for political authorities to distribute foreign exchange to preferred industries and firms, and would help to constrain the allocation of credit based on informal personal connections (Bomhoff, 1992: 454–5).

By the second half of the 1990s, it was common for external observers to contrast the length of time that it had taken West European economies to establish full current account convertibility after the end of WWII with the rapid moves that postcommunist states had taken towards convertibility. In the European centrally planned economies the change was particularly fast, with most countries adopting current account convertibility in the first year of market-based economic reforms (Stolze, 1997). The Baltic republics also rapidly established current account convertibility, in an attempt to take 'the fast track' from central planning to the world economy (Feldmann, 2001). In contrast to the post-WWII experience of West European economies, international actors such as the IMF encouraged a rapid transition to current account convertibility in postcommunist states primarily for two reasons. First, as discussed above, the international monetary order that the former Soviet republics and the European centrally planned economies sought to enter in the early 1990s was characterized by a strong normative commitment to current account convertibility. Because it had become a powerful symbol of economic openness and liberalization, postcommunist states were encouraged to adopt convertibility in order to send a credible signal to international and domestic audiences of the authorities' commitment to market-based reform. Liberalizing access to foreign exchange could also help to lock in policy reforms by making it costly for governments to change track. For example, if states were to subsequently renege on their commitment to convertibility they could expect to face major reputational consequences among key audiences (Simmons, 2000: 600–1). Second, a rapid move to establish currency convertibility in postcommunist states was widely seen as an important part of the solution to the specific economic problems they faced – especially the perceived need to force a shift from administered prices to international prices and the need to open centrally planned economies to external competition (Van Selm and Wagener, 1995: 30).

A new mission for the IMF

With the collapse of the Soviet economic system, the IMF faced an unprecedented challenge of overseeing systemic transformation and institutional change in a large number of economies at the same time. This required formulating advice on how to reconstruct economies of which the IMF had little or no prior knowledge, and in the case of the former Soviet republics advising on the construction of 15 new national economies from the rubble of what had previously been a single economic unit. It also involved overseeing systemic change in the world economy, with a rapid expansion of the international monetary order as the postcommunist economies sought to engage the international financial community. For their part, most of the centrally planned economies had little knowledge of the policies and functions of the IMF, while in Central Asia specialists in international affairs had been trained to denounce the international financial institutions as foreign policy tools of the capitalist powers rather than to see them as forums for multilateral economic cooperation (Gleason, 1997: 12). Throughout most of the Cold War period the majority of the Soviet bloc economies had little or no contact with the IMF. The organization continued to maintain a Central and Eastern European Division within the European Department, with staff occasionally conducting research on individual non-member centrally planned economies based on data that was available within the IMF (IMF, 1966), as well as researching specific policy issues common to centrally planned economies. For instance, during the 1960s the IMF explored the possibility of achieving currency convertibility and multilateralism in foreign trade within a communist economic system (IMF, 1965), and argued that there was no reason why IMF-friendly policies such as convertibility and multilateralism should be seen as exclusive to capitalist economies.

Nonetheless, throughout most of the Cold War era relations between the IMF and centrally planned economies – when they existed at all – remained frosty at best. The Soviet Union never joined the IMF, despite a Soviet delegation taking part in the deliberations at Bretton Woods at the end of WWII and signing the draft Bretton Woods agreements (Assetto, 1988: 62–3). Poland withdrew its membership of the IMF and the World Bank in 1950 following increasing tensions over access to the organizations' resources and disagreements over the country's economic policies. Other Soviet bloc countries that were members of the IMF during the Cold War included Czechoslovakia, which was expelled from the IMF at the end of 1954 after failing to consult with Fund staff before implementing restrictive currency reforms the previous year. Yugoslavia arranged loans from both the World Bank and the IMF throughout the Cold War, helped by the country's non-aligned foreign policy stance. In addition, Romania became a member of the IMF in 1972 after shifting its foreign policy away from Moscow (Assetto, 1988: 73–4, 86–7, 132–3, 144–5).

Several centrally planned economies began to express greater interest in becoming members of the IFIs during the 1980s, with China's representation in the IMF shifting from Taiwan to the People's Republic in 1980, Hungary joining in 1982, and Poland rejoining in 1986 (Boughton, 2001: 967). The Soviet Union also began to express interest in the IMF, and sent a delegation of senior officials from the State Bank of the USSR, the Ministry of Finance, and the Ministry of Foreign

Affairs on an informal three-day visit to the IMF in November 1988. The stated purpose of the visit was: (1) to learn first hand about the IMF's policies and activities; (2) to understand the obligations and responsibilities of IMF membership; and (3) to investigate the potential for establishing informal contacts between the Fund staff and Soviet officials and scholars (IMF, 1988). With the subsequent collapse of the Soviet system a rapid band-wagoning effect took place as the former Soviet bloc centrally planned economies, including the Soviet republics, sought to become legitimate members of 'international society' by joining the IMF and other multilateral organizations, which led to IMF membership increasing rapidly from 152 member states in 1989 to 178 in 1993 (James, 1996: 602–3).

By chance, the end of the Cold War coincided with the IMF's search for a new mission. The organization's role managing adjustments to the Bretton Woods exchange rate system had been superseded by the shift to floating exchange rates and regional currency arrangements from the early 1970s, and its role in the Latin American debt crisis diminished after the mid-1980s. With the Soviet system suddenly discredited as an alternative to a market-based economy, and with most of the centrally planned economies moving to build market mechanisms, the IMF was presented with a unique opportunity to oversee the expansion of the international monetary order and to solidify its international role as a key source of ideas for economic reform. Enlarging its membership also allowed the IMF to finally become a truly global organization.

The IMF's interest in carving out a new role for itself converged with the interests of major donor states that sought a vehicle to support and oversee structural economic reform in the centrally planned economies, preferably without having to provide large new aid outlays themselves (Zecchini, 1995: 117). While some observers called for large-scale direct financial assistance to the Soviet bloc economies similar to the post-WWII Marshall Plan for reconstruction in Western Europe, domestic political and economic considerations in major donor states meant that a similar-sized package would not be forthcoming. Moreover, because of its organizational identity as a pre-eminent source of technical economic expertise, the IMF was seen as capable of enforcing policy conditions and fostering an elite domestic constituency in favor of structural economic reform without attracting the same criticisms that could be expected if countries such as the US played a more direct hands-on role (Woods, 2006: 108; Rutland, 1999: 189).

Because of these propitious circumstances, the IMF quickly assumed a leading role in the early period of postcommunist economic reform as the primary international organization advising centrally planned economies on plans for a new economic framework. The IMF's central role was sponsored by the Group of 7 industrial economies, and was reinforced by the practice of cross-conditionality between multilateral and bilateral donors. In order to access financial support from other sources such as the World Bank, the European Investment Bank, the European Bank for Reconstruction and Development (EBRD), and major bilateral donors, policymakers in postcommunist states had to maintain good relations with the IMF and had to reach agreement with Fund staff on their strategy for economic reform. With IMF arrangements also necessary for states to access debt relief under the Paris Club process, the practice of cross-conditionality amplified the potential influence of the IMF's advice by increasing the symbolic and material benefits that would be gained by policymakers from establishing and maintaining a positive bilateral relationship with the IMF.

The IMF eagerly sought to expand into its new role as the chief international organization advising postcommunist economies on how to shift to a market economy, but in the process of taking on such challenging new responsibilities it risked what Pauly (1999) has called 'the perils of international organizational overextension'. In addition to lacking an in-depth knowledge of the Soviet system, the IMF was ill-prepared for the wholesale reconfiguration of state structures that countries had to undergo, in what constituted a historically distinct episode of political and economic transformation and state-building. The IMF's previous experience of advising on structural economic reform in 'distorted' market economies offered few lessons that it could use to model change in a context where the disintegration of the state-owned economy created a set of political, economic, and social pressures that worked against the likelihood of successful reform, especially in the short term.

At an elite level, the shift away from central planning stimulated a process of resource extraction from the state by 'predatory elites', creating a situation where the immediate interests of key players in postcommunist states were often diametrically opposed to the establishment of stable new state structures (Ganev, 2005: 435–7). In these circumstances the state risked becoming effectively privatized, thereby undermining the social bases for economic policy reform and institutional change and leading to the emergence of a 'rent-seeking state' (Van Zon, 2001: 75). For non-elites, who faced severe disruptions to their cash incomes and who struggled to maintain access to food and other basic goods, the imperative of day-to-day survival and the need to sustain a basic level of household welfare prompted individuals and groups to engage in everyday practices that further impeded attempts at structural economic reforms. With the breakdown of the existing economic system, non-elites who participated in the official economy that was the target of IMF-supported reforms were simultaneously active in non-monetized social economies, as well as illicit economies where cash payments avoided state regulations and taxes (discussed further in Chapter 3). These alternative forms of economic activity helped to provide an informal safety net for non-elites but worked against the achievement of macroeconomic goals – such as sustaining tax revenues, reversing demonetization, and increasing social spending to cope with unemployment – despite being wholly rational at an individual level as basic survival strategies (Rose, 1993: 420, 422). To illustrate the scale of the economic and social costs experienced by postcommunist states, the combined decline in official economic output experienced in the first five years of the transition by the 27 former Soviet bloc economies exceeded the contraction experienced by Western economies during the Great Depression (Bunce, 1999: 764). The precipitous decline of the official economy and the rising importance of social and illicit economies also impeded the analytical capacity of international organizations such as the IMF to evaluate what was going in postcommunist states. In particular, these trends made it difficult for Fund staff to quantify the impact of policy changes and to assess whether formal policy changes were being implemented in practice.

The IMF's monetary reform template

The IMF saw a complete overhaul of monetary institutions as vital to the goal of financial marketization in postcommunist economies. A staff paper prepared by the IMF's Research Department in November 1990 at the request of the Executive Board spells out the IMF's intellectual position on the shift towards currency convertibility in centrally planned economies and their integration into the international monetary system. The Research Department is the main unit of the IMF responsible for the production of the organization's in-house academic knowledge, and its research output has helped to shape the outcome of important policy debates within the IMF (James, 1996: 277). It is also responsible for 'keeping score' of major developments in the world economy by producing the IMF's flagship multilateral surveillance publication, the *World Economic Outlook* report (Boughton, 2001: 228). The Research Department staff considered the establishment of current account convertibility in transition economies important for achieving two purposes. First, it could help to reduce the costs of the administrative control of foreign exchange; and, second, because it had 'become a key symbol of openness and economic freedom', the establishment of convertibility would be 'important for the acceptability and credibility of difficult reform programs' (IMF, 1990a).

The establishment of convertibility for international transactions is not a one-way bet but implies both benefits and costs for an economy. Convertibility may help to increase a country's competitiveness and efficiency by exposing domestic producers to foreign competition and allowing firms to access foreign capital and intermediate goods, as well as expanding the range of choices available to domestic consumers. But it may also present a risk to employment rates and household incomes, and may exacerbate current account imbalances with a higher risk of macroeconomic instability. In the context of centrally planned economies that were embarking on a transition to a market-based economy, the IMF saw the potential benefits of convertibility in terms of helping to decentralize economic decisions over production and investment by increasing economic actors' reliance on prices rather than centralized production plans to coordinate the allocation of resources and economic behavior. The IMF also believed that convertibility would help blunt the market power of the large industrial monopolies that were common to both European and Soviet centrally planned economies through exposing them to international competitors, and would achieve efficiency gains through economies of scale by enlarging the export market available to domestic firms. However, Fund staff noted that in the short term convertibility might lead to high unemployment, a cut in wages, and a substantial decline in domestic production if consumers and firms switched to imported goods and services over domestic products. In a worst case scenario, Fund staff predicted that 'If the environment for domestic enterprises grows too harsh, the strains imposed on the population can become unsustainable, thereby undermining political support for a reform program' (IMF, 1990a).

In order to avoid the erosion of political support for market-based economic reform, the Research Department staff identified four preconditions before governments should attempt to establish currency convertibility. First, an appropriate exchange rate should be adopted to help maintain macroeconomic stability and to achieve a viable current account balance. Second, a country should have access to adequate foreign exchange reserves and external financing in order to endure possible balance of payments shortfalls or trade shocks that may be exacerbated by currency convertibility. Third, governments should have in place 'sound' macroeconomic policies – including fiscal restraint, the control of budget deficits, and an independent central bank that could stabilize economic activity and maintain monetary control through indirect market-based instruments. Fourth, transition economies must have instituted a program of price reform to enable economic actors to respond to the market incentives provided by changes in relative prices. The speed with which a government should establish current account convertibility was considered to depend upon how quickly they could achieve these four preconditions. For the Fund staff, this was not simply a matter of putting appropriate policies in place and engaging in institutional reform to help decentralize economic decisionmaking, but also depended on the level of popular support for a government's overall reform program (IMF, 1990a).

To help ameliorate the potential economic costs and political opposition that convertibility might generate, Fund staff outlined policy options for countries that might wish to adopt a transitional system that would help to establish some of the benefits of convertibility while allowing the government to maintain control over the amount of foreign exchange that was available for imports. The Research Department staff put forward two possible alternative currency systems that could be used for transitional purposes. First, countries could establish a licensing system whereby actors bid for the right to access foreign exchange, which could be funded by foreign exchange surrender requirements for exporters. A system along these lines, which would in effect create a multiple exchange rate regime, would regulate the balance between the amount of foreign exchange entering the country through foreign payments for the country's exports and the amount that was available for domestic importers to pay for foreign goods and services. Second, countries might quickly establish current account convertibility and a unified exchange rate while temporarily raising import tariffs to guard against a sudden and destabilizing switch in consumption from domestic products to imports. Currency convertibility combined with high trade tariffs, which Fund staff argued should be phased out according to a pre-announced schedule, would give domestic firms a temporary breathing space to restructure their businesses and to make new investments before being fully exposed to international competition, and would have the added benefit, from the IMF's perspective, of allowing countries to immediately accept Article VIII status (IMF, 1990a).

When the IMF Executive Board debated the conclusions of the Research Department's report on currency convertibility in transition economies in December 1991, executive directors voiced strong support in favor of the four preconditions for the successful establishment of current account convertibility. The main area of contention centered on the speed with which postcommunist governments ought to open their economies through currency liberalization. In particular, several members of the Executive Board emphasized the need for governments to make decisions regarding the timing of the introduction of convertibility based on their individual economic circumstances and the progress of their reform programs. For instance, J.E. Ismael, the executive director representing the Indonesian constituency, emphasized the need for the IMF to 'exercise due flexibility in urging members to move toward current account convertibility', in accordance with the stated goals of the IMF in the Articles of Agreement to achieve high employment and income levels and to promote exchange rate stability. To bolster this position, Ismael reminded the Executive Board that the IMF has the formal right to approve temporary currency restrictions where these are deemed necessary (IMF, 1990b).

Several executive directors, such as those representing the Netherlands, France, and Italy, argued in response that a rapid transition to current account convertibility would be the best way to aid the broader transition to a market-based economy. Renato Filosa, the Italian executive director, emphasized that establishing current account convertibility would help to send an 'internationally visible signal' that a country's authorities were committed to implementing market-based policies consistently in the future. Filosa argued against encouraging countries to resort to a gradual approach to current account convertibility, because the possible costs involved if reforms stalled would be much greater than the costs involved with a rapid move toward convertibility (IMF, 1990b). Striking a slightly different tone, the German executive director Bernd Goos argued that 'the adoption of a cautious and more gradual approach might be advisable' for transition economies. At the same time, his view – reinforced by the arguments from other directors – was that 'there was no risk-free or cost-free alternative to current account convertibility'. Most speakers suggested that capital account convertibility should come much later in the reform process, and directors reached a consensus view that despite the inevitable short-term disadvantages and risks involved, the transition economies did not have any viable alternatives available to them that would allow them to maintain inconvertible currencies in the long term (IMF, 1990c).

From the perspective of the Fund staff, systemic changes to the conduct and nature of monetary policy in postcommunist economies were essential in order for governments to communicate a clear commitment to market-based reforms to both external and internal audiences, as well as to help entrench a shift away from central planning mechanisms of economic governance within national policymaking communities. In response to several directors' requests for the IMF to tailor its advice to countries on the move toward current account convertibility on a case-by-case basis, Director of the Research Department Jacob Frenkel strongly emphasized to the Executive Board that 'The most important prerequisite for the success of a program of economic transformation was credibility'. Without establishing policy credibility, Frenkel argued, reforms such as the establishment of current account convertibility would be likely to result in policy failure. In this respect, he concluded that the authorities in transition economies would need to 'change fundamentally their attitude toward policymaking and how it was carried out' (IMF, 1990c).

In addition to currency reform, the IMF also believed that encouraging a shift within central banks from direct to indirect monetary instruments was crucial to the goal of achieving monetary restraint, as well as for the IMF's wider aims of changing the nature and scope of state intervention in postcommunist economies. Direct instruments of monetary policy – which tend to involve a 'hands on' regulatory role for monetary authorities – include credit controls, interest rate ceilings, and directed credits. Indirect instruments – whereby monetary authorities take a more 'hands off' role and rely instead on their ability to influence monetary demand and supply conditions – include the purchase or sale of financial securities by the central bank, central bank lending, credit auctions, and reserve requirements (IMF, 1994a). The IMF believed that the introduction of indirect monetary policy tools would help to overcome the Soviet legacy of centrally determining the allocation of financial resources without enforcing hard budget constraints on firms. However, the difficulties involved with shifting to indirect monetary instruments were particularly complex in the case of transition economies, which required far-reaching policy reforms and institution-building on a number of fronts simultaneously.

The primary benefit of using a system of direct monetary controls is that they can be used to determine the growth of credit in the economy and the level of domestic interest rates. The main drawbacks include the potential for direct controls to lead to an inefficient allocation of financial resources, the potential for controls to hamper competition among domestic financial institutions, and the possibility that banks and borrowers will find ways to circumvent controls. In contrast, the potential benefits of indirect monetary instruments include the introduction of greater flexibility, efficiency, and competition into a state's financial system by operating monetary policy through market-based mechanisms (Hilbers, 1993: 4, 8–9).

Although governments in industrialized economies had increasingly moved towards a reliance on indirect instruments of monetary control as they liberalized their financial markets in the 1970s and 1980s, the particular circumstances of postcommunist economies in the early 1990s meant that a successful transition to indirect monetary instruments could only be achieved gradually. Currency reform would have to be undertaken incrementally if political momentum and public support for market-based reforms was to be maintained. Compared with industrialized economies the postcommunist economies had much less developed markets, highly vulnerable financial institutions, and severe macroeconomic imbalances, all of which would mitigate against the successful implementation of indirect monetary instruments. Because of these important differences, as well as problems inherent to the politics of money in post-Soviet states that are discussed more fully in the following chapter, the successful introduction of indirect instruments of monetary control in the newly independent states of Central Asia was unlikely to occur in the short term after the breakdown of the Soviet system. Rather than facilitating a seamless substitution of market-based policy techniques for central planning mechanisms, Fund staff seeking to foster monetary change in Central Asia quickly found that this was an arduous process of trying to fit square pegs into round holes.

The demise of the Soviet Union

Some of the European centrally planned economies, such as Poland and Hungary, had a long history of policy experiments with economic decentralization. In contrast, the IMF faced a much greater challenge in the Soviet republics. First, the Soviet republics had undergone a much longer period of central planning than the East and Central European economies. Second, most of the Soviet republics had no experience with market-based reforms. Third, they were accustomed to having economic policy run entirely by Moscow, and it was initially unclear whether Soviet institutions would continue to guide economic policy or whether the republics would become independent. Finally, there were vital geopolitical interests involved with the possibility of the Soviet Union becoming a member of the IMF, and compared with many of the European centrally planned economies there was a greater likelihood that the organization's dominant member states such as the US would seek to directly intervene in its negotiations with the Soviet authorities.

During the second half of 1991, the IMF began providing policy advice and technical assistance at both the union and the republic level at the same time as the USSR experienced a range of sovereignty problems over the shape of future economic and political relations between the Soviet republics. The Fund staff had their first contact with the Central Asian republics during a mission to the Soviet Union in October 1991 with a visit to Kazakhstan. In his report to the Executive Board on the outcomes of this mission in early November, IMF managing director Michel Camdessus emphasized the need for the staff to organize early introductory visits to the other Soviet republics, in order to learn more about their local economic circumstances and to gauge the nature of their relationships with the central Soviet authorities. As an indication of the strain that the IMF's new activities were placing on the staff, Camdessus recommended a series of major short-term measures to cope with the increasing demand for the IMF's services. These measures included postponing a number of scheduled Article IV consultations, temporarily placing several countries on biennial consultation cycles, and shifting staff from other departments – including the non-European area departments and the Treasurer's and Research departments – to alleviate the increase in workload. Camdessus also called for the recruitment of additional Fund staff, seconding economists from member governments and from other international organizations, and hiring outside consultants (IMF, 1991a). This led to a surge in staff recruitment to the IMF in 1992 when the IMF almost doubled the number of graduate recruits to the Economist Program, and more than doubled the number of mid-career recruits in order to enlarge the pool of experienced economists, a trend which continued through 1993 (Momani, 2005b: 176). Later that same month the managing director reinforced the scale of the IMF's challenge to the Executive Board, noting that eight of the Soviet republics had made public commitments to design economic reform programs in consultation with the IMF in early 1992. Camdessus told the Executive

Board that 'with eight programs to prepare, the staff will almost be starting from scratch, except in Russia, in the sense of collecting economic data for the republics, establishing relationships with the key policymakers, and agreeing on economic programs with them' (IMF, 1991b). As this statement indicates, the IMF senior management recognized that establishing the conditions for IMF-friendly economic reforms in the Soviet republics was not simply a matter of presenting a fully-furnished model for policy change, but would depend upon building good face-to-face working relationships with local policymakers.

In short, the IMF's influence would depend on its capacity for effective *persuasion*. The notion that the influence of the IMF is conditioned by its capacity to persuade national actors of the merits of its arguments has been acknowledged by the organization itself, and has also begun to receive more attention in the scholarly literature on the IMF. For example, Woods (2006: 72–3) has argued that the IMF's success in influencing economic reform in its member states depends upon it finding 'sympathetic interlocutors' among a country's policymaking community, individuals who are willing to listen to what the IMF has to say and to put its ideas into practice. This does not simply involve the IMF seeking out officials who already agree with its ideas, but also fostering relationships with local policymakers that might encourage them to become sympathetic interlocutors, through a process of mutual learning, lesson drawing, and the persuasion of national policy elites into a shared way of thinking about economic problems.

Engagement with Russia was in full flight by November 1991, with IMF missions including staff from the Central Banking, Exchange and Trade Relations, European, Legal, Statistics, and Treasurer's departments as well as the IMF Institute. Missions also included representatives from the World Bank, the OECD, the BIS, and Eurostat, together with external consultants and staff seconded from member state central banks. Despite intensive engagement with Russia, however, relations with many of the other republics remained almost nonexistent. As the deputy director of the European Department pointed out to the Board, the staff lacked even basic information about the level of political support for economic reform in the individual republics apart from Russia (IMF, 1991b). The IMF began to realize that, if the trend towards separation continued, most of the other republics would face even greater difficulties than Russia when they were suddenly required to formulate macroeconomic policies that had been controlled by the Soviet authorities in Moscow and with which they had no previous experience.

As an initial step towards improving relations with the other Soviet republics, the staff conducted a series of brief missions during December 1991 to 'introduce the IMF' to the republics they had not yet visited. Events were moving fast, and with its staff and institutional resources under strain it is hardly surprising that the IMF struggled to keep up. At a meeting in Kazakhstan later that month, 11 communist party officials signed the 'Alma-Ata Declaration' announcing that the Soviet republics were now sovereign and independent and that 'the USSR shall henceforth cease to exist', and agreeing instead to set up the Commonwealth of Independent States (Gleason, 1997: 1). From the IMF's perspective this decision ended the uncertainty over whether the Soviet republics would re-establish a political union, but created new uncertainty over the nature of economic relations between what had suddenly become nominally-sovereign and independent states. As Michel Camdessus emphasized to the Executive Board in January 1992, 'In the area of monetary policy, it is painfully apparent that the republics are still feeling their way and do not have the institutional structures or expertise to design and implement an active monetary policy' (IMF, 1992a). In response, the IMF quickly made plans to send out new staff missions of around two weeks duration to discuss reform programs and IMF membership with policymakers in each republic. An exception was made in the case of Uzbekistan, where the authorities indicated a lack of interest in participating closely with the IMF, which foreshadowed the difficulties Fund staff would have in the future in their attempts to establish good relations with Uzbek policymakers.

Adapting the IMF to the post-Soviet transition

When the USSR was dissolved, the five Central Asian states of Kazakhstan, the Kyrgyz Republic, Tajikistan, Turkmenistan, and Uzbekistan had no previous experience of independent statehood and had only limited experience with economic management. Most of the important economic decisions for the Central Asian republics had been centrally determined in Moscow for the past 70 years. Moreover, policy experiments conducted elsewhere in the USSR during the Gorbachev era, such as in the Baltic republics and the Russian republic, had not been extended to Central Asia (Pomfret, 2006: 1–3). Predominantly agricultural producers, the Central Asian republics had been tightly integrated into a set of privileged trading relationships with the other republics of the USSR, exchanging mostly agricultural goods for overpriced manufactured goods and cheap oil and gas imports (Orlowski,

1993: 1007). The few manufacturing industries that were established in Soviet Central Asia had depended on the guarantee of state purchases and the extension of soft credit for their survival (Chavin, 1994: 161–2). These circumstances left the Central Asian republics with a very high level of trade dependence with the rest of the Soviet Union, and consequently in a poor position from which to build distinct 'national' economies. Although all five new states had identical formal political structures at independence, Central Asian policymakers faced the added challenge of imposing formal institutional change upon strong informal social networks that were accustomed to resisting attempts at top-down change by the Soviet state (Collins, 2006: 332).

The IMF quickly recognized that the process of economic transformation in the frontier economies of Central Asia would pose major new challenges for the organization. Unaccustomed to the complex set of problems this would involve, the IMF had to confront the cognitive and practical challenge of 'learning to learn' (see Haas and Haas, 1995). First, the IMF had to build a capacity to provide advice on day-to-day policy changes, as well as to help with the design of an overall grand strategy for economic transformation. Second, it had to provide extensive technical assistance to help policymakers adapt existing institutions or to build new ones in order to establish a new national structure of economic governance. Third, the IMF had to oversee a learning process to increase the level of understanding about market mechanisms among policymaking elites, through regular contact by staff missions and resident representatives as well as through the provision of economic training. The intended goal of these efforts was to create a reform corridor for the former Soviet republics, which would start with basic assistance on institutional design and crisis management advice and progress to more intensive cooperation to lock-in an IMF-friendly policy orientation. To respond to these challenges, the IMF implemented several organizational changes in an attempt to adapt its financial and intellectual resources to the unique needs of the former Soviet republics. Three of the main changes the IMF adopted involved measures designed to boost the organization's analytical, financial, and educational resources to foster market-based economic reform in the former Soviet Union. These included: (1) establishing a new area department dedicated to focusing on the former Soviet centrally planned economies; (2) creating a new temporary lending facility with low policy conditionality; and (3) cooperating with other international organizations to establish the Joint Vienna Institute to provide economic policy training to officials.

In an Executive Board meeting on 11 December 1991, Camdessus informed directors that he intended to establish a new area department drawn from units in the European Department to consolidate the IMF's work on the USSR, the individual Soviet republics, and the Baltic centrally planned economies (1991c). The creation of the new European II Department (disestablished in 2003) was unusual as it was the first that would initially deal entirely with states that were not yet members of the IMF. Because the IMF could not lend to states until they became members, in the short term it depended upon rhetorical action, policy advice, and technical assistance to shape the direction of economic policy in the newly independent states of Central Asia. As the director of the new department, John Odling-Smee, explained to the Executive Board in January 1992, the staff initially relied on the use of 'moral suasion' and intellectual arguments to influence the direction of economic policy in the former Soviet republics, rather than attempting to exercise more direct leverage (IMF, 1992a).

In a report on the design of reform strategies in the former Soviet republics in July 1992 (IMF, 1992b), the staff of the European II Department made it clear to the Executive Board that:

> ...the IMF must be <u>ready to adapt</u> its policy advice in response to unexpected developments. The enormous changes taking place in the societies and economies of the FSU [Former Soviet Union], the lack of experience of monetary and fiscal policy institutions, the weak statistical and information base supporting policy decisions, and the immature political institutions make the prediction of economic developments and the choice of appropriate instruments unusually hazardous. Mistakes, surprises and setbacks are inevitable, and changing circumstances may call for corrections in course along the way. Program objectives should not be cast rigidly, but should ensure that the process of economic transition maintains sufficient momentum for the FSU economies to achieve a return to stability and growth within a medium-term horizon.

Quoted here at length, this report indicates that the Fund staff with the primary responsibility for coordinating relations with the new Central Asian states recognized that they would have to adapt their advice to suit rapidly changing local economic circumstances. It suggests a recognition that the outcomes of policy actions would be difficult to predict, given the weak institutional capacity of the new states to design and implement macroeconomic policies and the uncertain political and economic environment in the region. Significantly, the above quote also shows that the staff accepted that unexpected setbacks would be an inevitable occurrence in the economic transformation of Central Asia, leading the staff to conclude that the policy benchmarks in loan programs should be flexible enough to maintain momentum for reform without setting the bar too high.

In order to foster the process of economic transformation and to encourage international economic integration, in early 1993 the IMF sought to devise a way to help the former Soviet republics cope with the severe economic shocks caused by the breakdown of existing trade, monetary, and credit relationships among the newly independent states. In the short term, most of the IMF's new member states were unlikely to develop economic reform programs that could be supported through its regular loan facilities. The IMF therefore sought to establish a temporary lending facility that would help governments to cope with severe balance of payments difficulties, and would constitute the first step towards developing comprehensive IMF-friendly reform programs.

Compared with standard upper credit tranche drawings or loans under the extended fund facility, the new lending window came with less strict policy conditions. The main qualification was the rather ambiguous stipulation that the IMF needed to be satisfied that states would cooperate with staff in devising solutions to their balance of payment problems and in formulating IMF-friendly policies that could qualify for financial support under the IMF's regular loan facilities. To establish whether member states met these qualifications, the IMF assessed economies on four criteria. First, the authorities were required to implement certain 'prior actions' in crucial policy areas, the use of which is discussed further below. Second, governments had to present a policy statement specifying their main macroeconomic objectives for the next year and expressing the intention to design a comprehensive reform program with the IMF. This policy statement also included an undertaking by policymakers not to tighten existing exchange or trade controls or introduce new multiple exchange rate practices. Third, the IMF required policymakers to move quickly towards putting in place a quantifiable quarterly financial program that could be monitored by the staff, which would enhance the IMF's ability to track changes in the growth of the money supply and credit allocation practices. Finally, policymakers had to adopt structural reforms aimed at facilitating the shift to market mechanisms, including price liberalization, the elimination of import subsidies, and exchange rate and trade liberalization. Under the proposed low conditionality loan facility, funds were to be phased in over two purchases, with the second purchase available after six months and subject to review by the Executive Board. Approval of the second purchase would be conditional upon a judgment of whether states had implemented agreed policy reforms and had maintained their commitment to cooperate with the IMF, which included making satisfactory progress towards a regular loan program (IMF, 1993b, 1993c).

In a low-trust environment, or when there is no history of contact between the IMF and national officials, Fund staff are often faced with a severe problem of information asymmetry because they lack sufficient knowledge to weigh policymakers' future intentions. To alleviate this problem, Fund staff commonly use the application of prior actions that states must fulfill before loans are approved to test the strength of policymakers' commitment to achieving IMF-friendly economic reforms, as well as to help safeguard the use of IMF resources. Prior actions therefore serve as a 'screening device' for the IMF, to help staff establish the credibility of a government's reform intentions before the organization commits financial resources to a loan program (Thomas and Ramakrishnan, 2006: 8). These constitute explicit benchmarks for states to achieve, and are often identified by Fund staff based on previous Executive Board discussions of a country's policy settings. At the same time, the use of prior actions also provides staff with an additional source of autonomy from the Executive Board, because they have the responsibility to define policy preconditions and to assess a state's compliance without requiring the Board's endorsement (Martin, 2006: 159–60). Insisting upon the implementation of prior actions provides a way for staff to get around the fact that policy reform can be a long and arduous process, which makes it difficult to achieve the IMF's policy objectives within the relatively short life cycle of a loan arrangement. As a 1996 report on the rationale for prior actions by the IMF's Policy Development and Review and Legal Departments makes clear, the IMF considers that the 'viability of most programs depends on certain policy measures being in place early in the program period'. Requiring governments to begin the reform process before a loan arrangement is underway is believed to enhance the chances of the program's success, and helps to increase the IMF's confidence in a state's policy intentions by demonstrating the level of 'the authorities' determination and political will to implement the program' (IMF, 1996a: 1–2).

The formulation of a timetable of specific prior actions that a state is expected to implement highlights once again the importance for states of maintaining good relations with Fund staff. While they are guided by previous Executive Board discussions on a country's policy settings, staff have the main responsibility for deciding on prior actions based on an assessment of the importance of a particular policy change, the feasibility of it being implemented before a program is in place, and a state's track record with policy implementation. However, the process of successfully progressing from prior actions to an IMF loan arrangement might simply involve states learning to use an IMF-friendly policy discourse rather than actually implementing policy changes in the way envisaged by the IMF. Unlike the strict quantitative performance criteria that are standard fare in loan arrangements, the staff primarily rely upon a state communicating to the IMF when prior actions have been implemented, although if prior actions include legislative changes documentary evidence of the new laws will usually be requested (IMF, 1996a: 2–3).

The main rationale for the relatively low level of policy conditions that were attached to the use of this new lending window was the need to balance the limited capacity of the former Soviet republics to design and implement rapid policy reforms with the IMF's desire to effect macroeconomic stabilization and institutional change (IMF, 1995a). Although the Iranian executive director, Abbas Mirakhor, questioned the need for a new loan facility when Michel Camdessus first brought the proposal before the Executive Board, most directors acknowledged a need for the IMF to develop a new form of assistance for the former Soviet republics (IMF, 1993d). The decision to establish a temporary systemic transformation facility to operate until the end of 1994 (later extended until April 1995) was subsequently adopted in April 1993 (IMF, 1993e).

Between April 1993 and December 1994, 18 countries borrowed SDR 3.4 billion through the systemic transformation facility. Although it was intended to play a catalytic role in facilitating other sources of external finance, a 1995 staff review of the systemic transformation facility found that the IMF's assumptions of the amount of bilateral and multilateral external financing that systemic transformation facility agreements would facilitate were often wide of the mark, leaving significant shortfalls that skewed the outcomes of the programs (IMF, 1995a). The systemic transformation facility did play a catalytic role in facilitating additional external financing for Russia, with up to US$10 billion of loans dependent upon the IMF's approval of a US$1.5 billion second tranche payment to Russia through the systemic transformation facility in late 1993. However, Russia's geopolitical importance relative to most of the other former Soviet republics in the early 1990s led the Clinton Administration to apply US pressure on the IMF to relax its enforcement of policy conditions, which softened the influence of the IMF's direct attempts to generate policy reform by delaying access to its resources (Stone, 2002: 128–9; Woods, 2006: 114–17).

A third way in which the IMF sought to adapt its organizational resources to the challenges of assisting economic transformation in the former Soviet republics was through the creation of the Joint Vienna Institute as a new international organization in 1992. As advisors who were on the ground in the former Soviet republics during the early years of independence have observed, a major problem facing local policymakers was that Soviet-trained economists had very little understanding of how market mechanisms worked (Pomfret, 2002: 122). The foundation of the Joint Vienna Institute established an important additional location for Fund staff to create a policy reform corridor that could help to gradually escalate the scope and intensity of market-based reforms in postcommunist economies, which complemented the bilateral technical assistance provided by the IMF.

The new organization was a joint venture sponsored by the Austrian central bank and Ministry of Finance as well as the IMF, the World Bank, the BIS, the OECD, the EBRD, and the European Commission. Since it was established in 1992, the Joint Vienna Institute has provided training to over 23,000 officials from former centrally planned economies. The organization has played an important role in the process of postcommunist economic transformation because the professional training individuals receive influences how they construct causal interpretations of how economies work, as well as how they conceive economies ought to be organized (see Broome, 2010b). While the IMF's technical assistance programs aim to encourage institutional change and the IMF's policy dialogue with national authorities aims to foster systemic change in postcommunist economies, the IMF sought to foster social learning and ideational change among individual postcommunist officials through the Joint Vienna Institute, as well as through other courses run by the IMF Institute.

Conclusion

The international monetary order that postcommunist states in Europe and the former Soviet Union sought to enter in the early 1990s was characterized by a strong normative commitment to the principles of currency convertibility and central bank independence. The IMF believed that the implementation of both major monetary changes would be a crucial part of the reform process, and would help to lock in the shift from central planning to a market-based economic system. Yet despite a clear preference for the rapid international integration of post-communist economies, the IMF's monetary reform template for transition economies was not simply a uniform blueprint for neoliberal reforms. Rather, Fund staff produced alternative policy strategies that states might adopt to guard against the severe economic costs that monetary reforms such as currency liberalization might entail, including the temporary use of high trade tariffs to give domestic producers time to adjust to changing economic circumstances.

During the 1990s, the IMF became a lightning rod for criticism of the policy failures resulting from the external advice given to states undergoing the transition from central planning to market mechanisms. Leaving aside for the moment the substantial domestic obstacles that the IMF faced in seeking to persuade policymakers to implement IMF-friendly economic reforms, however, the IMF suffered from severe organizational constraints that impeded its ability to do the job that member states expected of it. In response to these new challenges, the IMF created the systemic transformation facility as a new loan facility designed specifically to address the external financing needs of the former Soviet republics. The IMF also established the European II Department and collaborated in the creation of the Joint Vienna Institute to facilitate greater access to the organization's analytical and educational resources. While the Fund staff and the Executive Board recognized the need to tailor policy reform mixes to local circumstances, however, chronic staff shortages initially hampered its capacity to build the necessary country-specific knowledge that would make this possible. Staffing constraints also meant that the IMF had a late start in establishing working relationships with local policymakers in the Soviet republics, which would be essential for the persuasion of elites towards a consensus on adopting IMF-friendly policy reforms and institutional changes. These organizational constraints would prove detrimental to the IMF's ill-fated efforts to maintain a monetary union among the former Soviet republics in the wake of the Soviet Union's demise.

3
The Disintegration of the Ruble Zone

How money and credit are organized within a particular society and across societies has important implications for the institutional capacity of states, as well as for the life chances of the individuals who live within them. Because the right to issue and validate money provides an important power resource that can be used to expand national economic wealth and military strength, modern centralized states tend to place great importance on maintaining the privilege to control the organization of monetary arrangements within their borders (Dodd, 1994: 31–5; Cohen, 1998: 42–4). Moreover, because monetary arrangements influence how wealth is distributed throughout a society – as well as the extent of a government's policy autonomy from economic decisions taken by other countries – monetary policy choices continue to be regarded as sensitive aspects of state sovereignty despite moves toward the legalization of international monetary relations through the IMF after WWII (Simmons, 2000; Gold, 1983).

This chapter explores the regional context in which the IMF sought to persuade Central Asian policymakers to adopt IMF-friendly monetary reforms prior to and immediately following the demise of the Soviet Union. The political and economic environment in the region during the period in which the ruble zone common currency area was maintained was characterized by both a 'logic of appropriateness' and a 'logic of consequences'. Economic actors continued to act in accordance with extant social norms and relied on interpersonal trust for exchange, but these actions collectively helped to undermine macroeconomic stability. In these circumstances the politics of money became crucial to the process of institutional change in the ruble zone. This was a contest over economic ideas where the IMF's efforts to diffuse global monetary norms to the ruble zone economies failed to gain traction while the monetary union lasted, due to competing political pressures between the individual republics and ambiguity over the future role that Russia would play in the region.

The breakdown of Soviet monetary control

People's beliefs about money and ideas about how monetary rules should be organized have real effects. Monetary systems work best when money is commonly taken for granted as representing a 'true' measure of value, and when the system itself has strong collective legitimacy, but there is nothing natural about the contemporary uses of money in everyday life or the institutional frameworks governments devise to regulate such uses. Rather, the creation of money and debates over alternative regulatory frameworks and policy targets are intensely *political* processes at every step of the way. To borrow Jonathan Kirshner's (2003: 646) metaphor: 'Even if all the passengers on an otherwise sound plane don't think it will take off, it will. But if just enough of the holders of a given currency don't think an otherwise sound monetary reform makes sense, it won't fly'. Actors' intersubjective understandings about a currency – and the actions taken based on such understandings – therefore help to shape aggregate monetary outcomes (Widmaier, 2004: 436).

The shift from central planning to market mechanisms involved a fundamental clash between entrenched intersubjective understandings about the function of money in the Soviet economy and new monetary ideas supplied by the IMF. Unlike aspects of postcommunist economic transformation such as privatization and labor market reform, where other international organizations such as the World Bank played the central role, helping its member states to achieve monetary stability and to cooperate in response to international monetary problems is a core part of the IMF's mandate. One of the most pressing monetary issues during the early 1990s was the question of whether the ruble would be maintained as the common currency among the Soviet republics, or whether policymakers would choose to adopt independent national currencies with the associated risks of widespread disruptions to inter-republican trade and production networks. As one commentator observed at the time, decisions about the future of the ruble would be a key determinant of the future economic links between the constituent republics of the Soviet Union (Ellman, 1991: 495). With the rapid disintegration of the USSR during the second half of 1991, the politics of money became crucial to the IMF's ability to influence the process of postcommunist economic transformation.

The IMF quickly realized that transforming the structure of economic governance in the former Soviet centrally planned economies to market mechanisms would depend upon fundamentally changing the role that money and credit played in economic activity (IMF et al., 1990). Under the Soviet system, bank money functioned mainly as a passive unit of account to assess firm compliance with an economic plan designed in Moscow, with cash money mostly used to pay wages and to purchase the consumer goods that firms produced (McKinnon, 1993: 124–5). Interest rates played no role in determining the allocation of credit among economic actors. Instead, firms in the Soviet economy were accustomed to a financial system that set no hard constraints on the extension of credit, with the balance between supply and demand approximated by central planning (McKinnon, 1991: 110). The state savings bank (*Sberbank*) received household deposits at low rates of interest, most of which were transferred to the State Bank of the Soviet Union (*Gosbank*). Based on a credit plan and a cash plan decided by the central planning authorities, the *Gosbank* then determined the volume and allocation of credit to different sectors of the economy, as well as the volume and allocation of cash issuance (Pazarbaşioğlu and Willem van der Vossen, 1997: 27). The main function of the banking system was to 'lubricate' the economy with soft credit, to ensure that firms had access to enough funds to fulfill centrally determined production targets (Bigman and Leite, 1993: 3).

The uncertainty over future political and economic relations between the Soviet republics as well as their different rates of economic reform contributed to growing monetary disruptions in the Soviet economy during 1991, which only intensified following the political disintegration of the USSR and the emergence of the republics as nominally sovereign and independent states. The decline of central planning mechanisms and other Soviet institutions caused major disruptions to inter-republican trade, which hampered efforts to reach new agreements on economic relations between the newly independent states as well as creating incentives for policymakers in each republic to ignore the agreements that were already in place (Melliss and Cornelius, 1994: 5, 7). The acute uncertainty generated by the rapidly changing environment severely hampered the capacity of firms and households to cope with the ruptures of the economic transition. For example, Russia's liberalization of 90 per cent of prices in January 1992, which was quickly emulated to varying degrees by the other former Soviet republics, immediately led to rapid inflation. In this environment, firms faced a high 'inflation tax' on their bank deposits because policymakers continued to maintain nominal interest rates at a very low level.

Russia's price liberalization and subsequent inflation prompted growing macroeconomic instability in the three Central Asian cases examined in this study. Figures 3.1 to 3.5 trace the monthly rate of inflation in Russia, Kazakhstan, the Kyrgyz Republic, and Uzbekistan as well as the average inflation rate across the four countries from 1991 to 1995. As the figures show, inflation shot up following the shock liberalization of prices at the beginning of 1992, rising from under 15 per cent in December 1991 to between 100 and 300 per cent in January 1992. In most countries, monthly inflation rates did not fall below 10 per cent until 1995. Inflation trends in all four countries remained similar during 1991–2 but diverged during 1993–4, before gradually converging again in 1995.

The breakdown of monetary control in 1992 made a mockery of the IMF's demand for Russia to commit to achieving a monthly inflation target of 3 per cent in the second half of the year in order to help achieve macroeconomic stabilization and avoid a high inflation tax (Stone, 2002: 119). Instead, one study has estimated that Russia's inflation tax reached 31 per cent of Gross Domestic Product (GDP) in 1992 (Easterly and Vieira da Cunha, 1994: 13). The rapid rise in inflation contributed to widespread shortages of cash currency throughout the former Soviet Union during 1992, and the inability of firms to pay wages and governments to make pension and social welfare payments in cash prompted economic actors to purchase essential goods on credit wherever possible (Conway, 1997: 7). In such circumstances the exchange value of cash rubles (*nalichnyye*) and credit rubles (*beznalichnyye*) diverged, which further depreciated the value of household savings and firm deposits leading to rapid disintermediation, a lack of trust in the banking system, and a consequent growth in barter economies (Poser, 1998: 165). Although price liberalization was intended to stimulate a shift from the central allocation of resources among economic actors to the decentralized allocation of resources via relative price changes, rapid inflation initially impeded the potential for market mechanisms to function at all.

The growth of barter economies

As firms and households developed survival strategies in response to the crumbling Soviet financial system the newly independent states had inherited, their actions contributed to a swift process of

Figure 3.1 Monthly Consumer Price Inflation in Selected Former Soviet Republics, 1991

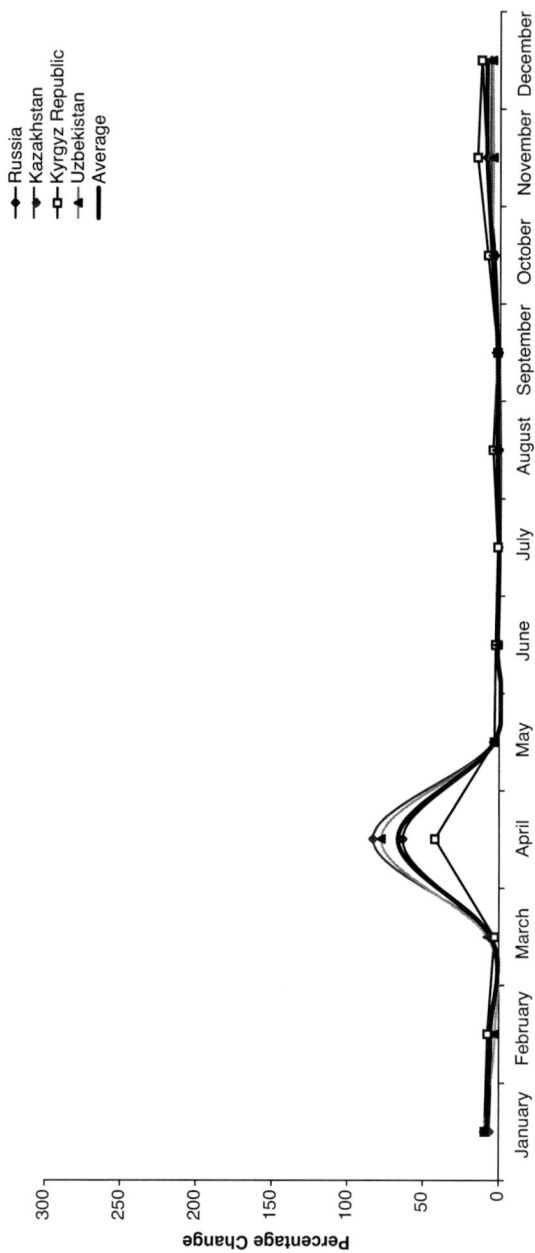

Source: Koen and De Masi, 1997: 27.

Figure 3.2 Monthly Consumer Price Inflation in Selected Former Soviet Republics, 1992

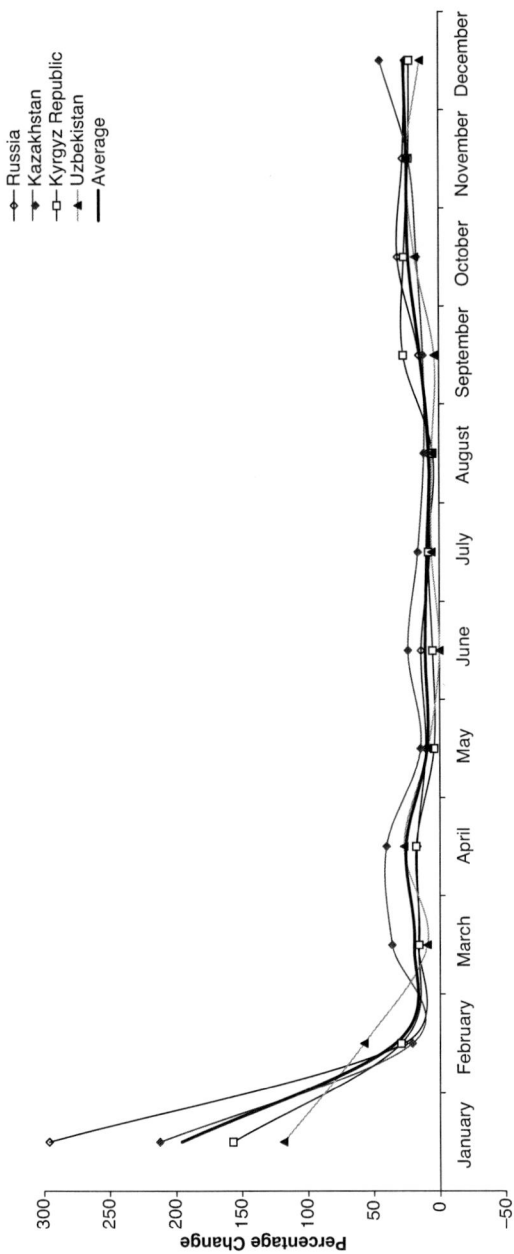

Legend:
- Russia
- Kazakhstan
- Kyrgyz Republic
- Uzbekistan
- Average

Figure 3.3 Monthly Consumer Price Inflation in Selected Former Soviet Republics, 1993

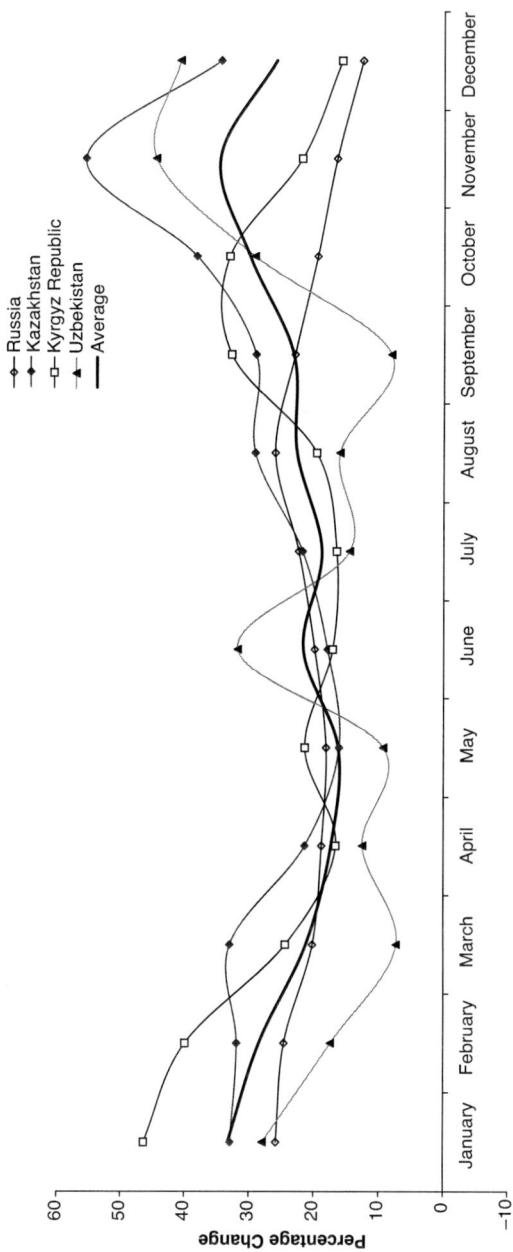

Source: Koen and De Masi, 1997: 27.

84

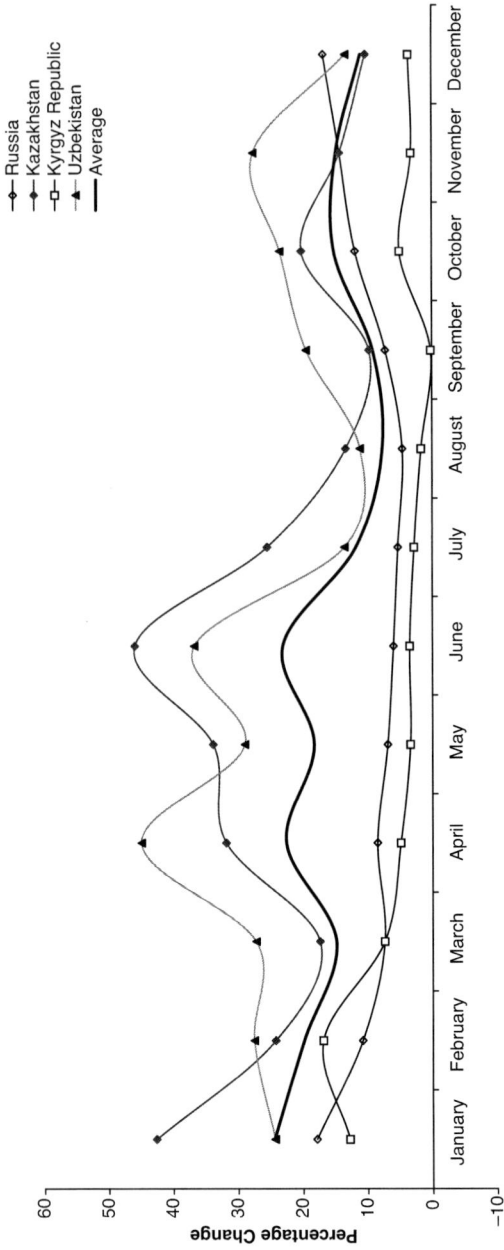

Figure 3.4 Monthly Consumer Price Inflation in Selected Former Soviet Republics, 1994

Source: Koen and De Masi, 1997: 27.

Figure 3.5   Monthly Consumer Price Inflation in Selected Former Soviet Republics, 1995

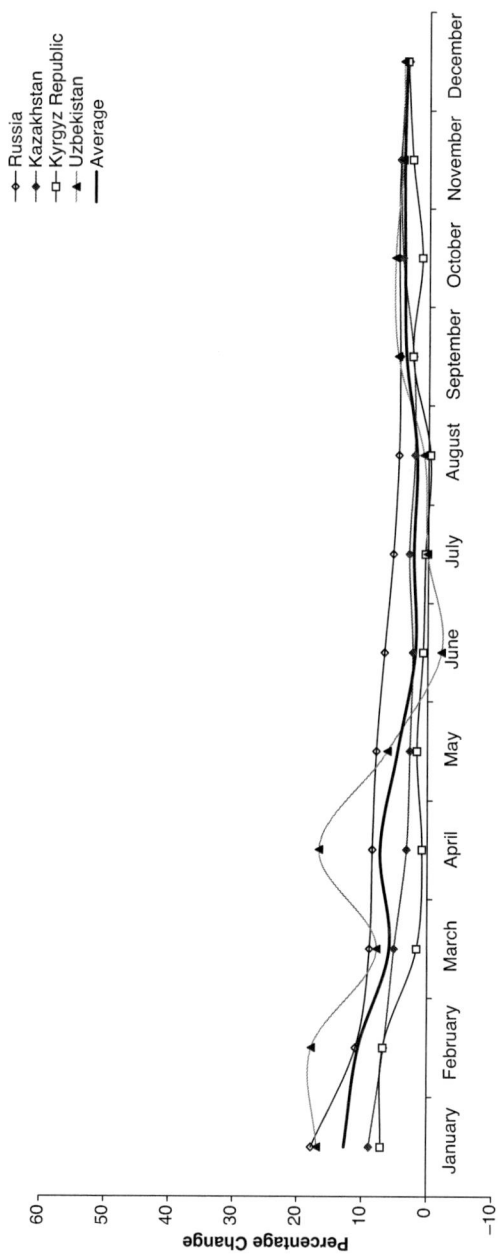

Source: Koen and De Masi, 1997: 27.

demonetization that worked against official efforts to achieve monetary stability. The contributors to Seabright's (2000a) *The Vanishing Ruble* show that demonetization and the rise of barter economies in the post-Soviet states stemmed from two interconnected factors. First, as firms became heavily indebted due to cash flow problems, banks had strong incentives to withhold new loans that might be used to repay other creditors rather than to enhance a firm's capacity to repay the bank by investing in productive activity. Large firms facing the problem of 'debt overhang' sought to induce their suppliers to extend credit for payment in kind, as a way to bypass the claims of existing creditors on cash revenue. Second, because of the uneven distribution of·credit constraints among firms in post-Soviet states, allowing some industrial customers to pay for goods through barter still enabled a firm to sell its products for a high cash price to those who could afford to pay with currency. While this strategy helped firms to prop up selling prices and thereby maintain cash revenue that would have been lost if a firm simply slashed its prices to a level that its credit-constrained customers could afford to pay, it hindered policymakers' efforts to control the rate of inflation (Seabright, 2000b: 5–6).

Post-Soviet production chains were highly conducive to the emergence of barter arrangements because the immediate economic interests of industrial partners in trading networks were interdependent. In addition to inhibiting official attempts to lower inflation, once barter economies had emerged they quickly became an entrenched feature of the economic environment, with firms limiting their operations to a virtual 'information island' shared by the members of their traditional trading networks. This phenomenon made the job of economic transformation even more difficult as firms sought to shelter from competition within the mutual interdependence of defensive trading networks, rather than reorienting their products toward new customers (Seabright, 2000b: 6–8). While barter trade had also played an important informal role in economic relations between firms during the Soviet era, the currency shortages following price liberalization and the authorities' subsequent attempts to impose hard constraints on bank credit prompted a rapid growth in barter economies. In a 1999 EBRD/World Bank enterprise survey, 64 per cent of Kazakh firms in the sample reported that they had resorted to barter and non-monetary exchange transactions for some sales. The figures were somewhat lower for other Central Asian states but still indicated the development of an extensive non-monetary economy, with 53 per cent of Kyrgyz firms and 32 per cent of Uzbek firms in the sample reporting that they had arranged barter transactions (Carlin et al., 2000: 214). Rather than embarking on a process of marketization, firms in the former Soviet centrally planned economies shifted toward the *barterization* of their economic relations, which worked against official efforts to achieve monetary stability and structural economic transformation.

Demonetization and rapid inflation in the post-Soviet economies hit most households even harder than firms because they were accustomed to paying for consumer goods with cash. Most households in the newly independent states of Central Asia experienced falling living standards and rising income inequality as the changes wrought by the breakdown of the Soviet system led to a redistribution of wealth between different social groups, radical changes in people's life chances, and the abolition of social benefits that people previously took for granted (Pomfret, 2006: 139). In these circumstances informal social organizations, or 'clans', became increasingly important as social networks that enabled individuals to meet basic needs and helped to provide the trust necessary for economic exchange in the absence of effective formal rules (Collins, 2006: 50). Like firms, many households relied on strategies of reciprocity to cope with the monetary chaos that characterized the early period after independence, epitomized in the popular Russian proverb 'better a hundred friends than a hundred rubles' (Kuehnast and Dudwick, 2004: 13). Such strategies included the reciprocal exchange of gifts consisting of cash money and other everyday necessities, the giving and receiving of help among relatives and friends similar to barter, as well as the exchange of illicitly obtained resources (Nazpary, 2002: 75–81; Coudouel et al., 1997). Similar to barterization among firms, the strategy of resorting to circuits of mutual obligation within social networks also worked against official efforts to establish new market institutions, as individuals struggled to survive by relying on informal social networks that were geared towards resisting or illicitly profiting from structural economic change (Nazpary, 2002: 89; Collins, 2006: 49). Household survival strategies further undermined the government's tax base, depreciated the value of firms' assets, and increased the process of demonetization when households faced with cash shortages withdrew from the formal economy by cutting consumption expenditure and engaging in non-taxable barter activities (Howell, 1996: 57–9; Clarke, 2000: 194–5).

Accompanying the emergence of barter economies among firms, the increase in a refusal to pay for goods led to a rapid build-up of informal inter-enterprise arrears, defined as the nominal value of 'payment demand orders' not executed by banks due to insufficient funds in the payer's account. Following price liberalization in Russia, for instance, firms faced a debt blowout as inter-enterprise arrears increased to 3 trillion ruble during the first half of 1992, at the same time as firms accumulated large arrears on bank loans and tax payments (Bigman and Leite, 1993: 1). Because the Soviet tax system was based on a firm's revenues and running up tax arrears did not attract interest penalties, firms had an incentive to reduce their taxable revenue through barter and to delay tax payments by reducing their bank balances to benefit from the surge in inflation shown in Figure 3.2 (Noguera and Linz, 2006: 721). This contributed to a severe budget crunch, as the newly independent states faced a precipitate decline in tax revenue at the same time as the demand for public spending increased (Pomfret, 2002: 37). In Russia, local governments began to accept 'non cash' tax payments by firms, a practice later accepted by the federal government that led to an estimated 25 per cent of state revenue accounted for by 'in kind' payments in 1996 (Abdelal, 2003a: 58–9).

The legacy of Soviet monetary norms

The growth of inter-enterprise arrears was accelerated via a chain of strategic actions by firms pursuing their immediate economic interests, a situation made worse by the inefficiencies and delays of the paper-based Soviet payments system. Some firms engaged in 'refusals to pay' as a necessary survival response to the new phenomenon of rapid inflation and the emergence of credit constraints following price liberalization, causing more firms to suspend their payments when customers refused to pay. Other firms that could afford to settle their accounts with suppliers then suspended payments with the expectation that, in line with existing monetary norms, the central bank would be forced to step in and cancel inter-enterprise debts to avoid a systemic economic collapse (Bigman and Leite, 1993: 5–6, 9).

Economic actors continued to exhibit a 'central planning mentality' in other ways. For example, firms maintained existing norms of reciprocity in an attempt to reduce the transaction costs of exchange. In particular, firms continued to supply goods and services to each other without expecting to receive payment, assuming that if they reached their production targets the authorities would help them to cover their wage costs (Bigman and Leite, 1993: 9). The erosion of the tax base made this unlikely as governments found themselves increasingly strapped for cash, while the monetary situation deteriorated further when firms began to seek innovative ways to convert rubles into dollars in order to avoid a depreciation of their capital through inflation. Some firms established their own insurance companies or small companies registered overseas as a way to export capital, while others founded their own banks in order to acquire a license to operate on foreign exchange markets where they could exchange their depreciating rubles for hard currency (Poser, 1998: 165). The weakening of Soviet institutions also led to the growth of 'uncivil' economies, where economic actors began to rely on private security forces and the threat of violence as a means to enforce contracts and protect their profits (Clarke, 2000: 178–9; Volkov, 2000).

These micro-level actions by firms collectively obstructed the ability of policymakers to achieve macroeconomic stability from which all 'viable' firms would have benefited, as well as generating even greater economic and social costs. In the variety of firms' responses to the radical uncertainty they faced following price liberalization in 1992, we see economic actors exhibiting different forms of economic rationality. Based on a 'logic of consequences', a rationalist approach suggests that it was in their material interests for firms to: (a) run up arrears in payments to suppliers and commercial banks, in the expectation of a systemic government bailout; and (b) to delay paying tax to take advantage of high inflation rates, which would rapidly decrease the real amount of tax owed (Bigman and Leite, 1993: 9). The strategy of using the threat of violence to enforce contracts and protect profits can be construed as instrumentally rational in the case of 'state failure' in the provision of basic public goods.

The practice of continuing to deliver goods to non-paying customers and thereby maintaining employment levels even when firms could not afford to pay cash wages can also be seen as an example of instrumental rationality. For instance, firms may have expected to receive government funds to reimburse wage costs they accumulated by continuing to produce and deliver goods to non-paying customers, so maintaining their existing workforce could be accounted for as a strategy to increase the likelihood of systemic debt cancellation by deliberately escalating the level of inter-enterprise arrears (Perotti, 1998). On its own, however, this explanation implies an unrealistic and highly asocial view of the environment to which Soviet firms were accustomed in 1992. A different interpretation is that at the same time as pursuing their immediate economic survival, the behavior of managers in many firms was also prompted by strongly held normative beliefs regarding their obligations to the economic welfare of workers and the role of the state as a provider of easy credit to maintain full employment.

Within the Soviet system, firms held tightly combined employment and social protection objectives, and were responsible for administering numerous social benefits. Many firms had also created implicit rules that determined what employees could legitimately steal from the workplace to supplement their cash wages (Clarke, 2000: 192). With the shift away from central planning, World Bank studies of the former Soviet republics found that many managers were initially reluctant to lay off workers due to long-standing social norms of full employment (see, for example, World Bank, 1993). Managers instead allowed employees to develop work-sharing arrangements, or to take unpaid vacations in order to maintain access to social benefits (Silverman and Yanowitch, 1997: 102; Broome, 2006). These normative routines suggest that the behavior of firms, as they responded to rapidly changing monetary conditions, can be understood by considering what would constitute socially legitimate actions based on a 'logic of appropriateness'. This does not mean that firm managers themselves necessarily believed that such benefits were legitimate, but rather they understood that workers considered them to be an integral part of workplace norms, the violation of which might generate material costs for firms if workers responded by engaging in greater theft or widespread industrial conflict.

The political economy of the ruble zone

These micro-level actions by firms and households collectively led to the breakdown of monetary control across all of the former Soviet republics. Despite widespread agreement among international actors on the urgent need to achieve monetary stability in post-Soviet states in the early 1990s, opinions diverged on whether this would be best achieved by maintaining the ruble zone currency union or the introduction of independent national currencies (Goldberg et al., 1994; Melliss and Cornelius, 1994). Increasing economic decentralization, driven by the lack of effective policy coordination, caused monetary conditions in the ruble zone to deteriorate rapidly following the formal dissolution of the USSR and Russia's subsequent price liberalization. In addition, the demise of the USSR created ambiguity among the newly independent states about the status of future economic relations with Russia. This led to local debates over whether post-Soviet states should seek to reintegrate into a common economic space with the Russian

Federation, or whether they should go down the nationalist route and seek greater economic sovereignty through monetary independence. The three Baltic states quickly took the latter choice during 1992. The Estonian kroon was introduced as sole legal tender in June, the temporary Latvian ruble was made sole legal tender in July, and Lithuanian talonas became sole legal tender in October.

Even among the post-Soviet states that continued to seek close economic cooperation with Russia, many governments were wary of Russia further strengthening its regional hegemony (Abdelal, 2003b: 913–14). As a result, when the Central Bank of Russia (CBR) assumed the responsibilities of the Soviet Union's *Gosbank* in January 1992, despite lacking the same power to make monetary policy across the newly independent states (Johnson, 2000: 77), governments in the other 14 post-Soviet states proved unwilling to cede effective monetary authority to the CBR. Formal declarations during 1992 from many of the former Soviet republics intending to continue to use the ruble as a common currency notwithstanding, the lack of appropriate federal institutions and the difficulties of achieving policy coordination among the newly independent states would eventually make this goal impossible to achieve in practice.

By taking over the responsibilities of the *Gosbank*, the CBR became the sole issuer of cash rubles in the ruble zone due to the location of all the Soviet printing presses in Russia. However, the 14 other central banks in the ruble zone at the start of 1992 – established from the republican branches of the *Gosbank* – were each able to create domestic credit denominated in rubles (Johnson, 2000: 78). As a response to the shortage of cash rubles and Russia's attempts to restrict the money supply, the other former Soviet republics began using their new central banks to extend a large volume of credit rubles to local commercial banks and firms during 1992 (Daviddi and Espa, 1995: 40). The authorities in each of the newly independent states in the ruble zone thus confronted a 'prisoner's dilemma' that inhibited effective cooperation, because each stood to gain by maximizing their own interests at the expense of other states (Åslund, 1995: 108). Without enforceable formal rules of the game, policymakers in each state had strong incentives to cheat by emitting domestic credit in order to maintain production, thereby enlarging their 'piece of the pie' in terms of ruble zone output. Rather than working towards policy coordination to achieve mutual welfare gains, the former Soviet republics engaged in competitive credit creation in response to what observers have described as a classic 'free-rider problem' (Pomfret, 2002: 83; Schoors, 2003a: 4).

Increasing credit creation in each of the newly independent states further contributed to rapid inflation across the ruble zone as a whole, which had an uneven impact on the fortunes of different economic actors. For instance, the scarcity of cash rubles and rising prices imposed hard budget constraints on most households as individuals' cash incomes declined (Silverman and Yanowitch, 1997: 84–5), further hastening the demonetization of post-Soviet economies. Among households, the initial 'winners' in the early post-Soviet period were workers in energy industries and the financial sector, as well as firm directors and senior managers, who saw their wages increase in both absolute and relative terms. The principal 'losers' were the already low-paid public sector workers such as teachers, manufacturing employees in the light industry, machine-building, and metalworking sectors, and workers in agriculture (Silverman and Yanowitch, 1997: 86–7).

For firms whose managers had good personal connections, however, the expansion of credit rubles allowed them to continue to operate within soft budget constraints. Rather than price liberalization enabling markets to allocate credit as the IMF had intended, commercial banks used their new financial freedom and their privileged relationship with the central bank to secure highly subsidized credit funded by the difference between high rates of inflation and low central bank refinancing rates. This was used to generate income by passing cheap credit on to favored clients (sometimes in return for bribes), extending credit to firms co-owned by the bank or senior bank managers, and in some cases engaging in financial speculation (Treisman, 1998: 251).

During the period in which the post-Soviet ruble zone was maintained, subsidized credit continued to be supplied to firms on a massive scale, although a firm's creditworthiness was determined by the quality of its managers' personal connections (Tompson, 1997: 1166). In response to underdeveloped market institutions and a lack of confidence that formal rules would be enforced, economic actors shunned 'identity-blind' transactions and instead chose to do business with well-known customers (Dinello, 1999: 25–6). For instance, a survey of the Russian financial sector in May 1993 found that 92 per cent of commercial banks were extending subsidized credit to favored clients with whom they had personal relationships (Treisman, 1995: 949–50). As a result, in early 1993 Russian firms were reportedly able to borrow credit from banks at interest rates that ranged from 30 per cent to 240 per cent per annum (cf. Figure 3.3 for monthly inflation rates at the time), with total subsidized credit equal to approximately 23 per cent of Russia's GDP in 1992 (Treisman, 1995: 950, 958). Even as the uncontrolled creation of bank credit undermined the sustainability of the ruble zone, many policymakers in the non-Russian republics still sought to remain in the monetary union in the hope of retaining the direct and indirect financial transfers from Russia and easy market access that had characterized the Soviet period (Åslund, 1995: 109).

Following the CBR's assumption of the *Gosbank*'s responsibilities, Russia made a number of changes to inter-republican monetary relations during 1992 in an attempt to achieve monetary stability. In the first half of 1992 inter-republican payments were channeled through 'correspondent accounts' set up by the CBR. While in theory the system of correspondent accounts would allow the CBR to limit the extension of bilateral credit to the non-Russian republics, in practice the other republics were initially able to overdraw their correspondent accounts without facing penalties due to delays and inefficiencies in the payments system. Russia had instructed commercial banks to process all inter-republican transactions through the CBR, but with 1,400 payments centers all processing paper records of transactions independently, the system was impossible to monitor. This initially led to the automatic financing of republic overdrafts by the CBR. When the CBR tried to restrict payments to its 82 main branches, continued slow reporting of payments meant that the system remained too congested to enable the CBR to impose restraint on the republics' correspondent account overdrafts (see Åslund, 1995: 120–4; Schoors, 2003a: 4–5).

Given, the strong material incentives for individual republics to cheat on their multilateral commitments, at first sight the political economy of the ruble zone might seem explicable solely by reference to rationalist theories, and game theory in particular. The benefits of competitive credit creation, in terms of maintaining employment and economic production in accordance with actors' prescriptive beliefs, accrued to each post-Soviet state individually, while the material costs of increased inflation were distributed evenly across all the ruble zone economies. These ambiguous monetary arrangements – whereby the CBR effectively subsidized inter-republican trade while raising 'seigniorage' revenue from the republics – resulted in Russia continuing to be a net contributor to the ruble zone economies. Indeed, the IMF and the Russian government estimated that Russia financed inter-republican trade to the tune of more than one trillion rubles in 1992 (Goldberg et al., 1994: 315, fn. 39). However, comprehending actors' motivations in this instance as driven primarily by material incentives in the face of an intractable 'prisoner's dilemma' and 'free rider' problems would be misunderstanding the social dimension of the politics of money in post-Soviet states. While material incentives, the distribution of benefits, and the potential for illicit financial gains were undoubtedly important factors shaping individual actors' behavior, an important additional feature of the ruble zone saga is its place as part of 'a long struggle over the nature and meaning of money' in the newly independent states (Woodruff, 2000: 459).

Two facets of this struggle are particularly important here. First, whether intersubjective understandings about the appropriate role of credit could be changed to make credit money symbolically and functionally equivalent to cash money, and hence crucial to attempts to restrain inflation despite the incommensurability of cash money and credit money in the Soviet economy (Woodruff, 2000: 453). Second, whether the role of the state should be circumscribed in such a way that credit would be withheld from 'unviable' firms, which would then be forced to make a definitive choice between labor retrenchment and reorienting their trade networks towards new markets or 'hitting the wall'. Both of these elements of the post-Soviet struggle over the meaning of money worked together, because the passive function of credit money had been tightly linked to employment and production objectives in the Soviet economy.

This is not to claim that norms matter more than material incentives in explaining the political dynamics of the ruble zone. Rather, the point is to place both a 'logic of appropriateness' and a 'logic of consequences' side-by-side in order to understand how both operate as symbiotic drivers of political economy outcomes. Along with material incentives, high stakes political struggles over normative beliefs provided an important impulse to monetary policy decisions, as well as non-decisions, regarding the future of the ruble zone during 1992–93. It is also probable that while Soviet-era monetary norms functioned as contextual variables that shaped the behavior of some actors, they functioned simply as utilitarian justifications for others who could appeal to an extant 'logic of appropriateness' to disguise their own self-interested behavior. For example, some commercial banks sought cheap central bank credit on the grounds of enabling industrial clients to maintain their labor force and production output, but delayed passing credit on to firms in order to engage in financial speculation (Tompson, 1997: 1171). In both cases, however, understanding actors' intersubjective beliefs is an important step in explaining what animated their behavior, without denying the centrality of self-interested conflict over the distribution of economic resources.

The end of the ruble zone façade

On 1 June 1992, Russia became a member of the IMF and became eligible to access loans, although disagreements over monetary stabilization targets delayed the IMF's approval of a stand-by arrangement until the beginning of August. While the IMF was unable to induce Russia to agree to collective action that could help to make the ruble zone viable, the government subsequently took new unilateral moves to restrict the flow of credit to the non-Russian republics. The CBR decided in July 1992 to enforce fixed limits on the financing of inter-republican trade, set at the amount of rubles the CBR had credited to the importing republic's correspondent account, with payments now processed centrally in Moscow in an attempt to insulate the Russian economy from ruble zone inflation (Schoors, 2003a: 5). Requiring republican governments to balance their correspondent accounts with the CBR created a market where firms bought republic rubles to pay for imports from each of the ruble zone members, which briefly limited the degree to which inflation fueled by domestic credit creation in one state was exported to other ruble zone members (Daviddi and Espa, 1995: 40). Instead, the rate of credit expansion in each republic contributed to an effective depreciation of the value of each republic's credit rubles, at the cost of restricting the non-Russian central banks' ability to access cash rubles or to accumulate seigniorage (Goldberg et al., 1994: 304).

To ease the process of adjustment and to support Russia's inter-republican exports, the CBR extended new credit lines in the form of 'technical credits', which allowed loans to the non-Russian republics to continue to grow from 325 billion rubles at the end of June to 1,545 billion rubles at the end of 1992. While the new credit lines helped to soften the blow of the July policy change for the non-Russian republics, the system still had a negative effect on inter-republican trade (Schoors, 2003a: 5–6). The shortage of cash rubles and the emergence of a spread between cash rubles and credit rubles – as well as differences between the exchange value of each republic's credit rubles – helped to stimulate the harmful speculation that a currency union is intended to mitigate (Conway, 1997: 7). By the end of 1992, the divergence between the respective values of what had become *de facto* multiple ruble currencies had created mounting pressure for states to establish *de jure* independent currencies, in order for each state to assert independent monetary control in place of what had now become the ruble zone 'façade' (*The Economist*, 1992). Following the example of the Baltic states, which had moved first to introduce independent currencies during the second half of 1992, most of the other former Soviet republics chose to exit the ruble zone and establish new currencies (or temporary 'coupons' leading to new currencies) between the end of 1992 and November 1993. As Table 3.1 shows, the Kyrgyz Republic was the first of the three Central Asian states that are at the center of the remaining chapters to introduce an independent currency in May 1993, followed by Kazakhstan and Uzbekistan in November 1993 after attempts to agree to new rules to resurrect the ruble zone with Russia had failed.

The killer blow to the ruble zone came in July 1993. On 24 July, Russia announced that a new Russian ruble would become sole legal tender inside Russia from September and the banknotes of old pre-1993 Soviet rubles would become invalid. The CBR had begun issuing the new banknotes in Russia at the beginning of 1993, but had not included them in cash shipments to the other republics (Abdelal, 2001: 53). Russia adopted this radical change in ruble zone policy unilaterally without discussing the move with the other ruble zone members or consulting with the IMF (IMF, 1993f), which immediately prompted Azerbaijan, Georgia, Moldova, and Turkmenistan to announce plans to introduce new currencies. Russia had used its dominant position of power as the other republics' main export market and the sole issuer of cash rubles to unilaterally change the monetary rules of the game, thereby altering the distribution of material benefits in the ruble zone. As each state introduced a new currency as sole legal tender and exited the ruble zone, it increased the inflationary pressure on the remaining members due to old Soviet rubles flowing out of the states that exited the ruble zone and into neighboring states where the ruble remained legal tender (Conway, 1995: 41).

If the intention of Russian policymakers was to force the other republics out of the ruble zone entirely, the July policy change did not immediately have this effect. Five post-Soviet states, including Kazakhstan and Uzbekistan, remained publicly committed to a 'ruble zone of a new type' (*rublevaia zona novogo tipa*). These states signed bilateral monetary agreements with Russia during September 1993, in which they effectively agreed to centralize the power to make monetary policy in Moscow. However, when Russia tightened the entry conditions for states wishing to use the new Russian ruble as a common currency even further in November, the cost of staying in a revamped ruble zone became too high. Russia proposed providing cash rubles to the republics that would be recorded as credits for an initial trial period

Table 3.1 IMF Membership and the Introduction of National Currencies in Central Asia

Country	Date of IMF Membership	Date of New Currency	Sole Legal Tender	Name	Conversion Rate	Initial Exchange System
Kazakhstan	15 July 1992	15 Nov. 1993	18 Nov. 1993	Tenge	T 1 = Rub. 500	Managed float through foreign exchange auctions.
Kyrgyz Republic	8 May 1992	10 May 1993	15 May 1993	Som	Som 1 = Rub. 200	Managed float through foreign exchange auctions.
Uzbekistan	21 Sep. 1992	15 Nov. 1993 1 July 1994	1 Jan. 1994 15 Oct. 1994	Sum-Coupon Sum	SC 1 = Rub. 1 Som 1 = SC 1000	Managed float through foreign exchange auctions.

Source: Snoek and van Rooden, 1999.

of six months, on which the non-Russian central banks would be required to pay interest and to deposit half the value of these 'credits' with the CBR in hard currency or gold for security. Pre-1993 Soviet ruble banknotes would be exchanged for the new Russian ruble banknotes at the unattractive rate of approximately three to one (Abdelal, 2001: 56–8). If the non-Russian republics had accepted the conditions that Russia set out for membership in the ruble zone, they would have greatly increased their monetary dependence on Russia. In particular, the new concessions Russia demanded for continued participation in a monetary union would reverse the republics' capacity to extract wealth from Russia through subsidized credit and domestic credit creation, and would consolidate monetary power over the ruble zone members in the CBR. These terms proved to be unacceptable to the governments of the five remaining non-Russian republics and the faltering ruble zone finally collapsed.

With the structure of material incentives working against inter-state cooperation and policy coordination on monetary reform, and the emergence of nationalist pressures for greater independence and monetary sovereignty in many of the post-Soviet states, the ultimate failure of the ruble zone seems from today's vantage point to have been almost inevitable. As Eichengreen (1996: 7) has observed, with the notable exception of the Bretton Woods system, monetary agreements do not usually result from inter-state negotiations but are the product of the individual choices that governments make, with policymakers 'constrained by the prior decisions of their neighbors and, more generally, by the inheritance of history'. The case of the ruble zone seems to bear out this point remarkably well, highlighting the importance of inherited monetary norms as well as the need for governments to react to the monetary policy decisions taken by neighboring states. It should also give pause to critics of the IMF who argue that the organization did not do enough to achieve monetary cooperation among the former Soviet republics. As the above discussion indicates, it is not feasible to suggest that the IMF should have sought to impose a solution to the unfolding ruble zone crisis on the former Soviet republics after the dissolution of the USSR in December 1991. With the emergence of nationalist pressures and the desire for greater independence and monetary sovereignty – or at least independence from the Russian Federation – in many of the post-Soviet states, it is unlikely that the IMF could have successfully coerced a critical mass of the ruble zone members to implement a new framework for effective monetary control and cooperation. In any case, its Articles of Agreement prevented the IMF from attempting to do so. Therefore, the important question to ask is not 'why didn't the IMF do more?', but rather, during the collapse of the ruble zone, 'what was the IMF's advice and how did it influence the post-Soviet states?' This is addressed in the following sections, which explore the evolution of the IMF's thinking and its advice on monetary developments to the former Soviet republics, and highlight how the IMF's influence was constrained by political realities on the ground as well as by the way that it interpreted the limits of its own authority over national governments.

The IMF and the ruble zone crisis

Sustained political support is a crucial ingredient for a monetary union to be successful. As Cohen (1998: 84) argues, in any attempt to achieve a successful monetary union 'economics may matter, but politics matters more'. Cohen suggests that two particular political factors are relevant here. First, whether there is a dominant state, such as Russia in the case of the ruble zone, which is prepared to act to maintain a monetary union based on conditions that each member state will consent to. Second, whether there is a sufficiently dense set of institutional linkages and a shared sense of 'community' among member states that compensates members for the loss of policy autonomy that a monetary union entails. Where these two political conditions are absent, it is likely that monetary unions will fail. As the remaining sections in this chapter demonstrate, these political imperatives help to explain why the IMF's efforts to maintain the ruble zone were unsuccessful, as well as why the common currency area lasted as long as it did despite the steep economic and social costs involved.

The IMF's initial advice on currency reform to the former Soviet republics was informed by two key assumptions. First, the IMF expected that regional monetary cooperation to maintain the ruble zone could be achieved, given the long-standing governance ties and economic interdependence between the newly independent states. Second, the IMF initially believed that maintaining the ruble zone would be the best possible outcome for the former Soviet republics because it would help sustain the level of economic production and trade, a belief that was also shared by other international actors such as the European Commission (Åslund, 1995: 110–11).

This second assumption was based on the theory of 'optimum currency areas' (Mundell, 1961; McKinnon, 1963), which hypothesizes that a currency union between multiple countries can help to improve the welfare of each country above the level that would be expected if states maintained independent currencies. For instance, a common currency area eliminates the uncertainties associated with currency risk to inter-state trade and investment among member countries, and enlarges the potential market available to all producers, thereby enabling firms to achieve economies of scale through product specialization. Deepening foreign exchange markets through a currency union can also help to alleviate the potential for harmful currency speculation and exchange rate fluctuations, as well as contributing to domestic price stability by providing a 'nominal anchor' for economic actors' price expectations and establishing a source of discipline on macroeconomic policies (Grubel, 1970: 319–21; Ricci, 1997: 33; cf. Willett, 1998).

The IMF's initial advice to ruble zone economies was also informed by an awareness that most of the new states lacked the necessary institutional capacity to design and implement independent monetary policies. In particular, Soviet-trained policymakers often had a poor grasp of how market-based monetary systems work. Many national officials in post-Soviet states initially failed to comprehend the dangers associated with inflation (Pomfret, 2002: 35), or saw no contradiction between attempting to restrain inflation at the same time as they extended a large volume of subsidized credit to firms because they were used to understanding credit as simply a unit of account that was distinct from cash money (Johnson, 2000: 79). With the establishment almost overnight of 15 new central banks, staffed by Soviet-trained officials who had little familiarity with market-based monetary policies, the IMF believed that officials should undergo an initial period of policy learning about market mechanisms before considering the introduction of new national currencies.

In hindsight, the IMF's initial assumption that there existed sufficient political will among the former Soviet republics to maintain and reform the ruble zone appears misjudged. However, because it is an organization with clear rules for engaging with its member states and a strict decisionmaking hierarchy, the IMF often finds it difficult to respond to unfolding events rapidly. This point is aptly illustrated by the Executive Board's discussions on the IMF's relations with the Soviet Union in late 1991. Although the IMF had been working on the assumption that the single economic unit of the USSR would remain intact, Michel Camdessus reported to the Executive Board in November that a mission to the USSR the previous month 'was struck by the accelerating deterioration and dismemberment of union-level economic structures, combined with growing republican assertiveness and expressions of national autonomy' (IMF, 1991a). In particular, the IMF managing director drew attention to the political difficulties of achieving agreement on inter-republican economic relations because of the declining authority of Soviet level institutions, with the non-Russian republics reluctant to accept the Russian Federation simply assuming control over the USSR's levers of power.

For Central Asian policymakers, the demise of the ruble zone and the introduction of independent currencies would involve a shift from strategic uncertainty, where actors knew what they stood to gain from ruble zone participation, to analytical uncertainty, where the distribution of costs and benefits from alternative policy decisions might be unknown (Iida, 1993: 433–4). Under analytical uncertainty, policymakers would be entering a 'brave new world' where both the rules of the game, and the potential outcomes from different policy choices, were unclear. However unsatisfactory the ambiguity of the situation was, the deputy director of the European II Department reported during the Executive Board debate on the future of the ruble zone in November 1991 that the IMF 'was approaching the immediate need for macroeconomic policies and economic reform on the assumption that the single currency might continue for a while'. The IMF's lack of knowledge about local conditions was a key factor here that inhibited its capacity to provide timely advice. In particular, the deputy director emphasized that the IMF 'did not have full information' about Russia's monetary policy intentions towards the other republics, and had even less information about the economic plans of the non-Russian republics (IMF, 1991b).

Monetary sovereignty versus multilateralism

Similar to the situation at the end of 1991, in 1992 the IMF continued to have difficulty evaluating monetary policy in Russia, and quickly found that effective credit control in some of the republics had almost entirely broken down in the absence of inter-republican monetary cooperation and policy coordination. The challenge of enhancing the IMF's understanding of monetary policy in Russia and helping the Russian authorities to establish monetary control would prove crucial to efforts to improve inter-republican monetary relations. As a result, and because of the continuing lack of information about economic policy decisions in many of the non-Russian republics, Executive Board discussions about the former Soviet Union focused predominantly on developments in Russia in the first quarter of 1992.

In February, the managing director reported positively on his face-to-face discussions with Yegor Gaidar, the First Deputy Prime Minister in charge of Finance and Economy for Russia, and noted that Gaidar himself 'had no difficulty with the prescriptions of the IMF'. Illustrating the perceived importance of the IMF's engagement as a way for states to signal their policy credibility to international audiences, Michel Camdessus communicated to the Executive Board that Gaidar 'was particularly knowledgeable of the central role that the IMF was playing in helping the international community to pass judgment on Russia's reform efforts and in catalyzing external support'. Significantly, Camdessus observed that 'It was not clear... that Russia's parliament enjoyed the same degree of understanding' (IMF, 1992e). The remarks by the managing director, which were reinforced by the UK executive director who had recently met Gaidar in London and the alternate executive director representing Austria who had met Gaidar in Vienna, indicate that the IMF saw Gaidar as a man with whom they could do business, in accordance with Woods's (2006: 72–3) concept of 'sympathetic interlocutors'. The Executive Board's discussions make clear that the IMF's governing body saw an important part of its role in the former Soviet republics as strengthening the hand of domestic reformers in debates over economic reform, by opening a gateway for reforming states to enter the capitalist world economy and become legitimate members of the international monetary order. As a further illustration of this point, the UK executive director suggested the IMF should 'send a signal to the reformers' in post-Soviet states that adoption of market-oriented policies would open up other forms of international assistance, such as debt relief through the Paris Club process and multilateral lending by the World Bank (IMF, 1992c).

To place the IMF's role in the protracted demise of the ruble zone in the wider political context, it is important to acknowledge the public commitments and rhetorical signals that the former Soviet republics communicated to the IMF regarding their monetary policy intentions, especially on the part of Russia. Here we discover one of the reasons the IMF had for continuing to explore the possibility of maintaining a ruble currency union during 1992, bearing in mind the IMF's stated position that the final choice over whether to remain in the ruble zone or to introduce separate currencies was a sovereign decision for the states themselves. For example, when the Executive Board met at the end of March 1992 to discuss the staff report on Russia's Pre-Membership Economic Review, a Russian delegation present at the meeting gave the IMF a clear indication that Russia intended to maintain the ruble zone through inter-republican monetary cooperation. The delegation was led by Konstantin Kagalovsky, the Plenipotentiary Representative of the Russian Government for Interaction with International Institutions (later appointed as Russia's first executive director at the IMF in November 1992), who clearly stated to the Executive Board that Russia wanted to 'maintain a common economic space' among the former Soviet republics (IMF, 1992d).

In the debate that followed, executive directors strongly emphasized the urgent need for Russia to establish an effective monetary framework. The main issue for the Executive Board was the need for the Russian authorities to establish monetary credibility by eliminating the policy ambiguity that characterized the current situation. The Board's recommendations on how to achieve this included measures to build public confidence in the CBR's willingness to exercise tight monetary control by establishing positive real interest rates and enforcing hard limits on the extension of central bank credit to the government and firms. In terms of the objective of maintaining a 'common economic space' in the former Soviet Union, executive directors highlighted Russia's unique role as a regional hegemon and reinforced the point that the Russian authorities had 'special responsibilities' to help coordinate monetary and exchange rate policies in the ruble zone (IMF, 1992d).

While the IMF officially elected to distance itself from the political decisions over monetary union versus monetary independence, the organization sought to use its analytical resources to shape the design of inter-republican monetary reforms. In May 1992, the IMF sent a staff team to Tashkent to participate in a meeting of the Interbank Coordinating Council of Heads of Central Banks, which had earlier been created at a meeting in Bishkek to provide a multilateral forum for discussion of monetary and credit policies in the ruble zone. The Fund staff helped to chair the Tashkent meeting, and presented central bankers with a set of proposed guidelines for monetary cooperation among the ruble zone members. The IMF's plan for the ruble zone envisaged inter-state policy coordination on four main fronts. First, the establishment of credit ceilings for individual central banks to restrict the growth of credit, as well as an aggregate credit ceiling for the ruble zone as a whole. Second, capping the credit extended by the CBR to the other central banks and reaching an agreement on the distribution of currency among the republics. Third, the establishment of uniform bank reserve requirements and central bank refinance rates, as well as movement towards a unified foreign exchange rate system. Finally, improving inter-state data collection and the transparent exchange of monetary and credit information among the ruble zone central banks (IMF, 1992e).

The Tashkent meeting began a pattern that dogged the IMF's efforts to establish inter-state monetary cooperation in the ruble zone. The heads of central banks failed to reach substantive agreement on any specific actions, while agreeing in principle that they *should* cooperate in the setting of monetary policy (IMF, 1992e). Even so, the IMF's efforts helped actors to frame potential policy agreements by suggesting boundaries on the efficacy of different options for policy coordination. The managing director informed the Executive Board that while it might prove difficult to translate the principles of the Tashkent agreement into substantive actions, the IMF had been able to use the event to improve the level of understanding among post-Soviet central bankers on the need for inter-state monetary policy coordination to reduce inflation. Camdessus also sought to use the IMF's experience at the Tashkent meeting to display the evenhanded approach the IMF was trying to take in providing advice on post-Soviet monetary relations. For instance, he noted that while representatives of the non-Russian republics had initially expected that the IMF would simply support the CBR's position, they were grateful that the IMF had instead encouraged Russia to take a more cooperative stance towards ruble zone negotiations (IMF, 1992e). Unfortunately, this approach only served to dissuade Russian policymakers from seeking a multilateral solution to the ruble zone's problems. The Russian authorities subsequently signaled that they had decided to formulate ruble zone monetary policy through bilateral negotiations with ruble zone members despite the proposals to achieve multilateral cooperation that were agreed in principle at the Tashkent meeting, bypassing the IMF through state-to-state discussions in which Russia would have a clear asymmetric power advantage (Odling-Smee and Pastor, 2001: 6–7).

The situation continued to change rapidly during the middle of 1992. On 24 July the deputy managing director reported to the Executive Board that there was 'a growing sentiment among all members of the ruble area other than Russia that their interests might be better served by introducing their own national currencies'. While Russia pushed ahead with bilateral negotiations with other ruble zone members conducted through a working group on ruble area issues, the Fund staff continued to seek to demonstrate their evenhanded treatment of the former Soviet republics by formulating advice for the Russian working group while transmitting the same advice to the non-Russian republics (IMF, 1992g). The dominant perspective among the Fund staff (as well as several executive directors) at this time continued to be based on the assumption that there were clear economic benefits from maintaining the ruble zone – at least until monetary stabilization was achieved and market-oriented reform was firmly on track. In providing advice on this process while formally seeking not to influence the choice between a common currency and monetary independence, the IMF continued to suffer from a lack of information about local economic conditions in many of the former Soviet republics. However, the IMF was quickly learning from experiences on the ground that the republics faced a wide variety of different economic circumstances, while pursuing diverse (and sometimes counterproductive) policy responses.

Divergent policies further worsened the prospects for multilateral monetary cooperation by sharpening the differences in monetary conditions between ruble zone economies. For instance, in July 1992 central bank refinance rates varied from 12 per cent in Azerbaijan and Georgia to 80 per cent in Russia (IMF, 1992h). In these ambiguous conditions, the IMF had to formulate its own advice based on assessments of policy intentions, national interests, and the political 'sentiment' among ruble zone policymakers. While this posed analytical difficulties for the organization, it also provided staff with a window of opportunity to shape how policymakers viewed the economic costs and benefits of alternative policy options. According to the Director of the European II Department John Odling-Smee and Gonzalo Pastor, the IMF's advice had changed to private support for independent currencies in the remaining ruble zone members by September 1992 as the costs of ruble zone membership continued to mount. In November, Odling-Smee wrote to the governments and central banks of the former Soviet republics to set out the IMF's view on the clear choice between maintaining a common currency managed by a single monetary authority and introducing independent national currencies. The IMF spelled out that it would not approve a loan program with a government until one of these two options had been firmly put in place (Odling-Smee and Pastor, 2001: 20, 41–4).

This choice between monetary sovereignty and multilateralism remained complicated by the lack of trust between Russia and the newly independent states. The non-Russian republics were unwilling to allow the CBR *de facto* control of ruble zone monetary policy, especially having witnessed the CBR's unilateral decisionmaking style during 1992, while Russia was unwilling (or, due to internal disagreements, unable) to agree to a cooperative multilateral arrangement. However, because of its dominant economic size and hegemonic role in the region, the IMF believed that the ball was squarely in Russia's court. Publicly defending the IMF's role in the former Soviet Union in an opinion article in the *Financial Times* in December 1992, Odling-Smee (1992) argued that inflation could 'escalate into hyperinflation unless the Russian authorities act vigorously to reimpose financial discipline'. Commenting on the delay in approving an upper credit tranche loan agreement with Russia, Odling-Smee suggested that the loan negotiations had been impeded by 'the authorities' inability so far to decide on firm monetary and fiscal policies'.

At a meeting in Bishkek in October 1992, the leaders of the former Soviet republics agreed to establish an inter-state bank involving the remaining ruble zone members (Åslund, 1995: 127). Like the outcomes of previous meetings, however, this remained an agreement in principle rather than a practical solution to the problem of policy coordination in the ruble zone that policymakers were committed to implementing. Because of the lack of success in generating agreement on a new multilateral monetary system among the former Soviet republics in 1992, Fund staff now concluded that individual republics should make contingency preparations to introduce new national currencies (IMF, 1992h). The internal processes within the IMF then began to shift gear from an official policy of non-intervention on the question of independent currencies to intellectual support for the construction of national monetary systems in the ruble zone economies.

Loan conditionality and monetary independence

Critics of the IMF could no doubt see the IMF's debate over the problems of the former Soviet Union as driven by neoliberal ideology, where getting the 'right' policy framework in place is prioritized above people's everyday economic and social needs. This may indeed be the case, but simply pinning the neoliberal label to the IMF provides little analytical purchase on the motivations for and the discursive justifications used to support the IMF's intellectual position. For instance, in addition to blaming the Russian authorities, a recurring theme in Executive Board debates over the problems of achieving monetary control in the former Soviet Union is an emphasis on the social costs of inflation. As the UK executive director stated to the Board: 'The real losers from hyperinflation would be the Russian people' (IMF, 1993g). The IMF correctly saw monetary expansion and soft central bank loans as mostly benefiting political and economic elites, especially commercial banks and large firms, while the high inflation they helped produce was seen as undermining public support for economic reform by hurting those who were already poor and further impoverishing large sections of the population.

During the first half of 1993, the IMF's willingness to supply loans to the former Soviet republics became more tightly linked to their choice between remaining in the ruble zone and introducing independent currencies. As the staff made clear in an April report on the new systemic transformation facility lending window, countries remaining in the ruble zone would only be allowed to access a systemic transformation facility arrangement after they took 'convincing action' to tighten monetary policy, with the emphasis on the need for tough monetary policy decisions by Russia (IMF, 1993c). The views of executive directors, expressed in a 21 April Executive Board meeting that discussed Russia's 1993 Article IV Consultation with the IMF, focused on continuing to push Russia to tighten monetary policy in the ruble zone. Daniel Kaeser, the Swiss executive director representing several Central Asian states including Uzbekistan and the Kyrgyz Republic, argued that Russia's policies had created a 'speculative inflation mentality' among economic actors and had undermined the credibility of the government's reform program (IMF, 1993h).

With the staff now concluding that 'attempts to coordinate monetary policies in the ruble area had failed' (IMF, 1993i), executive directors began to speak more categorically against further attempts to maintain or to resurrect the ruble zone. For instance, the UK executive director argued that the need to settle monetary arrangements in the ruble zone 'almost certainly means moving to separate currencies as quickly as possible' (IMF, 1993h). Within Russia, however, disagreements among different political actors amid vacillation over whether to prioritize the pursuit of monetary stability in Russia or the pursuit of Russia's geopolitical interests by maintaining a unified monetary system with the former Soviet republics hampered the ability of Russian policymakers to take a clear decision one way or the other. Fund staff believed that while most Russian officials were now in favor of the non-Russian republics introducing independent currencies, senior policymaking elites were concerned about how to best serve Russia's long-term political interests. In addition, the staff noted that several of the former Soviet republics had continued to pressure the Russian authorities to maintain the ruble zone. In the staff's view, the uncertainties over inter-republican trade and monetary relations had now 'placed in jeopardy the entire thrust of the reform program' in Russia (IMF, 1993i).

With the establishment of the systemic transformation facility, it became clear that a conclusive decision over ruble zone membership versus independent national currencies would be crucial for the approval of an IMF loan program for the non-Russian former Soviet republics, which further complicated the IMF's official position of leaving the choice over monetary arrangements up to the individual states themselves. The remarks by Oleh Havrylyshyn, the alternate executive director for the Netherlands constituency that included several former Soviet republics, illustrate the bureaucratic gymnastics involved in the IMF's attempt to avoid making a sovereign decision regarding monetary arrangements for its new members. On the one hand, Havrylyshyn observed that the IMF could find itself unable to approve systemic transformation facility programs for states that remained in the ruble zone because their monetary policy would remain harnessed to developments in Russia – although these were the very states that the systemic transformation facility was designed to assist. On the other hand, he argued that the IMF should refrain from overstepping the bounds of its authority by requiring a state to exit from the ruble zone as a prior action for a systemic transformation facility program. Havrylyshyn instead suggested that a rhetorical commitment to introduce an independent currency should be a sufficient criterion to allow ruble zone members to access a systemic transformation facility loan. In effect, this formula could provide incentives for states to exit the ruble zone without directly exposing the IMF to the charge of overriding the monetary sovereignty of its member states (IMF, 1993e), but prompted stiff resistance from Fund staff.

The proposal that the former Soviet republics should be allowed to access a systemic transformation facility loan once they had rhetorically committed themselves to introducing an independent currency was opposed at the Executive Board level by the Director of the Policy Development and Review Department, who sought to retain the staff's discretion to assess states on a case-by-case basis. Although the systemic transformation facility was designed to provide relatively easy access to the IMF's resources, for the staff simply allowing states to make a rhetorical pledge of their monetary intentions was a step too far in this direction. In particular, Fund staff were keen to retain the right to assess policymakers' reform intentions for themselves, which might increase the incentives for governments to intensify cooperation with the IMF on everyday policy decisions. While the IMF bases its claim to expert authority on providing top quality analysis grounded in hard statistical data, the final Executive Board decision on the creation of the systemic transformation facility nonetheless included a strong element of ambiguity in the assessment of a state's eligibility to use the new loan facility. Summing up the sense of the meeting, the managing director stated that 'Where there is a reasonable case for eligibility, but the statistical case is unclear, the member will be given the benefit of the doubt' (IMF, 1993e). This would enable the IMF to establish an initial loan program with states in uncertain circumstances, in order to allow staff to build a stronger case for intellectual persuasion and policy diffusion over time.

From April 1993, the tone of Executive Board discussions on monetary developments in the ruble zone changed and became for the most part in favor of the former Soviet republics introducing independent currencies. As late as September 1993, however, the Fund staff continued to attempt to formally maintain a neutral position on the question of whether states should exit the ruble zone (IMF, 1993j). The IMF's public position changed to categorical support for new currencies following Russia's policy changes in November 1993, which tipped the balance for the five remaining members of the ruble zone in favor of monetary independence. The IMF's stance was finally resolved when Michel Camdessus released a press release on 15 November, the same day that Uzbekistan and Kazakhstan introduced their new currencies, publicly spelling out the IMF's clear intellectual and financial support for monetary independence in the former Soviet republics (IMF, 1993k).

Conclusion

The monetary challenges facing the former Soviet republics as they attempted to construct a functioning new monetary union following the demise of the Soviet Union grew increasingly complex during 1991–93. With the breakdown of monetary control in the former Soviet Union, barter economies quickly emerged, as credit-constrained firms and households relied on reciprocal exchange arrangements informed by extant social norms, in response to rapid inflation and the shortage of cash rubles. The actions of firms and households further worsened the process of demonetization in post-Soviet economies, thereby undermining official attempts to establish macroeconomic stability and maintain tax revenues, leading to the growth of illicit economies. In these difficult circumstances, the governments of the newly independent post-Soviet states faced strong incentives to engage in competitive credit creation to help maintain production and employment levels and to secure material gains at the expense of other ruble zone members. Despite being rational responses to the immediate economic circumstances that governments faced and reflecting the inherited conventions and social norms that had shaped the operation of the Soviet system, these official actions gradually eroded the advantages of maintaining the ruble zone. When the Russian government sought to monopolize monetary power over the remaining ruble zone members in the second half of 1993, the material costs and the loss of policy autonomy generated by continued participation became too large a sacrifice for most of the non-Russian republics.

Both rationalist and constructivist approaches help to explain different dimensions of the political economy of the ruble zone during 1991–93, where developments were driven both by individual actors' immediate economic interests and their normative beliefs based on long-standing intersubjective economic norms. Specifically, the politics of money in the common economic space of the former Soviet Union was driven by the set of material incentives that different actors faced as well as by Soviet-era regulative norms regarding the appropriate role of the state and the passive function of money in maintaining production output and employment levels. While governments may implement the formal architecture for a new monetary system by fiat, actors' beliefs about how monetary rules should be organized and the survival strategies they employ in response to acute uncertainty in a rapidly changing economic environment can diminish the effectiveness of formal changes. This can quickly undermine the political conditions necessary for sustaining inter-state monetary cooperation.

Monetary developments in the ruble zone were characterized by acute uncertainty and policy ambiguity in the final two years before the monetary union finally collapsed at the end of 1993. While some states sought a quick exit from the currency union to establish monetary independence and to burnish their claims to national sovereignty, others were reluctantly pushed out of the ruble zone by rising economic costs throughout 1992 and 1993 and the adverse policy actions of the Russian government. The Central Asian states were among those that were most reluctant to exit the common economic space of the former Soviet Union. This was due in part to a complete lack of experience with running an independent monetary system, as well as policymakers' beliefs that they could expect to access greater credit subsidies and trade benefits by maintaining a common monetary system with Russia.

In reasoning through these challenges, the IMF had to rely on its assessments of actors' intentions rather than grounding its policy advice and decisions on economic data. In an unprecedented situation where the IMF was expected to provide quick fix solutions for countries that were strangers to independent statehood and the obligations of IMF membership, the IMF struggled to manage the simultaneous challenges that it faced. The IMF's role was especially complicated because it had to formally respect the newly established juridical sovereignty of its members, which the staff and the Executive Board initially interpreted as prohibiting the right of the IMF to categorically favor monetary independence over the maintenance of the currency union or *vice versa*.

It is clear that the IMF saw decisive action by the Russian authorities as the key to stabilizing monetary relations among the former Soviet republics. Yet the IMF's influence was blunted by internal conflicts within Russia's policymaking elite over whether to seek monetary independence to stabilize the Russian economy or whether to use the ruble zone as a foreign policy instrument to shore up its regional hegemonic role by maintaining monetary and credit links with the other republics. The IMF's capacity to exercise leverage over Russian policymakers by withholding loans was further inhibited by the geopolitical interests of the US, which pressured the IMF to extend financial support for Russian President Boris Yeltsin's administration. In addition, some observers have suggested that the IMF's negotiations with Russia during the early 1990s indicates that on monetary issues the IMF may have been 'willfully deceived' by their Russian interlocutors (Hedlund and Sundstrom, 1996: 908).

Despite these political constraints, the IMF was by no means marginal to monetary developments in the ruble zone, and its efforts to initiate multilateral cooperation and to develop bilateral relationships with policymakers in post-Soviet states helped to frame the range of alternative options that were on the table. At the same time, however, the IMF was forced to be a back seat driver, which often led to it proffering advice on what should or should not be done after the fact. In Central Asia, the IMF's influence was greater after the newly independent states chose to exit the ruble zone and turned to the IMF for advice on the construction of new national monetary systems. The final two chapters in this book explore how the IMF sought to influence the introduction of new currencies and the reform of central banks in the Kyrgyz Republic, Kazakhstan, and Uzbekistan after the ruble zone had finally collapsed.

4
Designer Capitalism in Central Asia

When they became members of the IMF in 1992, the Kyrgyz Republic, Kazakhstan, and Uzbekistan each initially maintained transitional currency restrictions, permitted under Article XIV of the IMF's Articles of Agreement, and continued to exercise direct political control over central bank operations. Despite their similar institutional starting points, however, the process of systemic economic reform varied markedly across the Central Asian region during the 1990s. By the end of the first decade of economic transition in the former Soviet Union, the Kyrgyz Republic and to a lesser extent Kazakhstan were widely considered to have been the leading market-oriented reformers among the post-Soviet states of Central Asia, with Uzbekistan lagging far behind. The Kyrgyz Republic became the first Central Asian state to formally break away from the ruble zone by introducing its own currency, the Kyrgyz *som*, in May 1993 with strong financial and rhetorical support from the IMF. Kazakhstan moved more slowly towards the introduction of a national currency, but Kazakh policymakers established a much more cooperative policy relationship with the IMF compared with their counterparts in Uzbekistan.

In the final two chapters in this book I investigate the following questions to assess the sources of the IMF's influence in its attempts to effect institutional change in post-Soviet Central Asia after the demise of the ruble zone monetary union. First, how did the initial circumstances of each country at independence impact upon its relationship with the IMF? Second, what strategies did the IMF use to change national actors' policy preferences over time? Through addressing these two questions, Chapters 4 and 5 establish how the IMF sought to influence institutional change in Central Asia after the collapse of the ruble zone, whether it was able to do so in each case, and the enabling factors that permitted it to achieve influence.

As the foregoing chapters have argued, reconstructing how actors perceive their interests, and therefore changing their policy preferences, is not simply a matter of providing material incentives for states to adopt headline-grabbing policy changes under IMF loan programs. How actors understand their material interests flows from how they interpret the social, political, and economic circumstances that they confront. Therefore, understanding the strategies that Central Asian policymakers adopted in response to the challenges of independent statehood, and establishing whether this aided or hindered their openness to the IMF's ideas for economic reform, requires an examination of how the IMF sought to shape actors' interpretations of the transitional context they faced. Seen through the eyes of the IMF, winning a strategic game over policy conditionality with states may allow the IMF to achieve a degree of loan program success in the short term if states formally adopt the IMF's preferred institutional changes. However, in an environment characterized by acute uncertainty – where the informal rules of the game shape economic behavior more than official regulatory changes – the IMF must achieve a change in a state's broader policy orientation in order to entrench an IMF-friendly path of economic reform over time. This depends on the IMF's efforts to change policymakers' intersubjective understandings about how the economy should work, the monetary policy options at their disposal, and the appropriate role of state intervention in the economy. In short, this involves repeated attempts by the IMF to succeed in strategic games over policy efficacy, through persuading policymakers to adopt a common framework for analysis to design solutions to their economic challenges.

Post-Soviet political regimes in Central Asia

With any attempt to build new formal institutions designed to achieve fundamentally different social and economic goals, the past matters. In a period of systemic change actors do not construct new institutions in a social vacuum, but are constrained by the legacy of previous institutional frameworks as well as shared understandings about how the economy works and how it *ought* to work. Historical legacies were especially significant in the post-Soviet states of Central Asia, where the political transition from the Soviet Union to national independence, concomitant with the need to construct a new national economic system, was carried out by decisionmakers who were accustomed to the rules and incentive structure of the old regime. At the same time, exogenous shocks – such as the political disintegration of the USSR and the subsequent dismantling of the inter-republican monetary relationships that had characterized the Soviet system – open up a window of opportunity for rapid institutional change. What national policymakers choose to do with this window of opportunity is shaped by their existing understandings of their interests, but these are mutable because of the acute uncertainty that actors face.

In postcommunist Central Asia, the IMF stepped into an uncertain environment offering a wealth of comparative policy knowledge and an ability to reduce transaction costs by designing reform templates that national elites could use to pilot institutional change. Because of the uncertainty and the historical contingency that characterize systemic economic and political transitions, 'Not only is the endpoint of the transition unclear, so is the process' (Luong, 2002: 104). This might suggest that although institutional legacies will continue to be an important determinant of change, we can expect reform templates provided by international organizations to have a significant impact when actors seek quick policy fixes to ameliorate immediate uncertainty. However, when individual actors are uncertain who the winners and losers from economic reforms are likely to be, this individual-specific uncertainty generates a bias in favor of maintaining the institutional *status quo* (Fernandez and Rodrik, 1991). In the early 1990s, Central Asian policymakers were unfamiliar with how market-based mechanisms would work, circumstances which made it difficult for elites to ascertain in advance who would benefit and who would lose from economic reforms. While the IMF was presented with a window of opportunity to effect large-scale formal institutional change with the collapse of the ruble zone, uncertainty regarding the effects of economic reforms on different social groups made it unlikely that governments would be either willing or able to fully abandon their existing institutional frameworks and informal practices in the short term. How open policymakers were to the IMF's ideas for economic reform following independence would therefore depend in large part on how they interpreted the immediate economic and political challenges they confronted.

All three states established strong presidential systems following independence that were commonly characterized as authoritarian patronage-based regimes, albeit with considerable variation in the degree of domestic political competition, media criticism, and social dissent that rulers tolerated (Katz, 2006; Roeder, 1994). In effect, the post-Soviet constitutional structure adopted in each of the Central Asian republics gave presidential rulers the power to pass laws by decree

(Gleason, 2004: 46; Matveeva, 1999: 27–8). In contrast to other post-communist transitions, where popular social movements demanded political independence and economic reform, official decisions over the scope and speed of economic change in Central Asia were largely determined by ruling elites rather than being forced upon them by social dissent. Political leaders in each country rhetorically embraced the aim of systemic economic reform to establish a market-based system, while pursuing different national strategies towards this goal (Gleason, 2004: 46; Pomfret, 2003a).

Despite these commonalities, there were also some important variations in the political dimension of the transitional context in Kazakhstan, the Kyrgyz Republic, and Uzbekistan. While each country established a strong presidential system with weak or simply 'rubber stamp' legislatures, the different approaches of Central Asia's post-Soviet presidents to the challenges of independent statehood informed the development of each government's relationship with the IMF. In these three cases, the Kyrgyz Republic's first post-independence president, Askar Akaev, was forced to step down in 2005, while the first post-independence presidents in Kazakhstan and Uzbekistan still remain in power today. Several observers have credited the Kyrgyz Republic's first post-independence president, Askar Akaev, with playing the key role in the direction of the country's market-based reform program after 1992 (Gleason, 1997: 95; Luong, 2002: 115). Akaev held a doctorate in physics and had a background as President of the Kyrgyz Academy of Sciences rather than within the Communist Party hierarchy (Pomfret, 2006: 73). As an indication of how Akaev interpreted the Kyrgyz Republic's policy options, during the debates over the future direction of economic policy that accompanied the demise of the Soviet Union, Akaev is reported to have argued that 'although it was true that there were both poor countries and rich countries among the market economies, in the socialist world there were only poor countries' (Gleason, 1997: 95). Such views contributed to the early identification of the Kyrgyz President by external observers as a committed supporter of the market transition. Indeed, according to Central Asia specialist Kathleen Collins (2006: 159), 'Akaev, alone of the Central Asian leaders, was personally committed to the goals of perestroika'. After the country gained political independence, Akaev quickly sought to establish the Kyrgyz Republic's international reputation as a rapid reformer in the region (Anderson, 1999: 75–6).

In comparison with the Kyrgyz Republic, the first Kazakh president Nursultan Nazarbayev had been a more prominent and longer-serving member of the Communist Party elite before the country gained independence (Blackmon, 2005: 398; Brooker, 2004: 140–1). In policy debates over the appropriate reform strategy for Kazakhstan following the demise of the Soviet Union, decisionmakers considered whether to adopt blueprints from the economic reform experience of countries such as South Korea, Turkey, and Hungary rather than follow the IMF's template for institutional change (Conway, 1994: 165–6). In addition, Nazarbayev brought in a team of high-level German economists in 1993 to advise on the country's economic transformation and to provide policymakers with an independent source of advice to the reform ideas put forward by the Fund staff (Hoffman, 2001: 1–3). Despite elite debates over whether to adopt a particular country's model of reform, however, in practice the government introduced most major economic changes through an incremental and sometimes erratic process of institutional change, with policymakers intermittently switching from the IMF's ideas for market-based monetary reforms to Soviet practices of directing cheap credit to firms to maintain production and employment.

Uzbekistan's post-independence president Islam Karimov was trained as a Soviet economist and worked for the Uzbek branch of *Gosplan*, a background that has been credited with influencing his heavy-handed approach to Uzbekistan's post-independence economic reforms (Blackmon, 2005: 396). Karimov aggressively sought to maintain regime stability and to build up an authoritarian state through the centralization of economic and political power in the office of the president (Collins, 2004: 251), with a particular focus on establishing and maintaining Uzbekistan's sovereignty from Russia (Kazemi, 2003: 208). Like Kazakhstan, Uzbek policymakers in the early 1990s eschewed simply accepting the IMF's advice and publicly discussed whether to adopt models for economic reform from countries such as South Korea and China (Ruziev et al., 2007: 11). These examples were usually used to justify the government's self-proclaimed 'gradualist' policy orientation, however, rather than as blueprints that the Uzbek authorities actively sought to follow.

Fiscal capacity in Central Asia

The economic legacy from 70 years of Soviet rule was critical in shaping the degree of Central Asian policymakers' openness to the IMF's ideas for market-based monetary reforms. At independence, the Central Asian republics inherited similar institutional legacies from their subordinate roles in the Soviet economic system, although each faced radically different economic prospects. Like the other former Soviet republics, the newly independent states of Central Asia were accustomed to receiving implicit financial transfers through the centralized Soviet trading system as recipients of cheap oil and gas imports. Estimates suggest that in 1990 these indirect subsidies amounted to approximately 2.72 per cent of GDP in the Kyrgyz Republic, compared with 1.26 per cent of GDP in Uzbekistan. Because of its greater endowment of natural resources in comparison with its neighbors (including rich reserves of oil, minerals, and natural gas), Kazakhstan received smaller indirect financial transfers from the other Soviet republics, estimated at only 0.5 per cent of GDP in 1990 (Orlowski, 1993: 1006–7).

Direct fiscal transfers from the central Soviet budget had long been an even greater source of support for Central Asian governments. In 1989 net direct fiscal transfers to the republics as a proportion of their total revenue were estimated to comprise 24 per cent of the republican budget in Uzbekistan, 20 per cent in Kazakhstan, and 17.8 per cent in the Kyrgyz Republic (Orlowski, 1995: 64). Figure 4.1, based on IMF calculations, indicates that direct fiscal transfers accounted for between 5 and 10 per cent of each republic's GDP in the late 1980s. This rose in 1990 and 1991 to nearly 20 per cent of GDP in Uzbekistan before the Central Asian republics were cut off after Russia took over the *Gosbank* at the end of 1991, although some fiscal transfers to Kazakhstan continued during 1992. The abrupt loss of fiscal revenue further compounded the enormous economic difficulties faced by the republics from price and trade shocks, rapid inflation, and demonetization during 1992 and 1993. As Figures 4.2 and 4.3 indicate, the end of Soviet

Figure 4.1   Net Union Transfers to Central Asia, 1988–92

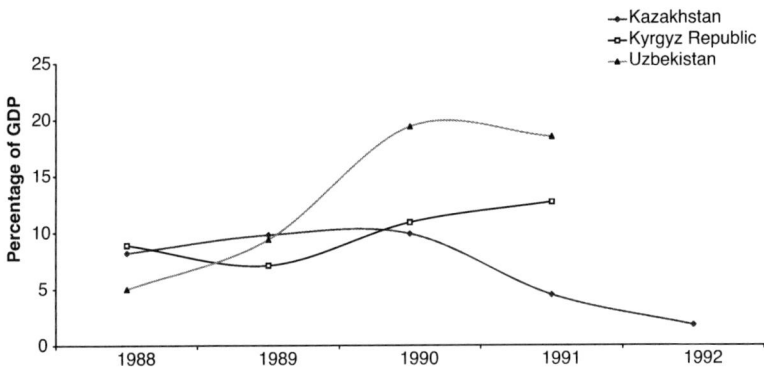

Source: IMF, 1992i, 1992l, 1992m, 1993o, 1994d, 1995b.

Figure 4.2   Government Expenditure in Central Asia, 1988–92

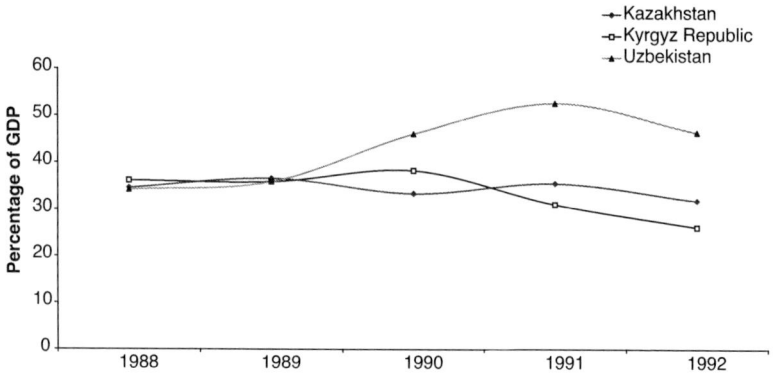

Source: IMF, 1992i, 1992m, 1992l, 1993o, 1994d, 1995b.

Figure 4.3   Net Budget Balance in Central Asia, 1988–92

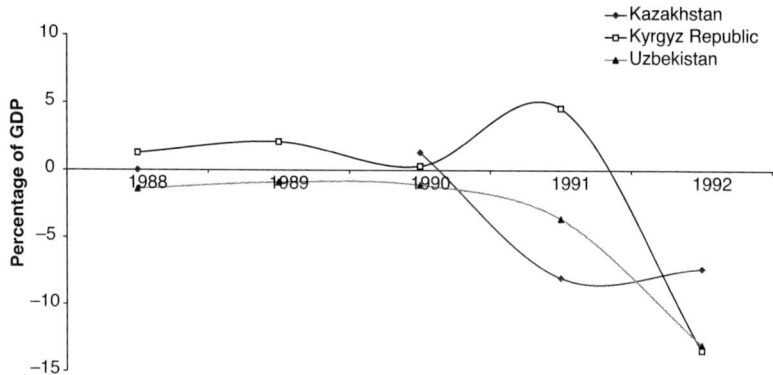

Source: IMF, 1992i, 1992m, 1992l, 1993o, 1994d, 1995b.

budget subsidies placed intense pressure on the fiscal capacities of the newly independent states. Public deficits rapidly increased at the same time as governments faced calls for greater subsidies to prop up domestic production and consumption and increased social spending to ameliorate the pressure on firms to maintain wage levels (Broome, 2006: 127, 129–30).

At the start of 1992, the monetary system in each of the newly independent states was dominated by the republican branches of the *Gosbank*, which were legally restructured as national central banks, as well as the specialized banks (*spetsbanki*) that had been created during the late 1980s as part of Mikhail Gorbachev's program of *perestroika*. The *spetsbanki* included the state savings bank (*Sberbank*), as well as the state banks that catered to particular sectors of the economy, such as foreign trade (*Vneshekonomobank*), agriculture (*Agroprombank*), industry and construction (*Promstroibank*), and housing and social development (*Zhilsotsbank*) (see Schoors, 2003b). All the Central Asian republics followed Russia's lead in liberalizing prices at the beginning of 1992, although the Uzbek government initially retained a much greater degree of administrative control over prices than either the Kyrgyz Republic or Kazakhstan (Pomfret, 2000: 737). Partly because of the continuation of price controls on a larger number of goods, the spike in Uzbekistan's inflation rate and the contraction of economic output following independence was markedly less than in the Kyrgyz Republic and Kazakhstan, as shown in Figures 4.4 and 4.5.

During 1992, the republics' central banks relied on two main instruments of monetary control. The first instrument was commercial bank reserve requirements based on the maturity of deposits, which were unremunerated and constituted a tax on the financial system. The second instrument was central bank refinance facilities for commercial banks and the government. In the Kyrgyz Republic and Kazakhstan, low interest rates on central bank financing for the budget were established in 1992 to replace the previous practice of providing the government with credit at no charge (IMF, 1992i: 34–5; IMF, 1992j: 8), while in Uzbekistan central bank credit to the government initially remained interest free (IMF, 1992k: 7). In each republic, the central bank's refinance rate for commercial banks was raised from 8 per cent to 12 per cent in mid-1991, and was further increased at varying rates during 1992 following increases in the CBR's refinance rate. However, interest rates in all three countries remained negative in real terms given the high rate of inflation. In January 1992 monthly inflation shot up following price liberalization to 157 per cent in the Kyrgyz Republic, 212 per cent in Kazakhstan, and 118 per cent in Uzbekistan, and remained in double figures each month for most of the next two years before a downward trend was established during 1994 (see Figure 3.4).

In each republic, the *spetsbanki* were heavily dependent upon central bank credit for loanable funds. Many Central Asian firms were either unable or were unwilling to service their debt during 1992 and 1993, while banks struggled to attract new savings in the high inflationary environment as the population became increasingly distrustful of the banking system (IMF, 1993l: 40–1). In these difficult circumstances a significant proportion of central bank lending to commercial banks

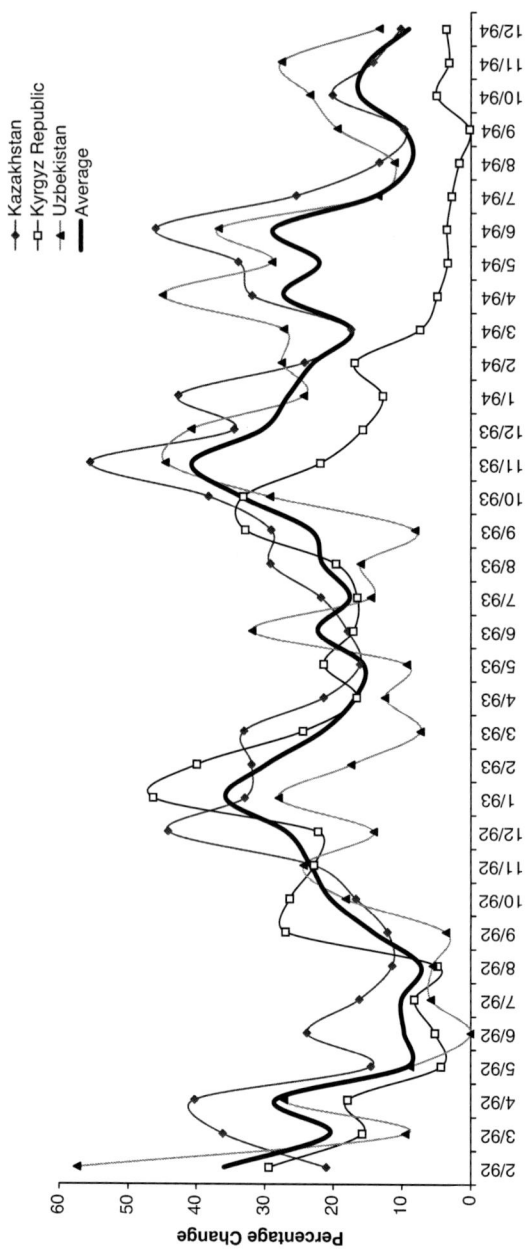

Figure 4.4 Monthly Consumer Price Inflation in Central Asia, 1992–94

Source: Koen and De Masi, 1997: 27.

Figure 4.5 Growth in Real GDP in Central Asia, 1989–2004

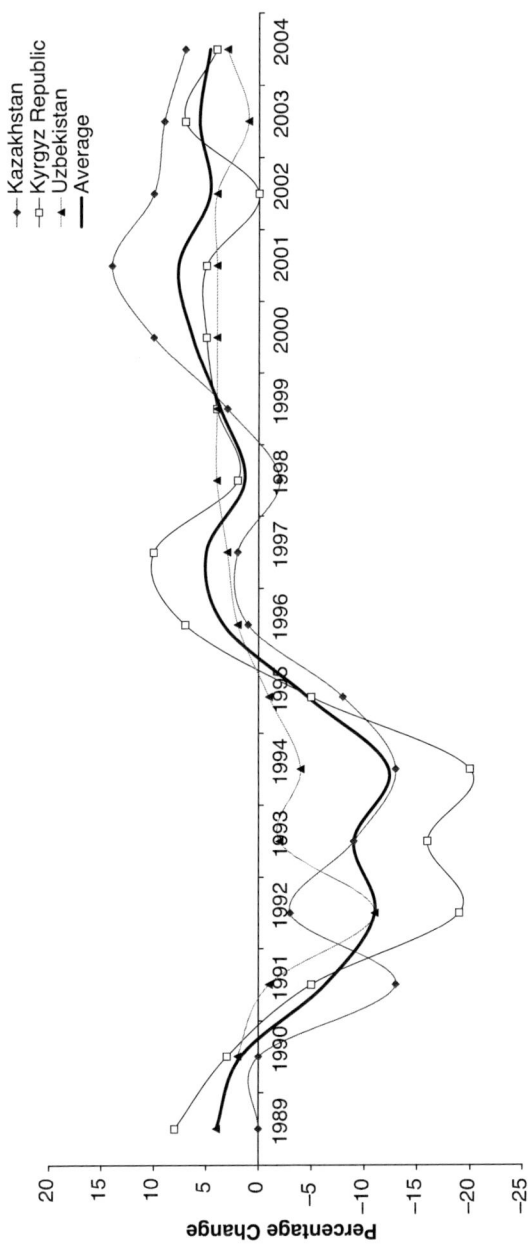

Source: EBRD, cited in Pomfret, 2006: 8.

took place on preferential terms well below the official interest rate. During 1992, refinance quotas and preferential refinance rates were commonly used by the republics' central banks as a way to allocate credit to particular sectors of the economy through the specialized commercial banks, in an attempt to maintain production and employment levels (IMF, 1992i: 34–5; IMF, 1992j: 8; IMF, 1992l: 15). In addition to direct methods of control through differential refinance rates, republican central banks also exercised moral suasion over commercial banks by insisting on discussing with bank managers the purposes for which credit would be used before approving loans, which ensured that a high proportion of refinancing credit was tied to specific goals (IMF, 1993l: 36–7).

The economic environment in Central Asia

Despite inheriting similar economic challenges at independence, there were also important economic differences in the transitional context each state faced. For instance, households in Kazakhstan were significantly wealthier compared with households in Uzbekistan or the Kyrgyz Republic. During the late 1980s Kazakhstan ranked in the middle-income group of Soviet republics, well above the poorest republics such as Uzbekistan and the Kyrgyz Republic, while still substantially below the much wealthier Baltic republics. In contrast, the average income level in Uzbekistan was estimated to be among the lowest of the Soviet republics in the 1980s, with Uzbekistan ranking as the poorest Central Asian republic next to Tajikistan (Alexeev and Gaddy, 1993: 31).

Kazakhstan's economic legacy from the Soviet era shaped its prospects for economic transformation in a distinct way compared with its Central Asian neighbors. At independence, the Kazakh economy was much more tightly integrated with the Russian economy than other Central Asian republics, especially in terms of physical infrastructure such as its systems of electrical power, coal production, and oil pipelines (see Blackmon, 2005). Despite having the advantage of inheriting a very favorable endowment of natural resources, it would take Kazakhstan most of the 1990s to reorient its economy and the physical infrastructure for exploiting its natural resources away from total dependence on Russia.

The attempt to establish a greater degree of economic independence by Kazakh policymakers, which involved the construction of a national economy within geographical boundaries that were previously irrelevant to economic planning and production, required substantial external financing. Given the higher degree of integration between Kazakhstan's economy and Russia's, compared with its Central Asian neighbors, in the early 1990s the Kazakh authorities faced a choice between maintaining their subordinate position within Russia's production system and undertaking an expensive reorientation of the economy towards new markets. The government subsequently chose the latter option, and decided to engage with the international financial community to access the foreign investment and technological expertise necessary to develop the potential of the country's petrochemical sector (Blackmon, 2005: 395). Kazakhstan was less dependent than the Kyrgyz Republic on cooperation with the IMF as a means of securing ODA because of the attractiveness of its natural resources to foreign investors. Yet establishing a good working relationship with Fund staff provided a means through which the authorities could signal their policy credibility to foreign investors as a safe and predictable environment for multinational businesses (Libman, 2006: 281–2; Bayulgen, 2005: 63; Esanov et al., 2001: 9).

To a far greater extent than either Kazakhstan or the Kyrgyz Republic, Uzbekistan's economy in both the Soviet and post-Soviet eras centered on cotton production, referred to in Central Asia as 'white gold'. By the late 1980s, Uzbekistan produced almost two-thirds of the total Soviet cotton output, accounted for around one-third of the Soviet Union's gold production, and was the third largest producer of natural gas among the Soviet republics, most of which was utilized by local industries (Blackmon, 2005: 395–6; Lubin, 1989: 622). Therefore, despite the country's low per capita income level among the Soviet republics, Uzbekistan could rely on the country's cotton and gold exports in the early 1990s as a ready source of foreign exchange.

As one economic advisor to the president observed, in the early 1990s Uzbekistan remained 'tied to Russia by thousands of strings' (Kangas, 1994: 182). Compared with Kazakhstan, however, Uzbekistan's infrastructure was less tightly integrated with the Russian republic, which enabled the Uzbek authorities to exercise more control over local energy supplies and to maintain a higher level of economic production following independence (Blackmon, 2005: 396; Ruziev et al., 2007: 12). Moreover, due to Uzbekistan's much smaller military industries than Kazakhstan, the economy did not suffer as much from the collapse in demand for military goods prompted by the end of the Cold War. With favorable terms of trade in the early 1990s for its main exports of gold and cotton, which could easily be sold to new markets,

Uzbekistan faced independence with much more promising economic circumstances in the short term than either the Kyrgyz Republic or Kazakhstan (Agzamov et al., 1995: 33).

Compared with the economic dimension of the transitional context in both Kazakhstan and Uzbekistan, the Kyrgyz Republic faced independence with very poor economic prospects. In particular, the country lacked an identifiable source of revenue to maintain fiscal solvency, to substitute for its heavy reliance on existing Soviet trade and monetary arrangements, a legacy which Kyrgyz economist Turar Koichuyev described as leaving the country with a 'psychology of dependence' on external support (Lloyd, 1993). The Kyrgyz Republic inherited a domestic economic structure that lacked either a ready source of foreign exchange or an endowment of raw resources that could attract large-scale foreign direct investment in the short term (Pomfret, 2003b: 444–5). In these unfavorable circumstances, external financing by the international financial institutions and other major official donors was the most readily accessible option that was available to Kyrgyz policymakers to alleviate the enormous economic and social costs associated with the breakdown of the USSR and national independence. However, in order to expand access to official sources of external finance, the Kyrgyz Republic had to cultivate and to consistently maintain a good relationship with the IMF due to the widespread use of cross-conditionality by major bilateral and multilateral donors.

To sum up their initial conditions, the three Central Asian states examined here each inherited similar institutional frameworks at independence but faced very different economic prospects in the immediate post-Soviet period. As a resource-poor country, the Kyrgyz Republic's political and economic circumstances left policymakers in need of significant external financing to fill the hole left by the withdrawal of direct and indirect Soviet subsidies to avert a full-blown fiscal collapse and to mitigate political opposition to the post-independence regime (see Esanov et al., 2001: 14). These circumstances suggest that Kyrgyz political leaders had little choice but to go cap-in-hand to the IMF for policy advice and loans, a decision also influenced by President Akaev's strong public commitment to enacting market-based reforms. Kazakhstan, by contrast, was much wealthier at independence than either the Kyrgyz Republic or Uzbekistan. In general, states with considerable resource wealth combined with weak formal institutions are likely to face less pressure to enact market-based economic reforms, especially where there is also a long legacy of central planning (Auty,

1999: 9, 27; Auty, 2003: 257). In the case of Kazakhstan, however, the country's geographical proximity and integrated physical infrastructure with Russia inclined Kazakh policymakers to seek good enough relations with the international financial community to secure the foreign investment that the country would require in order to take full advantage of its significant resource wealth (Esanov et al., 2001: 9). Unlike the Kyrgyz Republic, Kazakhstan could offer numerous investment opportunities to foreign businesses once the basic elements of a foreign investment-friendly environment were established, anchored by cooperation with the IMF (Esanov et al., 2001: 20), which would generate rents that could enable Kazakh policymakers to buy off potential sources of political opposition. Uzbekistan suffered the most from the loss of Soviet budget subsidies in the early 1990s, as indicated by Figure 4.1, but faced initial circumstances that enabled the country to maintain a higher level of economic production compared with its Central Asian neighbors. In particular, Uzbekistan's crop-based resource wealth was easier to exploit and to redirect to new markets than Kazakhstan's energy and mineral wealth (Auty, 1999: 28; Esanov et al., 2001: 9; Luong and Weinthal, 2001: 378–9). Combined with the authorities' ardent concern with maintaining economic and social stability, these conditions predisposed the government of Uzbekistan to be less open to the IMF's ideas for economic reform than either the Kyrgyz Republic or Kazakhstan.

Establishing an IMF loan program with the Kyrgyz Republic

Before the Fund staff would support loan applications from the Central Asian centrally planned economies, policymakers had to demonstrate to the IMF that they were serious about abandoning Soviet-era monetary practices and adopting IMF-friendly monetary reforms. As discussed in the foregoing chapters, the general monetary reform template that the IMF constructed for postcommunist economies focused on establishing current account convertibility as a means of decentralizing economic decisionmaking, increasing the role of relative price changes in determining the allocation of financial resources, and encouraging greater competition to breakup the monopolistic trading arrangements among domestic firms. The IMF saw the establishment of an independent central bank and the development of indirect market-based monetary instruments as key preconditions for the establishment of current account convertibility, which could help to enforce monetary restraint and provided a means of altering the financial relationship between the government, the central bank, commercial banks, and state-owned firms. These reforms would also allow states to signal their policy credibility to the international financial community, and conformed with the IMF's reputation for diffusing economic ideas that promote 'sound money' and 'sound public finances'.

As discussed in Chapter 2, the IMF relies on the application of prior actions as a means to test the strength of policymakers' commitment to achieving IMF-friendly economic reforms. The early demonstration of Kyrgyz policymakers' willingness to implement the IMF's advice from technical assistance missions enabled the government to move rapidly to finalize the terms of a loan arrangement with Fund staff. In March 1993, only ten months after becoming a member of the IMF, the staff supported the government's request to the Executive Board for a stand-by arrangement amounting to SDR 40.2 million. In the intervening period, Fund staff had successfully persuaded the Kyrgyz authorities to adopt numerous prior actions, which encompassed the IMF's four preconditions for establishing current account convertibility.

Of the eight prior actions adopted by the Kyrgyz authorities when they applied for a stand-by arrangement, five related to monetary reform. First, Kyrgyz policymakers had nearly completed a process of price liberalization, which the IMF wanted in place prior to the introduction of a new currency. Second, the government adopted a budget for 1993 that restricted public deficits from the point when the new currency was introduced, which the staff encouraged on the basis that it would help to shore up confidence in the value of the new currency by enforcing hard credit constraints and would signal an end to credit subsidies. This followed the extension of credit to enterprises at very low interest rates in the first quarter of 1993, which accounted for an estimated 17 per cent of the country's GDP. Third, the government had passed new legislation governing the role of the central bank and commercial banks, which legally established the central bank's independence from the government and stipulated an arms-length relationship between the National Bank of the Kyrgyz Republic (NBKR) and commercial banks. Fourth, from February 1993 the government began to allocate a proportion of central bank credit to commercial banks through credit auctions. This was a key change that the IMF wanted on the basis that it would help to create incentives for banks to act in accordance with market principles. Combined with increases in the central bank refinance rate, the introduction of credit auctions reduced the monetary benefits that had previously been available to state-owned firms in three ways. First, by increasing the cost and restricting the availability of bank credit; second, by stabilizing the value of enterprise debts that had declined because of negative real interest rates; and, third, by shifting the central bank towards a more arms-length relationship with commercial banks. Finally, the government centralized the control of foreign exchange reserves and gold in the central bank, which the IMF promoted in an effort to depoliticize decisions over the distribution of foreign exchange (IMF, 1993m: 21–2).

Based on the staff report on the Kyrgyz Republic's application for a stand-by arrangement, Fund staff believed that the government had in general accepted their policy advice on monetary reforms during 1992. In particular, Fund staff hailed the introduction of credit auctions as a key mechanism for phasing out the administrative allocation of credit to commercial banks, and praised the government's decision to introduce a convertible currency based on a free-floating exchange rate regime without intervention to influence the exchange rate by the NBKR. Fund staff nonetheless remained critical of the government's loose credit policies in the second half of 1992 and early 1993, and urged the government to resist demands from the agriculture sector and state-owned enterprises for the continued extension of easy credit (IMF, 1993m: 21, 23).

The performance criteria the staff proposed to the Executive Board for the first and second reviews of the stand-by arrangement, which were scheduled to be held in September and December 1993, centered on assessing the Kyrgyz Republic's implementation of the policies set out in its Memorandum of Economic and Financial Policies to the IMF that defined the government's key reform objectives. Following the IMF's advice, the government's reform objectives were redesigned to include establishing quarterly limits on commercial banks' access to refinance credit from the NBKR, discontinuing the practice of directed credits, and allocating all refinance credit through competitive auctions. The government committed itself to discontinuing the practice of automatically rolling over refinance credit upon maturity by the end of 1993. In addition, the maximum maturity period for central bank credit would be halved to six months in order to encourage commercial banks to use the NBKR's refinance facility only to meet short-term cash flow requirements, rather than as their main source of loanable funds (IMF, 1993n).

Through the application of prior conditions and the loan performance criteria designed by the staff for the Kyrgyz Republic, the IMF attempted to persuade Kyrgyz policymakers to set new institutional parameters that could help to change actors' preferences in favor of a market-based monetary system. In particular, Fund staff wanted to change the behavior of Kyrgyz banks by encouraging them to attract domestic savings as their main source of loanable funds, thereby increasing domestic financial intermediation and the allocation of finance based on market prices and creditworthiness assessments rather than administrative discretion and banks' traditional financial relationships with firms. To help achieve these objectives, Fund staff persuaded the government to commit to removing controls on commercial banks' interest rates. The authorities also agreed to meet the IMF's quantitative performance criteria, which included targets for domestic credit ceilings, a minimum level of convertible currency reserves, and limits on the growth of the money supply, as well as a prohibition on assuming further non-concessional debt (IMF, 1993m: 33).

Based on recommendations made by the IMF's technical assistance missions, the NBKR also introduced changes to commercial banks' 'risk concentration ceilings', which lowered the percentage of capital that banks could lend to a single customer or an individual bank shareholder (IMF, 1993m: 15). Because of the close relationship that had existed between the central bank and the *spetsbanki* in the Soviet system, such changes would radically alter the central bank's role in the domestic economy. This would also provide incentives for economic actors to adapt to a new market-based environment rather than resisting pressures for change by sheltering within traditional financial relationships. Fund staff believed that this was crucial for the long-term maintenance of a market-based policy orientation. As the IMF had learnt from the ruble zone crisis, achieving *de facto* central bank independence in the former Soviet republics of Central Asia would require not only embedding an arms-length relationship between the central bank and the government in the everyday operation of monetary policy, but also establishing an arms-length relationship between the central bank and commercial banks. Because of the impact that these changes would have on the capacity of commercial banks to continue to extend large credit flows on preferential terms to their traditional industrial customers, central bank reform became a key focus of the IMF's attempts to break up the close financial arrangements that existed between commercial banks and major public enterprises. Fund staff argued for these policy changes on the basis that they would help to reduce the segmentation of credit markets and were in line with best practice international prudential norms. Moreover, if they were fully implemented such changes would diminish the bargaining power of individual economic actors to lobby for continued access to 'easy money' based on inherited monetary norms. This would help to consolidate the political dominance of policymakers who were willing to support the IMF's approach, which was one of the major challenges for the IMF's intellectual role in Central Asia.

Before the Executive Board debated the Kyrgyz Republic's application for a stand-by arrangement, the government made an additional request for IMF resources at the beginning of May 1993 under the newly established systemic transformation facility. Fund staff supported this move because it would allow the authorities to build up their foreign exchange reserves in preparation for the introduction of a new convertible currency. The Kyrgyz authorities applied to reduce their stand-by arrangement purchase to SDR 27.09 million in combination with a proposed purchase of SDR 32.25 million under the systemic transformation facility because the systemic transformation facility funds were lent on concessional terms. The two requests for access to the IMF's resources added up to a total of 92 per cent of the Kyrgyz Republic's quota in the IMF. It is a measure of the Kyrgyz Republic's close policy relationship with the IMF that the staff supported the country's application for a stand-by arrangement in conjunction with a systemic transformation facility loan, when the other Central Asian states had to successfully graduate from a systemic transformation facility loan before the staff would support applications for a stand-by arrangement.

The Executive Board and the battle of the *som*

Following intensive technical assistance and training provided by the IMF, as well as technical assistance provided by consultants from the central banks of Estonia and Slovenia in early 1993, policymakers moved to introduce a new national currency, the Kyrgyz *som*, following parliamentary approval by a large majority on 3 May. The government announced on 7 May that the *som* would enter circulation on 10 May, with the conversion period lasting until 14 May. All Kyrgyz citizens as well as non-residents were permitted to convert an unlimited amount of cash rubles into *som* at the rate of 200 rubles per *som*. Deposits in the Savings Bank would be converted at the more favorable rate of 150 rubles per *som* to partly compensate account holders for the depreciation of their bank balances due to high inflation. Because the Kyrgyz authorities had insufficient foreign exchange reserves to defend a fixed or a semi-fixed exchange rate regime, the government took the IMF's advice and chose to introduce a free-floating exchange rate regime for the *som*. As a further demonstration of the government's willingness to listen to and implement the IMF's advice – even when this might severely disadvantage politically-important domestic industries such as agriculture – policymakers also took the bold step of establishing full currency convertibility by removing all restrictions on both current account and capital account transactions (IMF, 1993o: 61–2).

As the first Central Asian state to establish monetary independence from the ruble zone and to adopt full currency convertibility, the Kyrgyz Republic received strong support from the majority of directors on the Executive Board. The Board's debate on the Kyrgyz Republic's application for a stand-by arrangement and a systemic transformation facility arrangement with the IMF took place on 12 May 1993, when the country was halfway through the process of converting from the ruble to the *som*. In his introductory remarks, Daniel Kaeser, the executive director representing the Kyrgyz Republic, argued that the IMF should support the country's reform program 'because of the seriousness of the commitment and the competence shown by the Kyrgyz authorities'. Kaeser drew particular attention to the need for the IMF to offer strong support for the introduction of the first national currency in Central Asia, especially because of initial distrust of the currency amid local press reports that the *som*'s value 'was worthless because it was without backing' (IMF, 1993p: 29). The initial response from the Kyrgyz Republic's neighbors had added to domestic uncertainty about the new currency, with Uzbekistan closing the Kyrgyz-Uzbek border, freezing monetary and trade transactions, and shutting off the country's gas supplies (Lloyd, 1993). In response, Kaeser called for the IMF to perform an intermediary role through signaling strong rhetorical support for the new currency by communicating to the Kyrgyz press that its value 'was guaranteed mainly by the economic program that the authorities had agreed on with the IMF' (IMF, 1993p: 29).

Despite broad support for the Kyrgyz Republic, not all executive directors shared this rosy assessment of the Kyrgyz authorities' commitment to market-based reform. The new Russian executive director, Konstantin Kagalovsky, questioned the strength of the Kyrgyz authorities' commitment to maintain tight credit policies given the large expansion of central bank credit in the first quarter of 1993. Drawing attention to the outstanding bilateral differences between the two countries, Kagalovsky pressed for a resolution of the Kyrgyz Republic's outstanding debt that was owed to Russia before the Russian government would consider the extension of new bilateral credit to bridge the government's financing gap. Although he concluded his remarks by supporting the country's application for a stand-by arrangement and a systemic transformation facility arrangement, the Russian executive director indicated that supplementary financing from Russia for the Kyrgyz Republic's loan program would be withheld until the debt issue was resolved. As Kagalovsky stated to the Board: 'My authorities are ready to consider Russia's contribution to the gap coverage the day after such an agreement [on the outstanding debt] has been signed; however, we cannot commit to giving even a penny today' (IMF, 1993p: 36).

With the exception of the Russian representative, most other executive directors extended a high level of praise for the Kyrgyz authorities' commitment to implement a market-based reform program in cooperation with the Fund staff. Some directors even questioned whether the Kyrgyz Republic had gone too far too fast in pursuit of an IMF-friendly program of economic reform, although their views were in the minority. The Japanese alternate executive director, Naoki Tabata, questioned the staff over whether the IMF should consider recommending the introduction of new exchange restrictions if the *som* became unstable, possibly including the re-introduction of exchange surrender requirements for exporters or restricting internal currency convertibility by not permitting residents to hold foreign currency-denominated bank deposits. In addition, Giulo Lanciotti, the executive director representing the Italian constituency, questioned the staff over whether the authorities might have been better to rely on bank-specific credit ceilings rather than non-discriminatory credit auctions for allocating central bank refinance credit in the short term. Lanciotti argued that this would help to ensure that commercial banks with a high level of bad loans did not simply outbid more creditworthy banks to gain new finance. The temporary alternate executive director representing France, Patrice Bonzom, also mooted the potential for greater use of direct instruments of monetary control to achieve macroeconomic stability (IMF, 1993p: 38, 41, 47).

Kaeser's request for the IMF to attempt to play a greater role as a reputatational intermediary by providing a strong public demonstration of its confidence in the soundness of the Kyrgyz authorities' reform program as well as the new currency itself was reinforced by the comments of Oleh Havrylyshyn, the alternate executive director for the Netherlands constituency. Havrylyshyn argued that 'the soundness of the som is a reflection of the soundness of the economic stabilization and reform program'. He urged the IMF's management to express its strong confidence in the program through a press release in support of the currency, with the 'hope that someone locally can then shout this from the rooftops of Bishkek to offset the early skepticism shown toward the som' (IMF, 1993p: 50). The Executive Board hoped that the IMF's capacity to act as a reputational intermediary for its borrowing member states among international audiences could also help to shore up local confidence in the new Kyrgyz currency. Among Western commentators, the introduction of the *som* was subsequently described by the financial press as a crucial test case not only of the strength of the Kyrgyz authorities' commitment to market-based economic reform, but also of the credibility of the IMF itself. For example, John Lloyd (1993), writing in the *Financial Times*, suggested that the 'battle of the som' would determine 'the future of the state itself, the viability of new currencies in the post-Soviet world and the reputation of the multilateral financial institutions'.

With regard to the broader objectives of the loan program, other executive directors reinforced the need for the Kyrgyz authorities to signal their intention to maintain a strong commitment to market-based reform by consistently implementing the policies that had been designed in cooperation with the Fund staff. The temporary alternate executive director for the US, John Abbott, urged the Kyrgyz authorities to 'stand firm on intentions to harden the budget constraints of public enterprises' by refusing to allocate credit on preferential terms. In this regard, Abbott praised the decision to move towards the market-based allocation of credit through Central Bank auctions and the enactment of legislation to establish central bank independence. Commenting on the fact that the Kyrgyz Republic would be the first state to access the IMF's brand new systemic transformation facility lending window – and in a nod to the Russian authorities playing hardball in negotiations with the IMF over the terms of their own systemic transformation facility arrangement (Stone, 2002: 126) – Abbott stated that 'as a cooperative IMF member that has earned this access, Kyrgyzstan clearly provides an apt example for the others that will follow' (IMF, 1993p: 54–5).

Justifying the staff's policy advice in response to questions from the Board, a representative from the European II Department explained that the staff had explicitly advised the Kyrgyz authorities against introducing direct monetary controls such as credit ceilings for individual banks. This was based on the staff's view that encouraging a reliance on market-based monetary instruments, beginning with credit auctions, would quickly enable interest rates to become positive in real terms, and corresponded with the need to make a decisive break with policymakers' past practices of directing credit to specific industries and firms. In response to the Japanese executive director's suggestion of the possible use of additional exchange restrictions, the staff representative argued that such a move would be inappropriate and that the free-floating exchange rate regime would provide the necessary flexibility for the *som* to quickly reach an appropriate level. A staff representative from the Policy Development and Review Department reinforced this view, arguing that the introduction of bank-by-bank credit ceilings would constitute a 'second-best solution'. Following the Board's request for the IMF to offer rhetorical support for the country's program of monetary transformation, the staff representative from the European II Department agreed that an IMF press release communicating the Board's decision on the loan applications should signal strong endorsement of the new currency and approval of the authorities' policy settings in general (IMF, 1993p: 57, 60–1).

Executive directors subsequently approved the Kyrgyz Republic's two applications for access to the IMF's financial resources through a stand-by arrangement and a systemic transformation facility arrangement, based primarily on the staff's assessment of the strength of policy-makers' commitment to enacting market-based reforms. In making their decision, directors cited in particular the government's early track record of implementing policy reforms in cooperation with the IMF, as indicated by the rapid achievement of the staff's prior actions and technical assistance recommendations. Most directors agreed that while the economic outlook for the Kyrgyz Republic was very poor, they supported granting the country access to loan arrangements based on the reasoning that the authorities' demonstrated commitment to reform deserved the IMF's financial and rhetorical support (IMF, 1993q). As this case suggests, the way the Executive Board sees a government's track record of cooperation and constructive policy dialogue with the staff is significant for a state's capacity to access IMF loans. In particular, the Board's deliberations help to illustrate the greater importance that can be attached to the quality of a country's policy dialogue with Fund staff – at least when this is backed up with observable policy changes – compared with its actual economic circumstances (and hence the capacity to repay IMF loans).

The Kyrgyz Republic's first IMF loans

The best laid plans of international organizations and governments often go awry, which repeatedly proved to be the case for the IMF in Central Asia during the early 1990s. The evidence quickly suggested that the IMF had been overly optimistic about the willingness, or the political capacity, of the government to sustain its early market-based reforms given the scale of the economic crisis that the country faced. For example, the IMF's first review of the Kyrgyz Republic's progress under the stand-by arrangement, which took place in July and August 1993, indicated mixed success in the implementation of agreed policy changes. While the Kyrgyz authorities had successfully signaled a pro-market policy orientation to the IMF, in practice the government adopted several policies that the IMF opposed and failed to achieve several key performance criteria under the stand-by arrangement.

The IMF concentrates primarily on tracking and providing advice on formal institutional change, but this can quickly be derailed when actors seek to mediate uncertainty by operating through informal processes. Although the Kyrgyz government adopted the majority of the IMF's recommended reforms to legislation and to the institutional design of monetary arrangements, a degree of what the IMF terms 'policy slippage' occurred with regard to the quantitative targets that aimed to constrain the growth of cheap credit through traditional financial relationships. For instance, the government failed to meet the IMF's performance criteria for increasing the net domestic assets of the central bank, limiting bank credit to the government, and limiting non-concessional debt, while inflation rates continued to exceed program targets. Moreover, the banking system continued to function in practice according to informal monetary norms, with commercial banks channeling the bulk of credit to traditional customers, especially the large state-owned industrial and agricultural businesses that were bank shareholders (IMF, 1993r: 18). In addition, despite winning strong praise from the IMF as a model of successful post-Soviet currency reform, everyday monetary practices initially undermined the introduction of the new national currency. Due to a lack of trust in the currency among the population, only one-quarter of the cash rubles that were estimated to be in circulation when the *som* was introduced were converted into the new currency (Melliss and Cornelius, 1994: 68). Consequently, the high level of cash rubles remaining in the domestic money supply constrained the NBKR's capacity to breakup the existing monetary arrangements between commercial banks and their traditional customers.

Seen from the IMF's perspective, however, Fund staff notched up some important successes in their efforts to persuade policymakers to stick with market-based reforms when policymakers indicated an intention to defect on their policy commitments to the IMF. While the Kyrgyz authorities failed to meet some of the key performance criteria under the stand-by arrangement, in several policy areas where decision-makers had seemed likely to waver in their commitment to market-based reforms the staff successfully persuaded the government against taking policy actions that were seen as backward steps. Because the IMF had been able to establish a good working relationship with national policymakers, this enlarged the scope for Fund staff to have input into the country's day-to-day decisionmaking process and strengthened their hand in ongoing debates over policy efficacy. This can be illustrated by the success of Fund staff in persuading policymakers to follow their advice with respect to the increasing problem of inter-enterprise arrears, a major source of concern for the Kyrgyz authorities. Policymakers initially wanted to provide significant credit assistance from the government in order to diminish the threat to the economy and the government's revenue base posed by the growth of inter-firm debt. However, Fund staff persuaded policymakers to agree that any solution to the arrears problem would resist the strong domestic pressure for a further credit bailout in order to signal their commitment to monetary restraint (IMF, 1993r: 10).

Similar examples of IMF-friendly policy actions to address the steep challenges the country faced helped to assuage doubts among the Fund staff about the willingness of Kyrgyz officials to implement market-based reforms. Despite ongoing economic difficulties and instances of policy slippage, Fund staff remained convinced of the authorities' commitment due in large part to their success in persuading the Kyrgyz authorities to adhere to the original policy intentions set out in the government's Memorandum of Economic and Financial Policies. In particular, the authorities maintained their commitment to an open current account and capital account (with the exception of restrictions on the settlement of outstanding correspondent account balances with several of the other former Soviet republics), and Fund staff judged that officials had maintained a constructive relationship with technical assistance missions. During the loan review, Fund staff also took into account as mitigating factors the unexpected economic challenges the country had faced since the approval of the loan arrangement. These included worsening trade relations with the country's traditional trade partners in the former Soviet republics, as well as unforeseen shortfalls in the amount of external financing made available to the government. The staff therefore recommended that the Executive Board approve the government's requests for waivers of the non-observance of performance criteria and modifications of future targets under the stand-by arrangement (IMF, 1993r: 17).

In reaching their decision to support the Kyrgyz Republic's applic-ation for waivers of the loan performance criteria in September 1993, executive directors emphasized the substantial progress that the country had already made. They also took into account that economic targets had been missed by relatively small margins, and believed that these shortcomings were related to the unforeseen economic challenges the country faced rather than weaknesses in policy or political will. These unforeseen circumstances included a large shortfall in external financing, especially from Russia which had extended only one-fifth of the approx-imately US$100 million of financial support it had initially promised to commit in April 1993, energy price shocks, and trade disruptions arising from worsening relations with neighboring states. Despite these mitigating circumstances, Oleh Havrylyshyn, the Netherlands' exe-cutive director, drew the Board's attention to the continued allocation of credit according to the country's inherited informal monetary norms. He argued that the creation of a market-based monetary system would continue to be hampered if commercial banks maintained close con-nections with their traditional customers and continued to auto-matically extend them new credit. Havrylyshyn suggested that the Kyrgyz authorities could help to change these monetary relationships by expanding the proportion of central bank refinance credit allocated to commercial banks through auctions. In addition, other directors called on the Kyrgyz Republic to establish positive real interest rates as soon as possible to aid the transformation of the monetary system (IMF, 1993s: 9, 11, 13, 18, 20).

Despite these criticisms, the Executive Board singled out for praise the government's decision not to extend a general credit bailout to resolve the problem of inter-enterprise arrears. The temporary alternate executive director for the US, Jeremy Wire, praised the authorities' 'tremendous vision and courage' in pursuing market-based economic transformation. In addition, the Japanese representative, Toshio Oya, praised the government's decision to eliminate export and import licensing requirements despite most other former Soviet republics main-taining trade and exchange restrictions in the face of strong domestic resistance to change (IMF, 1993s: 12, 16). Because the Executive Board accepted the staff's assessment that the missed targets were mostly the result of economic circumstances that were beyond policymakers' con-trol, they saw the high degree of compliance with the broad thrust of the loan program as further evidence of the authorities' strong com-mitment to market-based economic reform and their willingness to maintain close cooperation with the IMF. In the first stage of the IMF's relationship with the Kyrgyz Republic, therefore, the organization achieved some important successes in persuading policymakers to adopt its ideas for formal institutional changes (see Table 4.1). Nevertheless, these achievements were partly undermined by the unfavorable economic environment the country faced, and the readiness of banks and firms to resist formal changes and instead to mediate the uncertainty they produced by continuing to maintain their traditional financial relationships.

Establishing an IMF loan program with Kazakhstan

After Kazakhstan became a member of the IMF in July 1992, Kazakh monetary officials faced substantial political difficulties that hampered attempts to restrain domestic credit expansion. For instance, although the National Bank of Kazakhstan (NBK) raised its official refinance rate to 65 per cent in July after the Russian central bank had raised its rate to 80 per cent, the bulk of central bank refinancing credit for commercial banks continued to be allocated on preferential terms in response to political pressure from the parliament and the government. Following widespread domestic resistance to its efforts to constrain credit growth by raising the refinance rate, the NBK extended a high proportion of credit to commercial banks at interest rates between 0 and 25 per cent in 1992, well below inflation, over half of which was allocated to the agriculture sector to mitigate social dissent. Like the Kyrgyz Republic, the IMF attempted to persuade Kazakh policymakers to set new institutional parameters that could help to change actors' preferences in favor of a market-based monetary system. To circumscribe the potential for political interference in the distribution of financial resources, Fund staff urged the central bank to adopt measures that would help to shift the financial system towards the allocation of credit via interest rates rather than administrative discretion. In particular, Fund staff sought to persuade policymakers to make greater use of auctions as an impersonal way of pricing and allocating credit (IMF, 1993t: 14–15).

In their efforts to shape the conduct of monetary policy in the early period of Kazakhstan's independence, Fund staff faced the problem of sharp disagreements between the parliament, the government, and the newly established central bank over whether to continue the practice of allocating credit to particular sectors on preferential terms. While a new constitution adopted in January 1993 enshrined legal independence for the NBK from both the parliament and the government,

Table 4.1 Chronology of Key Monetary Reforms in Central Asia, 1992–96

	Kyrgyz Republic	Kazakhstan	Uzbekistan
1992	*Introduction of interest charges on government debt *Price liberalization *Legal central bank independence	*Introduction of interest charges on government debt *Partial price liberalization	*Price liberalization
1993	*Introduction of credit auctions and quarterly credit ceilings *Central bank control over foreign exchange *Introduction of a national currency as sole legal tender *Current account and capital account convertibility *Liberalization of commercial interest rates *Introduction of foreign exchange auctions	*Legal central bank independence *Introduction of credit auctions and quarterly credit ceilings *Introduction of a national currency as sole legal tender *Partial current account convertibility *Partial liberalization of commercial interest rates *Introduction of foreign exchange auctions	*Legal central bank independence *Introduction of credit auctions and quarterly credit ceilings *Introduction of a temporary national currency *Partial current account convertibility
1994	*Positive real interest rates	*Expansion of credit auctions *Liberalization of commercial interest rates *Positive real interest rates	*Introduction of a national currency as sole legal tender *Partial liberalization of commercial interest rates *Introduction of foreign exchange auctions
1995	*Acceptance of Article VIII status		*Expansion of credit auctions and introduction of quarterly credit ceilings *Positive real interest rates *Current account convertibility *Legal central bank independence
1996		*Current account convertibility *Acceptance of Article VIII status	*Introduction of new exchange restrictions

the parliament had the formal right to supervise the central bank's operations, and in practice the government remained able to exert a high degree of informal influence over the central bank. The IMF wanted subsidies to enterprises to be fully costed and made explicit by incorporating them into the budget. However, the government continued to extend subsidies implicitly by allocating cheap money to firms through the banking system, although policymakers did agree to the IMF's request to limit the overall volume of preferential credit (IMF, 1993t: 16–17). In addition to the problem of building a political consensus on monetary reform among different actors within Kazakhstan, Fund staff continued to see the lack of regional monetary cooperation and policy coordination between the former Soviet republics in the ruble zone as the most urgent monetary challenge facing the Kazakh authorities in 1992 and early 1993.

Prior to the IMF's Article IV consultation with the authorities in early 1993, Fund staff had visited Kazakhstan to help foster a constituency in favor of economic liberalization, and to discuss the possibility of designing a reform program that could be supported by an IMF loan arrangement, on four occasions during 1992 (IMF, 1993t: 34). Although the symbolic advantages of the authorities agreeing on an IMF-supported reform program would greatly exceed the specific monetary value of any IMF loans, these earlier staff visits had produced only gradual progress towards the development of an IMF-friendly reform program for Kazakhstan. As with the other former Soviet republics, approval of a loan arrangement with the IMF would enable Kazakhstan to access loans from other bilateral and multilateral donors such as the World Bank, starting with a World Bank import rehabilitation credit of US$180 million. Discussions subsequently proved more fruitful during a staff team visit to Almaty in May 1993, at a time when the Kazakh authorities found themselves under greater financial pressure following a decision by the Central Bank of Russia to suspend its unlimited credit line to the National Bank of Kazakhstan. In negotiations over the development of an upper credit tranche stand-by arrangement, the principal sticking point for the IMF remained the inability of Kazakh policymakers to establish greater control over inflation and the exchange rate while the country remained within the ruble zone. However, for the Kazakh authorities the importance of the country's 'unique political relationship with Russia' limited the possibility of rapid movement to establish an independent currency (IMF, 1993u: 1, 3, 12).

In order to lay the foundation for a future stand-by arrangement application, following further negotiations over policy reforms with the staff, in July 1993 the government applied to the IMF for a loan under the systemic transformation facility of SDR 61.875 million (IMF, 1993u: 24). Although the systemic transformation facility loan did not entail the same level of policy conditions that would be attached to a stand-by arrangement, the government agreed to comply with a series of quantitative targets and structural reform benchmarks. The IMF's quantitative targets included quarterly ceilings on the extension of credit by the central bank to commercial banks and on total lending to the government, as well as floors for the level of convertible currency reserves. The principal monetary reform benchmarks included raising the refinance rate to equal the rate set by the Russian central bank, temporarily raising the foreign exchange surrender requirement on export earnings in order to shore up international reserves, and progressively increasing the proportion of new central bank lending that was allocated through competitive credit auctions. Fund staff successfully persuaded the authorities to agree that the central bank's refinance facility would only be used to meet the short-term cash flow needs of commercial banks rather than to selectively allocate credit to particular industries on preferential terms. Policymakers also agreed that the use of market-based mechanisms would be gradually increased by allocating 20 per cent of new central bank credit via competitive auctions in the second half of 1993, rising to 50 per cent of new credit during the second quarter of 1994 (IMF, 1993u: 33, 36). In the context of the proposed systemic transformation facility arrangement with the IMF, bilateral and multilateral donors pledged to support Kazakhstan's economic reform program to the amount of around US$400 million. In addition to loans from the World Bank, this included credit of 150 billion rubles from Russia, ECU 300 million from the EBRD, and around US$50 million from Austria, Belgium, Canada, Germany, and the US (IMF, 1993v: 32).

Establishing monetary independence in Kazakhstan

An important factor that influenced how easily the Central Asian republics could gain access to IMF financing was the judgment formed within the organization about the pace of economic reform in different countries – especially with respect to the marketization of the financial system and monetary policy. In the Executive Board's debates over Kazakhstan's application for a systemic transformation facility arrangement, for example, executive directors extended a more positive endorsement of the authorities' policy stance than during the first Article IV consultation with Kazakhstan only a few months earlier. The US executive director commented that 'There can be no doubt at this point that Kazakhstan is in the front ranks of the reforming countries of the former Soviet Union'. The US representative also observed that 'The National Bank of Kazakhstan has become a pacesetter among the countries of the former Soviet Union in using credit auctions to allocate central bank credit' (IMF, 1993v: 3–4).

The emphasis the IMF placed on transforming the way financial resources were distributed – in particular the objective of shifting to a system of competitive credit allocation based on interest rates – was driven by a belief that changing the role of money in post-Soviet economies was essential for changing people's behavior and their expectations of the role of the state. The IMF's approach was shaped by the emerging consensus among economists that monetary reforms are most likely to be successful when governments provide clear and credible signals to their domestic and international audiences that reforms will be consistently maintained (see Grabel, 2000; Hall, 2008). A statement by the representative for the Italian constituency, Enzo Quattrociocche, helps to illustrate the connection the Executive Board saw between monetary reform and the task of economic transformation in the former Soviet Union. Quattrociocche (IMF, 1993v: 6) argued that:

> The creation of a market economy requires fundamental changes in the institutional setting and in people's habits. Coherent and firm implementation of economic policies during the transition period is therefore essential in order to validate the expectations of economic agents... Dispelling the uncertainties surrounding the monetary arrangements [in Kazakhstan] is crucial in order to provide a clear signal of the future course of the stabilization process.

The Board's main concern thus continued to be the need to achieve greater macroeconomic stability by moving towards the establishment of monetary independence in Kazakhstan. Executive directors cited the steps already taken by the government towards relying on market-based mechanisms to allocate credit and recent increases in interest rates as positive changes that informed their decision to approve the country's application for a systemic transformation facility arrangement. Nevertheless, most directors agreed that a new currency would have to be introduced in order for Kazakhstan to qualify for an upper credit tranche stand-by arrangement with the IMF.

The government subsequently introduced a new national currency, the *tenge*, on 15 November 1993, in response to the tough conditions that Russia had set out for continued membership in a new ruble zone, as discussed in Chapter 3. Following the substantial preparations made by the authorities in consultation with technical assistance missions from the IMF, including financial penalties for any business that refused to accept payment in the new currency or which sought to take advantage of the change to raise prices, the conversion process was relatively trouble-free. The ruble was converted at the rate of 500 *tenge* to 1 ruble, with individuals allowed to convert up to 100,000 cash rubles from 15–20 November. The limit on the amount of cash rubles that could be converted to the new currency was an attempt to cope with the flood of old Soviet rubles that had flowed into the republic from elsewhere in Central Asia. However, in practice these controls were often circumvented, with individuals able to breach exchange limits by paying a premium to residents who had less than the full 100,000 rubles to convert (IMF, 1994b: 26).

Following its establishment as sole legal tender on 18 November, the authorities introduced a managed float exchange rate regime for the *tenge* with the currency traded on a new Interbank Currency Exchange. The National Bank of Kazakhstan initially intervened extensively in foreign exchange auctions to help establish sufficient liquidity for the new market to function effectively, prompting the Fund staff to negotiate the terms of an 'appropriate intervention policy' with the central bank (IMF, 1994c: 26). The introduction of the *tenge* cleared away the final major hurdle preventing Kazakhstan from accessing an upper credit tranche loan with the IMF, and the authorities applied for a stand-by arrangement as well as a second purchase under the systemic transformation facility in December 1993 (IMF, 1994b: 1–2, 5). In comparison with the Kyrgyz Republic, therefore, the IMF's progress during the first stage in the development of its relationship with Kazakhstan was much more uneven during 1993. This was in large part due to Kazakh policymakers' reluctance to move quickly to establish monetary independence because of their more intensive political and economic ties with Russia. However, the IMF was able to persuade the Kazakh authorities to adopt key formal monetary reforms – such as the introduction of credit auctions and quarterly credit ceilings – that the staff wanted in place in order to harden the budget constraints on commercial banks and firms (see Table 4.1).

The difficult case of Uzbekistan

While policymakers in the Kyrgyz Republic and Kazakhstan faced steep political and economic obstacles to implementing IMF-friendly reforms they were open to persuasion by the IMF on how to construct national monetary systems, whereas the Uzbek authorities were much less receptive to the IMF's advice for market-based monetary reforms throughout 1993. In the IMF's first Article IV consultation with Uzbekistan in October 1993, Fund staff strongly encouraged the government to restrain the rapid expansion of domestic credit, which the IMF calculated had increased enormously by 97 per cent of GDP in 1992 and 72 per cent of GDP in 1993. By comparing the CBU's refinance rate with the commercial bank rate in Russia (both of which remained negative in real terms), Fund staff estimated that the growth of preferential credit in 1992 had amounted to an interest rate subsidy equal to 22 per cent of Uzbekistan's GDP (IMF, 1994d: 39).

The financial system continued to operate within soft budget constraints throughout 1993, and was geared towards achieving the government's objectives of maintaining production and employment levels rather than achieving the changes in financial behavior sought by Fund staff. For example, the Central Bank of Uzbekistan (CBU) continued to channel credit to priority areas of the economy through commercial banks, which were permitted to run up large overdrafts to ease the pressure of repayments, and chose not to enforce the formal rules on banks' reserve requirements. The IMF persuaded the authorities to introduce credit auctions for the first time in August 1993, which the staff interpreted as marking 'a significant change of policy direction', but this was more a symbolic gesture by policymakers as initial auctions amounted to less than 5 per cent of total credit expansion (IMF, 1993w: 6–7).

In response to the harsh terms for continued ruble zone participation set down by Russia, the Uzbek authorities opted to introduce the *sum* coupon as a temporary currency on 15 November at the same time as Kazakhstan introduced the *tenge*. However, the *sum* coupon continued to circulate in addition to both old Soviet rubles and the new Russian rubles introduced by the CBR in July. Moreover, the introduction of the *sum* coupon was undertaken without the IMF's advice and assistance. The IMF had previously provided Uzbek officials with substantial information on how to prepare for the introduction of a new currency, but most of this advice was ignored. The uncertainty generated by the conversion process contributed to a lack of acceptance of the new currency among the population, and caused further disruptions in inter-republican trade when other former Soviet republics refused to accept the *sum* coupon at the government's official exchange rate as payment for goods (IMF, 1993w: 7).

During discussions in Tashkent with Uzbek officials for the 1993 Article IV consultation, the IMF nonetheless found some reasons to anticipate that the authorities' attitude towards economic reform might slowly be changing as a result of the final breakdown of the ruble zone and the monetary problems associated with the introduction of the *sum* coupon. For instance, officials in the government and in the central bank agreed with Fund staff that the expansion of credit had been too large during 1993, although this was justified on the grounds that it had been necessary to finance the year's cotton harvest. In addition, CBU officials agreed to follow the organization's advice to tighten credit growth and to channel a larger proportion of central bank lending through credit auctions – policy changes that the IMF was also pushing for in the Kyrgyz Republic and Kazakhstan. While Fund staff 'welcomed this apparent determination to strike out a new path', they sought to persuade CBU officials that the best way to demonstrate the credibility of a change in policy direction was to institute a large increase in the central bank's refinance rate to close the gap between the refinance rate and the credit auction interest rates. The staff also wanted the central bank to institute a single price for all credit, so that new lending to the government and commercial banks would take place at the interest rate determined by credit auctions. But decision-makers wished to retain administrative control over credit allocation and the price of central bank lending, and told the staff that they intended to continue their program of allocating preferential credit to the agriculture sector (IMF, 1993w: 11).

Despite some evidence that the Uzbek authorities were gradually becoming more receptive to the IMF's advice, this led the staff to conclude that 'it was not clear from the discussions whether there is a convergence of views within the government on either the scope or the direction of reform, and the policy stance remains highly interventionist' (IMF, 1993w: 11–12). In addition to the policies detailed above, the government introduced various measures to subsidize domestic consumption with the aim of maintaining social stability, which included an overvalued exchange rate, external borrowing, gold sales, widespread administrative controls, and large domestic credit expansion. The IMF mission therefore concluded its report with the stark assessment that 'The staff regards this approach as having no chance of success in bringing about sustained economic growth'. Instead, Fund staff argued that 'The Government's economic reforms... have reached a critical stage, and policies urgently need to be reoriented' (IMF, 1993w: 14–15).

Fund staff found so little to be positive about in Uzbekistan that they recommended the IMF's technical assistance missions should not be repeated in the future unless the government took concrete steps to demonstrate a commitment to market-based economic reform. Before Uzbekistan would be able to apply for a loan arrangement with the IMF, the staff wanted to see a significant demonstration of the government's commitment to adopting market-based reforms, measured by the implementation of the IMF's earlier technical assistance recommendations. In this regard, Fund staff urged the government to use the planned introduction of a new currency in 1994 to replace the *sum* coupon as an opportunity 'to demonstrate a new commitment to strong and credible adjustment policies'. In particular, staff wanted to see the introduction of the new currency accompanied by the establishment of a unified floating exchange rate regime, the development of a competitive domestic market for foreign exchange, and the adoption of full current account convertibility (IMF, 1993w: 15, 17). Whereas Kyrgyzstan moved very rapidly to adopt full currency convertibility, and Kazakhstan gradually but steadily reduced its exchange restrictions, the Uzbek authorities' policies instead intensified a *de facto* system of multiple exchange rates. Among other exchange restrictions that the government had continued, the *sum* coupon, old Soviet rubles, and new Russian rubles were all circulating in the economy simultaneously with multiple rates of exchange. An official exchange rate was set by the CBU, which was used to record trade transactions, to estimate taxes, and for debt servicing. A second commercial exchange rate was set by the National Bank for Foreign Economic Activity, the former Uzbek branch of the Soviet *Vneshekonombank* that continued to maintain control over the management of international reserves, which the IMF wanted the government to transfer to the CBU's control (IMF, 1994d: 35–6). In these conditions, policymakers continued to rely on central planning instruments to regulate economic activity, while keeping the IMF at arm's length.

Developing the IMF's policy dialogue with Uzbekistan

Despite starting off on the wrong foot with Uzbekistan, on several occasions a negative assessment by Fund staff helped prompt the authorities to make more of an effort to improve their relations with the IMF. Following the poor report from the 1993 Article IV consultation with the IMF, for example, the Uzbek authorities submitted a statement to the staff on their reform program for the coming year, with the aim of furthering discussions on a possible systemic transformation facility loan arrangement with the IMF in the near future. For the Fund staff, the government's policy intentions for 1994 signaled the potential for a substantial shift in policy orientation, although the staff demanded clarification on the timing and extent of particular reforms.

Especially promising for the IMF, the new program envisaged a significant change in credit practices. This included commitments that the CBU would cease to extend credit to banks on preferential terms from 1 January 1994 and the bulk of central bank refinance loans would be allocated through credit auctions (although this had not yet occurred when the staff prepared a supplementary report on the new program for the Executive Board in mid-January). The program set a target of reducing inflation to a monthly rate of 5 per cent by the middle of 1994, and committed the government to introducing several of the IMF's key technical assistance recommendations. These changes included a revision of central bank legislation, reversing the CBU's centralization of control over cash operations, and the establishment of a foreign currency auction. Although Fund staff stuck to their original evaluation in the Article IV consultation of the poor quality of the government's overall policy orientation, they cautiously commended the new program of reforms as 'a necessary and welcome shift in the right direction'. The staff continued to hold the door open for the Uzbek government to intensify its cooperation with the IMF, suggesting that they would 'offer to reinforce technical assistance missions in several areas, if there are indications that earlier recommendations are being implemented'. The staff also set benchmarks that would be used to assess the strength of the government's commitment to its new program, noting that the efficient introduction of a new national currency to replace the *sum* coupon 'would be important for the credibility of the Government's reform efforts' (IMF, 1993e: 3–5).

When the Executive Board discussed the country's first Article IV consultation with the IMF the following week, directors heavily criticized the Uzbek authorities' track record of resisting the implementation of market-based economic reforms and continuing to rely on 'the methods of the command economy'. The US executive director, Karin Lissakers, stated unambiguously that 'Uzbekistan appears to have made little real progress toward adoption of the macroeconomic policies and institutions necessary for a market economy', and had instead embraced a policy orientation 'that can barely be deemed "gradualistic"'. Lissakers concluded that 'The staff seems to have been kept at arm's length, even as the Uzbek authorities express interest in financial support from the IMF'. Moreover, the Executive Board judged that the Uzbek authorities appeared to have deliberately hindered the IMF's access to the government's economic statistics, which obstructed the staff's ability to conduct effective policy surveillance and constituted a violation of a key obligation of IMF membership. In this respect, the US executive director warned the Uzbek authorities that a loan arrangement with the IMF would only be forthcoming 'if the authorities work urgently, in cooperation with the staff, to bring their policies in line with their rhetoric'. In order to achieve this, Lissakers continued, 'the Government needs to undergo a major philosophical shift in attitude regarding its role in the economy and the pace of reform' (IMF, 1994f: 20, 28–9).

With regard to monetary policy reform, Lissakers stated categorically that the government should abandon the use of cheap credit to maintain production and employment levels. The US executive director also called for the establishment of greater political autonomy for the central bank, a shift towards the use of indirect instruments of monetary control, and the establishment of positive real interest rates. Lissakers applauded the government's stated intentions to adopt further moves towards market-based reform, but urged the authorities to follow this through with concrete actions in cooperation with Fund staff (IMF, 1994f: 30). The US executive director's comments were echoed by most other members of the Board, who called for a change in Uzbekistan's economic policy orientation in the strongest possible terms, toward a greater reliance on market-based mechanisms. Despite the substantial criticism of the Uzbek authorities' policy orientation, however, executive directors did not take issue with the social goals that formed the government's public justification for adopting a gradual approach to market-based reforms. Rather, they disagreed that these goals could be achieved by the policy measures the government was using and argued that, contrary to what national decisionmakers believed, the government's policy settings were more likely to prove detrimental to their stated economic and social goals (IMF, 1994f: 42–7). In response to the US executive director's strongly worded comments, a representative from the European II Department pointed out that staff were not yet recommending the adoption of indirect instruments of monetary control in either Uzbekistan or Kazakhstan. Due to the undeveloped nature of state institutions and credit markets in both countries, Fund staff instead recommended that central banks allocate credit through auctions as an alternative to the administrative allocation of credit on preferential terms, in order to help develop local credit markets and to establish a market price for central bank lending (IMF, 1994f: 37).

Establishing an IMF loan program with Uzbekistan

It took the whole of 1994 before Fund staff were sufficiently satisfied with the Uzbek government's economic policy reforms to recommend approving an IMF loan, even under the relatively low policy conditionality of the systemic transformation facility. The staff had visited Tashkent in March–April and in October–November 1994 for negotiations over the government's application for a loan agreement with the IMF. In the intervening period the IMF had substantially increased the level of its technical assistance support to Uzbekistan, with missions from the Monetary and Exchange Affairs Department (May), the Fiscal Affairs Department (January, June–July), the Statistics Department (January, March, April–May, May–June, and November–December), and the Legal Department (April). From the staff's perspective, the Uzbek authorities were now showing greater willingness to implement the policy recommendations of technical assistance missions. In addition, the IMF Institute had provided a further course on macroeconomic policymaking for senior officials in May, and the IMF had arranged for a resident advisor within the CBU to provide ongoing advice on monetary policy reforms from November 1994 (IMF, 1994g: 32–3).

The improvement in relations between the IMF and the Uzbek authorities followed a decree issued by President Karimov on 21 January 1994, which set out a series of concrete measures to increase the pace of economic reforms. This was deemed sufficient for the Fund staff to enter into negotiations with the authorities over whether to put in place a systemic transformation facility arrangement to support the planned introduction of the new national currency, the Uzbek *sum*, in July. Yet when the authorities failed to implement key prior actions required by the staff, such as substantially increasing interest rates, depreciating the exchange rate, and introducing auctions for the allocation of foreign exchange, plans for a systemic transformation facility arrangement to support the new currency were put on hold. After the introduction of the *sum* in July, however, the authorities implemented several of the prior actions that the staff had been promoting since October 1993. These changes included increasing the refinance rate of the CBU from 150 to 225 per cent and aligning it more closely with the credit auction interest rate, increasing the deposit rates of the Savings Bank, and unifying the official and the cash exchange rate for the *sum*. From mid-October 1994, the government also implemented the IMF's advice requiring that all payment transactions within Uzbekistan be undertaken in *sum* as the country's sole legal tender. For the first time, Fund staff judged that Uzbek policymakers had 'cooperated fully with the staff in establishing a comprehensive systemic and macroeconomic program' for the rest of the year and for 1995. While the staff still sought to convince the authorities to further increase the pace of economic reforms, the authorities justified their stance to the IMF on the grounds that 'it would not be feasible politically and institutionally to speed up the process further at this stage'. Despite this continued caution, the Uzbek government signaled to Fund staff that they were interested in preparing the ground for an upper credit tranche stand-by arrangement with the IMF as soon as possible (IMF, 1994g: 2, 5–8).

Fund staff finally supported the Uzbek government's application for a systemic transformation facility loan of SDR 49.875 million in December 1994 (which constituted a relatively low 25 per cent of the country's quota in the IMF, indicating continued caution regarding the authorities' policy intentions). Under the systemic transformation facility arrangement, the Uzbek government agreed to adopt several key IMF-friendly monetary policy reforms. These included commitments to increase the CBU's refinance rate in line with inflation in 1995, to increase the proportion of new central bank refinance allocated through credit auctions to 40 per cent in the final quarter of 1994 and all new credit in the first half of 1995, and to allow the credit auction interest rate to play a greater role in determining the interest rate structure of the financial system. Policymakers also agreed to the IMF's request to limit the central bank's intervention in the exchange rate to allow the *sum*'s value to be determined through weekly currency auctions (IMF, 1994g: 10–11). Like the Kyrgyz Republic and Kazakhstan, the IMF required Uzbekistan to agree to quarterly ceilings on total credit to the government and central bank credit to commercial banks, a floor for international reserves, and a ceiling on new non-concessional external debt. Among other structural benchmarks for the systemic transformation facility program the authorities also committed to introducing new foreign currency regulations in consultation with the Fund staff by the end of the first quarter in 1995, which staff hoped would move the authorities closer to the establishment of current account convertibility.

Despite agreeing to these reforms, the country still had a long way to go to reverse its early post-independence reputation in the international financial community. As executive directors stated when the Executive Board approved Uzbekistan's systemic transformation facility application in late January 1995, the systemic transformation facility program was 'only the first step in a long process' (IMF, 1995c: 2). But for the Fund staff a more intensive reform process was finally in train with the approval of the systemic transformation facility loan arrangement, following which Uzbekistan became eligible for a US$160 rehabilitation loan from the World Bank (IMF, 1994g: 1). Although the country lagged well behind both the Kyrgyz Republic and Kazakhstan (see Table 4.1), the next step for Fund staff was to reach an agreement on a reform program for Uzbekistan that would be eligible for an upper credit tranche stand-by arrangement with the IMF, which could provide an opportunity to lock in the IMF's gradual policy gains in the country.

Conclusion

The Central Asian republics inherited similar political and economic institutional frameworks following the breakdown of the Soviet Union, but each faced very different economic prospects. The Kyrgyz Republic was an example of a resource-poor country in need of significant external financing to ameliorate the loss of Soviet budget and trade subsidies, which predisposed President Akaev to seek good relations with bilateral and multilateral donors by establishing a strong relationship with the IMF. For the Kyrgyz Republic, good relations with the IMF helped to pave the way for the country to access ODA from other official sources during circumstances where it was unlikely to be able to access private financing and had few options for earning hard foreign exchange. While the conventional wisdom suggests that resource-rich countries are better able to resist pressure for economic reform, Kazakhstan also needed to access ODA in the short term to meet balance-of-payments shortfalls, and sought to draw on the IMF's reputation to help establish a foreign investment-friendly environment and attract private financing to develop its energy and mineral industries. Uzbekistan, by comparison, provides an example of a resource-rich country that was better placed to resist pressure for reform. At independence, Uzbekistan's energy sources were already geared towards domestic production, while its heavy reliance on cotton production initially provided the authorities with a ready source of foreign exchange and enabled the government to maintain greater fiscal capacity than its neighbors.

These differences in countries' initial circumstances were reflected in policymakers' openness to the IMF's ideas for economic reform when the organization began sending technical assistance missions to Central Asia to lay the groundwork for market-based reforms. The Fund staff's policy surveillance in each country, and the Executive Board meetings where their findings were debated, also reveal early differences in how the IMF saw the potential for enacting market-based institutional reforms in the Kyrgyz Republic, Kazakhstan, and Uzbekistan, based on the speed of each state's initial progress and staff assessments of policymakers' reform intentions. In the Kyrgyz Republic, Fund staff found that policymakers were open to the recommendations of technical assistance missions, as well as the staff's advice on policy changes that would form the basis of prior conditions for an initial loan program. While Kazakhstan did not receive the same high level of praise from Fund staff and the Executive Board as the Kyrgyz Republic, the IMF saw the country as an intermediate case where policymakers could be persuaded to pursue IMF-friendly policy changes over time, once outstanding issues such as Kazakhstan's participation in the ruble zone had been resolved. In Uzbekistan, however, the IMF found a government it perceived to be distinctly 'IMF unfriendly' from the start, which prioritized the goal of achieving 'stability at any cost' well above the goal of structural economic reform. As the following chapter illustrates, these early differences in the degree of influence that the IMF was able to achieve in Central Asia continued to define the parameters of policy dialogue between the IMF and with national officials throughout the 1990s.

5
The Scope of the IMF's Influence in Central Asia

Following the establishment of loan programs with the Central Asian economies, the IMF's main objective was to build on the initial steps to construct national market-based monetary systems in order to sustain an IMF-friendly program of institutional change over time. By increasing compliance with the new formal rules of the game, the IMF sought to bring about a permanent change in actors' financial behavior, regardless of the informal political and economic order in Central Asian societies. The foregoing chapters have illustrated that the IMF's concentration on achieving formal institutional reforms also generates new informal outcomes as decisionmakers respond to domestic uncertainty. This can affect how policymakers translate economic reform ideas into domestic contexts, and whether such reforms will be sustained over time. As this chapter shows, the informal context of institutional change in Central Asia helped to shape the results of the IMF's efforts to persuade policymakers to sustain IMF-friendly reforms in each country, especially in the difficult case of Uzbekistan.

Formal institutional changes adopted as part of an IMF loan program are never final, and may not even be particularly stable. Instead, policymakers continue to engage in a process of institutional change, which may lead them to build institutions that more closely resemble what the IMF wants or they may maintain a greater degree of similarity with inherited institutional forms. In Central Asia, despite the IMF's intellectual efforts to persuade policymakers to adopt a common framework for analysis, the common result of the IMF's influence was hybrid reform outcomes – where institutions emerged that exhibited a mix of central planning and liberal market principles and practices. Hybrid outcomes were not simply pathologies that resulted from a lack of political will or from checks on reform imposed by domestic veto players, but derived from actions that made sense to the actors involved with executing institutional change in each country as they sought to translate the IMF's ideas into local contexts. Table 5.1 provides a simple snapshot of the IMF's overall influence on key monetary reforms in each case. Here we see that the IMF achieved a strong degree of influence over formal monetary reforms, including *de jure* central bank independence, the marketization of domestic credit allocation, and acceptance of current account convertibility.

Informally, the story is quite different. Although changing informal practices was essential to achieve the implementation of formal reforms through changes in everyday economic behavior, the IMF's influence altered over time across the three cases. As the final chapter shows, the IMF's influence over informal monetary practices was strongest in the Kyrgyz Republic and weakest in Uzbekistan, with Kazakhstan an intermediate case (but closer to the Kyrgyz Republic than Uzbekistan). Although each state achieved hybrid institutional outcomes, the different transitional contexts that the Kyrgyz Republic, Kazakhstan, and Uzbekistan faced continued to shape the degree to which the IMF was able to mould institutional change over time.

Despite some setbacks, the IMF was able to persuade policymakers in the Kyrgyz Republic and Kazakhstan to embed an IMF-friendly policy orientation with respect to monetary practices through back-to-back loan programs. Establishing a policy reform corridor that stretched over multiple years gradually led to the acceptance of Article VIII status in the Kyrgyz Republic in 1995 and in Kazakhstan in 1996, which the IMF viewed as a key milestone in the process of locking in market-based monetary reforms. The IMF faced much greater difficulties in seeking to persuade the Uzbek authorities to sustain an IMF-friendly policy orientation over time, especially when the country's economic circumstances deteriorated during 1996. Uzbekistan's domestic circumstances differed in important ways from the Kyrgyz Republic, which needed to maintain good relations to the IMF to maintain access to ODA, and from Kazakhstan, where the construction of an IMF-friendly monetary system helped the country to establish a foreign investment-friendly environment that increased the opportunities for elites to extract resource rents. In contrast to its neighbors, the construction of an IMF-friendly monetary system in Uzbekistan threatened the interests of powerful elite groups that were accustomed to extracting rents from the financial system and from the foreign exchange earned by the country's cotton exports, which complicated the IMF's efforts to use material incentives to prevail in a series of strategic games over policy efficacy with Uzbek decisionmakers.

Table 5.1 Overall IMF Influence on Key Monetary Reforms in Central Asia

Policy Reforms	Kyrgyz Republic		Kazakhstan		Uzbekistan	
	Formal	Informal	Formal	Informal	Formal	Informal
Central Bank Independence	Strong	*Strong*	Strong	*Moderate*	Strong	*Weak*
Marketization of Credit Allocation	Strong	*Strong*	Strong	*Moderate*	Moderate	*Weak*
Current Account Convertibility	Strong	*Strong*	Strong	*Strong*	Moderate	*Weak*

Changing monetary norms in the Kyrgyz Republic

Following the completion of the Kyrgyz Republic's first stand-by arrangement in April 1994, the authorities applied to the IMF for a further three-year loan arrangement amounting to SDR 70.95 million (110 per cent of the country's IMF quota) on concessional terms from the IMF's enhanced structural adjustment facility. The IMF intended the new program to build on the government's monetary reforms under the stand-by arrangement and systemic transformation facility loans, in particular the need to make further progress in reducing inflation and to increase the pace of reform of the banking system. This would involve efforts to increase compliance with the new formal 'rules of the game', including persuading officials to take disciplinary action against commercial banks if they continued to run up large overdrafts with the NBKR (IMF, 1994h: 7).

In the government's Memorandum on Economic and Financial Policies for the enhanced structural adjustment facility application, the IMF persuaded the authorities to re-commit to channeling all central bank refinance credit through credit auctions and to completely refrain from directing credit to specific areas of the economy. The government had successfully maintained open current and capital accounts following the introduction of the *som* in 1993, and policymakers signaled to the IMF that they intended to adopt Article VIII status before the end of the scheduled Article IV consultations in 1995. With regard to the recurrent problem of inter-enterprise arrears, in early 1994 the government had adopted a severe method with which to harden the budget constraint on firms through requiring businesses to prepay for goods prior to delivery, despite the harsh cash flow constraints that this would place on all firms. In May, based on the IMF's advice, the government ramped up the pressure on firms even further, by limiting vital energy supplies to firms that had not moved to reduce their level of inter-enterprise arrears. Once more, the government reaffirmed to the IMF that they would resist domestic pressure for a generalized credit bailout for firms struggling with a high level of inter-enterprise debt, which suggests that the authorities had been persuaded by the IMF's arguments for hardening the budget constraints on firms. Similar to the 1993 stand-by arrangement, the proposed performance criteria devised by the IMF for the enhanced structural adjustment facility loan consisted of a floor for convertible foreign exchange reserves, domestic credit ceilings, and ceilings on non-concessional debt. Policy benchmarks also included further decreasing the limit on commercial bank lending to individual customers from 35 to 30 per cent of a bank's capital, and decreasing the limit on lending to 'related parties' from 20 per cent to 15 per cent of capital (IMF, 1994h: 8, 12). The IMF sought these changes because they were squarely aimed at circumscribing the close monetary relationships that existed between the major sectoral banks and their traditional customers, especially major customers that were also bank shareholders.

A crucial test of the central bank's new role in trying to generate a durable change in monetary norms occurred under the stand-by arrangement in the final months of 1993. In an effort to tighten credit policies in accordance with the IMF's advice, the government suspended regular refinance credit auctions in October, which led commercial banks to accumulate large overdrafts with the central bank when major enterprises refused to repay maturing bank loans. A few months earlier, the growth in inter-enterprise arrears and commercial banks' overdrafts with the NBKR had motivated the government to simply extend further credit to banks to allow the enterprises to continue to rollover their debts, with a large credit expansion in the first quarter of 1993, an action that was strongly criticized by the IMF. The method the NBKR chose to deal with the arrears problem at the end of the year helps to demonstrate the progress the IMF had achieved in persuading the central bank to adopt a new institutional role in the financial system. Following the advice of Fund staff the central bank responded by suspending auctions for refinance credit until April 1994, when the NBKR rescheduled commercial banks' outstanding debts over three years, including overdue interest penalties, and instructed the banks not to extend any new credit to state-owned firms facing financial difficulties (IMF, 1994i: 4). Furthermore, with technical assistance from the IMF the central bank moved to strengthen its prudential supervision of the financial system by conducting audits of most commercial banks in 1994, with the NBKR revoking the licenses of three banks that failed to meet the new standards. The authorities also announced that they would establish direct credit controls over any bank that continued to run up large overdrafts with the NBKR, and if necessary would implement disciplinary action against the bank's management (IMF, 1994i: 12).

From the IMF's perspective, Kyrgyz policymakers had for the most part been receptive to their advice, but had faced significant economic challenges that had compromised the country's performance under the initial stand-by arrangement and systemic transformation facility loans. As an indication of the difficult economic circumstances the Kyrgyz authorities faced during 1993, and as a forewarning of future debt problems, the country's external debt in convertible currency had rapidly increased from almost nothing at the beginning of the year (after the Kyrgyz Republic's share of the Soviet Union's debt had been assumed by the Russian Federation) to 18 per cent of GDP, most of which was used to finance imports (IMF, 1994i: 5). In a report to the Executive Board on the government's application for an enhanced structural adjustment facility loan, Fund staff sought to apply the lessons they had learned from the unexpected economic challenges that had plagued the Kyrgyz Republic under the stand-by arrangement. In particular, the staff built in contingency plans to guard against the risk of the new enhanced structural adjustment facility program going 'off track' due to similar circumstances that were largely outside of the government's control. For instance, the staff included automatic adjustments to the enhanced structural adjustment facility performance criteria and quantitative benchmarks in the case of any unexpected developments in external financing. If external balance of payments assistance managed to exceed the program's targets, the floor for the NBKR's convertible foreign exchange reserves would automatically rise upwards by 50 per cent. In addition, if supplementary financing for a planned World Bank loan fell short of the IMF's projections, the ceiling on domestic bank credit for the government would rise by one-third of the financing gap. Fund staff had also agreed in advance to the temporary tax changes the government would make in the event of unexpected shortfalls in government revenue (IMF, 1994i: 15).

Despite this more flexible approach to the use of conditionality, the IMF did not excuse all the problems associated with the stand-by arrangement program as the result of exogenous circumstances. The staff report to the Executive Board on the enhanced structural adjustment facility application makes clear the ongoing difficulties the IMF faced in persuading policymakers to maintain a consistent approach to the implementation of IMF-friendly economic policy reforms, even though policymakers had continued a cooperative relationship with the Fund staff. For instance, following a successful review of the stand-by arrangement in September 1993, the Kyrgyz authorities had delayed the introduction of important reforms and had also switched back to looser credit policies to support domestic production and employment (although monetary policies were quickly tightened the following month). Fund staff concluded that 'These slippages reflected an ill-considered reaction by the authorities to the unavoidable but sharp decline of the economy and, in particular, the deteriorating performance of public sector enterprises' (IMF, 1994i: 19).

Although the stand-by arrangement had gone 'off track', staff supported the Kyrgyz Republic's application for an enhanced structural adjustment facility loan on the basis that the authorities had subsequently followed the IMF's advice and tightened their monetary and fiscal policies in late 1993 and early 1994. The government's tightening of monetary policies also resulted in deposit interest rates at most banks becoming positive in real terms in early 1994, thereby realizing one of the key policy outcomes the staff and the Executive Board had strongly encouraged all of the Central Asian centrally planned economies to achieve in 1993. As a consequence, Fund staff judged that 'in early 1994, there was... strong evidence of a renewed impetus to structural reforms' (IMF, 1994i: 19). Policymakers also continued to take a cooperative approach towards implementing the advice of technical assistance missions, and, in addition to the IMF's resident representative, the authorities welcomed a long-term advisor for the NBKR as well as a long-term budgetary advisor for the Ministry of Finance (IMF, 1994i: 36). Fund staff warned, however, that the main risks to the country's progress under an enhanced structural adjustment facility loan would come 'from the uncertainty regarding the strength of the political support for the reform and stabilization efforts'. They therefore urged the government to put in place a social safety net that could help to alleviate some of the political pressures that had impeded the success of reforms during 1993. In another area where the Fund staff had drawn lessons from their experiment with the 1993 stand-by arrangement, staff recommended to the Executive Board that the IMF should 'backload' the provision of finance under the enhanced structural adjustment facility in the first year compared with the 'frontloading' of finance under the previous stand-by arrangement. This had left the staff with relatively weak short-term financial incentives at their disposal to persuade the Kyrgyz authorities to maintain their policy intentions when the program had begun to go 'off track' in September/October 1993, because the bulk of the stand-by arrangement credit had already been disbursed (IMF, 1994i: 21).

In the Executive Board's debate on the Kyrgyz Republic's application for an enhanced structural adjustment facility loan, the country's representative on the Executive Board noted that in late 1993 the authorities had not been able to resist political pressure for access to credit from state-owned enterprises, but had established a greater degree of monetary control since the beginning of 1994 (IMF, 1994j: 3). This assessment was generally shared by other executive directors, with many expressing the IMF's disappointment with the Kyrgyz authorities' performance following the positive review under the stand-by arrangement in September 1993, noting that poor policy performance had undermined credibility in the government's commitment to market-based reform in the international financial community. But directors also praised the government for tightening monetary policies from the end of 1993, and in particular welcomed the government's recent success in achieving positive real interest rates. Because the authorities had successfully maintained their early decision to establish open current and capital accounts, policymakers were encouraged to accept Article VIII status as soon as possible (IMF, 1994j: 7, 10). In approving the enhanced structural adjustment facility loan, the Executive Board strongly emphasized to the Kyrgyz authorities that the success of the program would depend upon a high level of 'political will' to implement unpopular policy decisions that would generate significant domestic resistance, especially from banks and major state-owned firms. In response to the Board's debate, the executive director representing the Kyrgyz Republic suggested that the authorities had learned from their experience with 'policy slippages' in September. He argued that the government was now 'seriously trying to regain the lost momentum in its economic transition', indicated by the large number of prior actions that policymakers had implemented before staff brought the enhanced structural adjustment facility application to the Executive Board for approval (IMF, 1994j: 31).

Embedding IMF-friendly policies in the Kyrgyz Republic

Under the enhanced structural adjustment facility loan, the Kyrgyz Republic subsequently achieved a high degree of compliance with the program's performance criteria, including the landmark achievement of being the first Central Asian state to accept Article VIII status in the IMF in March 1995 (IMF, 1994k: 23). During a mid-term loan review in early 1995, Fund staff praised the government's success in doubling the level of convertible foreign exchange reserves, achieving a stable exchange rate for the *som*, and maintaining tight credit policies. Yet deviations from the program had still occurred, including a higher rate of credit to the government and lower tax revenue than program targets. Fund staff had also experienced disagreements with *Goskomstat*, the government's statistical agency, over how the country's GDP was calculated. Overall, however, staff were satisfied with the government's policy performance in very difficult economic conditions, with GDP declining by an estimated 26.5 per cent in 1994 as a result of ongoing trade disruptions between the former Soviet republics when the loan program had initially projected only a 5 per cent decline (IMF, 1994k: 26, 48).

In line with the IMF's advice and loan performance criteria, the NBKR continued to rely predominantly on market-based instruments of monetary policy, with central bank refinance credit allocated through competitive auctions conducted on a weekly basis. Following recommendations from the IMF's monetary technical assistance missions, the NBKR closed three poorly performing banks and put six other banks under direct supervision. The government also altered its approach to exchange rate management, with the central bank intervening to help establish an informal exchange rate target of approximately 10.6–10.8 *som* to the US dollar, a policy objective endorsed by Fund staff due to the improvement in the country's level of convertible foreign exchange reserves. Indicating the IMF's recognition that the country still faced a high degree of economic uncertainty and that program targets remained vulnerable to unexpected shocks, the IMF again agreed to establish provisions for automatic adjustments of benchmarks, such as the NBKR's credit ceilings and bank financing to the government, if economic circumstances changed. Fund staff judged that the IMF's ongoing technical assistance missions were 'well received by the authorities and cooperation with IMF experts is excellent'. Once again, staff determined that where the authorities had failed to meet the performance criteria agreed under the enhanced structural adjustment facility loan, this in part reflected economic conditions outside the government's control. In particular, staff were satisfied that the authorities had adjusted their policies in close consultation with the IMF in order to get the program back 'on track' (IMF, 1994k: 21).

Building on the country's performance in the mid-term review, a staff report on the Kyrgyz Republic's application for a second annual arrangement under the enhanced structural adjustment facility in November 1995 praised the Kyrgyz authorities for making significant progress in implementing market-based reforms with close policy surveillance by the IMF. In particular, staff praised the government for maintaining a fully convertible currency in exceptionally difficult economic circumstances. Because the Kyrgyz government had achieved a high degree of success in complying with IMF program targets, or consulted with the IMF before adjusting policies in response to unforeseen changes in economic circumstances, staff recommended a continuation of the enhanced structural adjustment facility loan in order to lock-in the direction of reforms over the medium term (IMF, 1994l:

16). The IMF's repeated interactions with Kyrgyz policymakers during 1993 to 1995 neatly capture the importance of sustaining a constructive dialogue between Fund staff and national officials. On the one hand, this is essential in order for the IMF to gain opportunities to reorient a country's economic policy framework. On the other hand, a good relationship with Fund staff improves the ease with which member states can access the organization's financial resources.

As the Kyrgyz Republic's experience demonstrates, however, being an exemplar case of IMF-friendly policy reforms is no guarantee of future economic success. Despite policymakers' efforts to maintain a high degree of cooperation with the IMF, the Kyrgyz Republic continued to experience lackluster economic performance during the 1990s, with the exception of achieving a sharp decline in inflation during 1994, as indicated in Figure 4.5. The country's poor performance is illustrated in Figure 4.4, which shows that the Kyrgyz Republic experienced a severe contraction in economic output during the 1990s – recording the worst output decline of the three Central Asian cases examined here. The country's GDP in 1999 has been estimated as constituting only 63 per cent of its 1989 level, which increased to 78 per cent of its 1989 GDP by 2003 (Pomfret, 2006: 8). By 2002, the Kyrgyz Republic was putting its case to the Paris Club of official bilateral creditors for a debt rescheduling agreement (Pomfret, 2006: 82–3), and in 2006 the country was granted Heavily-Indebted Poor Country (HIPC) status by the World Bank and the IMF (IMF, 2006). Gaining HIPC status has cemented the country's position as a poor 'frontier' economy for the foreseeable future, and has frustrated the country's ambitious goal of becoming the 'Switzerland of the East' that was often talked about by Kyrgyz political leaders in the early 1990s (Anderson, 1999: 65). This also shows the potential downside for states of using the IMF as a reputational intermediary. By enabling the Kyrgyz Republic to access additional sources of external finance, this allowed the country to build up an unsustainable level of sovereign debt over the course of the 1990s. Policymakers then turned to the IMF to play another dimension of its intermediary role, as a gatekeeper to enable heavily indebted states to access debt relief through the Paris Club process.

Changing monetary norms in Kazakhstan

With the adoption of a new national currency in November 1993, the IMF expected the Kazakh authorities to be able to achieve much greater macroeconomic stability and monetary control, with Fund staff projecting a decline in GDP of only 3 per cent in 1994 and the achievement of single digit monthly inflation rates by the middle of the year (IMF, 1994b: 8). The IMF was satisfied that Kazakhstan had now implemented most of the prior actions specified for the country to be eligible for a stand-by arrangement loan. In addition to the introduction of the *tenge*, the authorities had removed further administrative controls on prices and profits, increased the amount of central bank credit that was allocated through competitive auctions, raised the central bank's refinance rate to the market level established through credit auctions, and expanded the weekly foreign exchange auctions. Again, the main quantitative performance criteria that the authorities would have to meet under the stand-by arrangement centered on quarterly credit ceilings on central bank credit as well as domestic and external government borrowing, and floors on the level of international currency reserves. The government also committed itself to further liberalizing the trade and payments system, and agreed not to modify or adopt any new exchange and trade restrictions that were incompatible with the provisions of Article VIII (IMF, 1994b: 14).

In their report on Kazakhstan's application for a stand-by arrangement, Fund staff noted the substantial progress the government had already made in moving towards a market-based economy, but concluded that 'structural reforms must be accelerated if the improvement in financial performance is to be durable and accompanied by the stabilization and subsequent recovery of output'. Staff were satisfied that the reform program they had negotiated with the government for the stand-by arrangement would help to achieve these goals (IMF, 1994b: 16). The program was also supported by significant financial support from bilateral and multilateral donors to bridge Kazakhstan's expected external financing gap of US$450 million in 1994, including a US$145 million parallel financing loan from Japan that was linked to the IMF's loan arrangement (IMF, 1994m: 3).

When Kazakhstan's stand-by arrangement application came before the Executive Board, most executive directors voiced strong support for the authorities' renewed commitment to an IMF-friendly program of economic reform. In particular, directors endorsed the country's strong track record under the systemic transformation facility arrangement in the difficult monetary conditions accompanying the final collapse of the ruble zone in late 1993, which the Executive Board blamed for undermining the authorities' attempts to lower inflation. Before the Executive Board had begun discussions on Kazakhstan's stand-by arrangement application, executive directors briefly debated whether the IMF should publicly respond to recent press reports – most notably Jeffrey Sachs's article 'The Reformers' Tragedy' in the *New York Times* three days earlier – which heavily criticized the IMF's approach to economic transformation in the Russian Federation (IMF, 1994c: 3–4). Sachs, along with Anders Åslund, had resigned his position as an advisor to the Russian government on 21 January, citing Prime Minister Viktor Chernomyrdin's decision to apply the breaks to economic transformation, but placing most of the blame on the IMF for the collapse of elite support for rapid reforms (Erlanger, 1994: 4). This direct criticism of the IMF's role in the former Soviet Union by a prominent American economist partly colored the Executive Board's debate on Kazakhstan. For example, the French executive director Marc-Antoine Autheman suggested that the approval of Kazakhstan's stand-by arrangement application would 'demonstrate that... IMF support is not irrationally conditioned on the achievement of overly precise numerical targets or on the implementation of a specific model, but that it is in fact dependent upon the steady and firm pursuit of stability oriented policies'. These remarks were reinforced by Daniel Kaeser, the Swiss executive director representing both Kyrgyzstan and Uzbekistan, who concluded that 'Judging from the number of IMF missions and the volume of technical assistance to Kazakhstan, it is clear that Kazakhstan has been put under intensive care' (IMF, 1994c: 17, 23–4, 46). In a context of growing controversy over the IMF's role in the region, and with most directors extending a favorable endorsement of the Kazakh authorities' policy stance and their level of cooperation with Fund staff, the Executive Board subsequently approved the government's applications for a one year stand-by arrangement loan of SDR 123.75 million and a second purchase under the systemic transformation facility arrangement of SDR 61.875 million.

Embedding IMF-friendly policies in Kazakhstan

Despite the IMF's high hopes of achieving a permanent shift in the Kazakh authorities' policy orientation, the government's policy performance and the quality of its cooperation with the IMF under consecutive stand-by arrangements over the next two years was mixed at best. In the first review of the stand-by arrangement in mid-1994, staff judged that 'impressive progress was achieved in many areas', but several key performance criteria and quantitative targets had not been met. Missed program objectives included the targets on credit ceilings, following a rapid monetary expansion in the first half of 1994 in response to a significant growth in inter-enterprise arrears that had been generated by the tight credit policies the authorities had established when they introduced the *tenge* the previous year (IMF, 1994n: 1–2). Unlike the Kyrgyz Republic, the IMF had not been able to persuade Kazakh policymakers to resist political pressure for a credit bailout of indebted firms.

Kazakhstan continued to face severe economic challenges on a number of fronts that impeded the IMF's efforts to achieve a sustained change in policy orientation, which illustrate the difficulties the organization faces in accurately predicting future economic performance under an IMF loan program in an uncertain environment. For instance, the IMF's indicative targets for inflation were not even close to being met, with monthly inflation rising by over 30 per cent in April and May and nearly 50 per cent in June, rather than the single digit monthly inflation figures that the program had envisaged. Furthermore, economic output continued to decline rapidly, with a 30 per cent decline in GDP from January to May compared with the ambitious initial estimate by Fund staff of a 3 per cent decline in GDP for 1994 as a whole (IMF, 1994n: 1–2). As these figures show, in difficult circumstances the IMF failed to accurately predict the short-term outcomes of formal institutional reforms, which served to increase Kazakh policymakers' uncertainty regarding the social and economic costs associated with implementing IMF-friendly reforms.

One area where the authorities complied more closely with the stand-by arrangement conditions was the implementation of institutional changes relating to the conduct of monetary policy, in particular the expansion of the use of interest rates to allocate credit. In addition, the government continued to allow the unified exchange rate for the *tenge* to be set by weekly foreign exchange auctions and built up the level of international reserves, although reserves remained below the program's initial targets. During ongoing negotiations between the authorities and Fund staff during May–July 1994, Kazakh officials emphasized to staff that the policy slippages that had occurred were temporary, and were the result of one-off problems requiring a quick response in the early stages of the loan program. The authorities reiterated to Fund staff that both the government and the National Bank of Kazakhstan were fully committed to implementing the loan program's key objectives (IMF, 1994n: 7–9). As an indication of the strength of this commitment, from May policymakers significantly tightened monetary policies in an attempt to bring the program back 'on track'.

In response to the mixed results of the authorities' compliance with program conditions in the first half of 1994, Fund staff proposed to push back the date when Kazakhstan would be able to make another purchase under the stand-by arrangement until the second loan review was completed. Fund staff also recommended extending the length of the program by four months to May 1995, with additional funds to be made available in January and April 1995 based on future program compliance. Fund staff sought to use both the purchase delay and the program's extension as material incentives to strengthen their case for normative persuasion, a task made increasingly difficult by the rapid deterioration in the country's economic performance (IMF, 1994n: 16–18). In particular, Fund staff strongly criticized efforts by the government to pressure the NBK to extend credit to clear domestic inter-enterprise arrears and to defer repayments on loans to the agricultural sector, arguing that the government's decisions had circumscribed the central bank's capacity to act autonomously.

In the second review of the country's performance under the stand-by arrangement in September and October 1994, Fund staff praised the authorities' greater degree of success in adhering to tight credit policies and achieving positive real interest rates. Fund staff believed these measures had helped to change financial behavior among banks and firms that had previously worked against the success of the program. In particular, from the perspective of the Fund staff these changes had broken the country's high inflation-exchange rate depreciation cycle that occurred in the first half of the year, whereby commercial banks had borrowed central bank credit on preferential terms only to use the funds to speculate against the exchange rate of the *tenge* (IMF, 1994o: 8). Banks had initially continued to exploit inherited financial norms as a means to pursue their own material gains under the guise of an extant 'logic of appropriateness', an example which Fund staff were able to use to discredit the government's soft credit practices and bolster their case for adherence to market-based monetary norms.

Furthermore, Fund staff strongly supported the government's efforts to develop the foreign exchange market, as well as limited exchange rate intervention by the central bank in accordance with an agreement previously reached with the IMF. The NBK had also gradually increased its convertible currency reserves and increased the amount of refinancing credit allocated through auctions, and agreed with Fund staff that credit auctions would be used to allocate 80 per cent of total central bank lending to commercial banks by the end of the year (IMF, 1994o: 10, 18, 44). While the government had removed most of the exchange restrictions that were initially maintained under Article XIV when Kazakhstan joined the IMF, some restrictions remained in place for export proceeds that were deposited in non-resident bank accounts denominated in *tenge*. Rather than recommend that the Executive Board approve the maintenance of these exchange restrictions, however, Fund staff opted to rely on their continuing efforts to persuade the government to set in place a timetable to remove the controls, which would pave the way for Kazakhstan to accept Article VIII status in the IMF.

In their assessment of the government's overall performance, Fund staff praised the authorities for taking tough policy decisions in the face of stiff domestic opposition, and commended the government for successfully making up for the ground that had been lost under the first half of the stand-by arrangement. Evaluating the country's reforms since the first Article IV consultation with Kazakhstan in April 1993, Fund staff concluded that 'a great deal of progress has been made in the overall direction and pace of economic reform policies' (IMF, 1994o: 19). Towards the end of 1994, however, the government again failed to achieve some of the stand-by arrangement performance criteria, largely due to firms refusing to meet their payment obligations on government-guaranteed debt.

Despite the government's ongoing difficulties with generating changes in firms' financial behavior, these policy slippages had little negative impact on the authorities' relationship with the IMF. This was due to the tough actions taken by the central bank to tighten the flow of credit to commercial banks and to maintain positive interest rates, which enabled inflation to decline to a monthly rate of 10 per cent in December 1994 and helped to stabilize the exchange rate of the *tenge* against the US dollar. The central bank's stance on credit to the banking system was further tightened in early 1995 when the NBK's total refinancing credit to commercial banks decreased by 20 per cent, with almost all new lending to banks passing through the central bank's credit auctions held three times each week. Because of this evidence of behavioral changes in the conduct of monetary policy, staff assessed that the country's 'performance during the year was uneven although the momentum of reform was generally maintained' (IMF, 1994d: 3, 12).

Fund staff subsequently supported the authorities' application for a new stand-by arrangement loan of SDR 185.6 million in May 1995 in order to encourage the government to continue the process of economic policy reform in cooperation with the IMF (IMF, 1994d). Kazakhstan continued to require waivers for the non-observance of some performance criteria, specifically with regard to the accumulation of government-guaranteed external debt by firms. But staff supported these moves because of the authorities' overall success in complying with the stand-by arrangement conditions as well as satisfactory evidence of an ongoing change in the authorities' economic policy orientation, especially with regard to the role and operations of the central bank (IMF, 1994o: 21, 1994e: 6, 1996b: 1–2).

Staff also welcomed the authorities' intention at the end of 1995 to remove remaining exchange restrictions and to move towards the acceptance of Article VIII status in the near future, an aim which led staff to recommend that the Executive Board approve the retention of existing exchange restrictions until the middle of 1996 (IMF, 1994f: 26). Following a technical assistance mission from the IMF's Legal Department and Monetary and Exchange Affairs Department in November 1995 to advise the authorities on Article VIII compliance requirements (IMF, 1996c: 36, 39), Kazakhstan subsequently removed the remaining exchange restrictions on non-residents' bank accounts in June 1996. After the completion of Kazakhstan's second stand-by arrangement loan the country applied for its first loan under the enhanced structural adjustment facility in June 1996. The Executive Board approved the new loan application, which began the following month the day after Kazakhstan became the second Central Asian state to accept Article VIII status in the IMF on 16 July (IMF, 1996d).

While Kazakhstan never quite achieved the same degree of close cooperation with the IMF compared with the Kyrgyz Republic, the country's policymakers invested considerable time and energy in implementing key IMF-friendly policy changes and reaching compromises with the Fund staff in other areas where reforms required greater adjustment in order to be translated into the difficult informal environment. From the date when the IMF approved Kazakhstan's first application for a systemic transformation facility loan in July 1993, the country remained under back-to-back loan programs with the IMF until 2002. During this period, Fund staff continued to use loan reviews, new loan applications, and waivers for quantitative targets as a series of opportunities to foster a durable change in the government's monetary policy orientation. Despite the uneven progress towards establishing an IMF-friendly policy orientation during the early period of IMF membership, the country subsequently fared much better than the Kyrgyz Republic in terms of its economic outcomes, largely because of its greater natural resources.

After the shock of the Russian financial crisis in 1998, Kazakhstan devalued its currency and benefited from a substantial increase in oil revenues, with oil production doubling between 1998 and 2003 at the same time as the world price of oil more than doubled (Pomfret, 2006: 42). In contrast to the other Central Asian states, Kazakhstan was recognized by the United States as a market economy in 2002, and in the same year graduated from speculative- to investment-grade status with a credit rating of Baa3 by Moody's Investors Service (Junisbai and Junisbai, 2005: 385). Among all 15 former Soviet republics, Kazakhstan was second only to Russia in the total amount of foreign direct investment the country received during the 1990s, which reached US$1 billion in 1996 and 1997 (Meyer and Pind, 1999: 205). The far greater level of foreign investment, export revenues, and oil-driven economic growth that the country experienced compared with other Central Asian republics enabled Kazakhstan to graduate early from the IMF's 'tuition' compared with the Kyrgyz Republic, with the Kazakh authorities choosing to repay their outstanding debt to the IMF ahead of schedule in May 2000 (IMF, 2000). When a 1999–2002 enhanced structural adjustment facility loan expired without the government choosing to make any purchases under the loan, the IMF decided that there was no longer a need to maintain its resident representative office in the country, which closed at the expiry of the last resident representative's term in August 2003.

The challenge of changing monetary norms in Uzbekistan

For the Fund staff, it finally seemed as though Uzbekistan might have turned a corner in 1995. While the country was still considered to be lagging well behind the Kyrgyz Republic and Kazakhstan, Uzbek policymakers achieved a relatively high degree of policy cooperation with the IMF under the country's systemic transformation facility loan during 1995. This enabled the authorities to successfully apply for an upper credit tranche stand-by arrangement with the IMF of SDR 124.7 million and a second purchase under the systemic transformation facility of SDR 49.9 million in November 1995 (IMF, 1995b: 37). Under the systemic transformation facility program, the CBU had further tightened monetary policy in line with the IMF's advice, increasing the refinance rate to 250 per cent in February 1995 and then to 300 per cent in March, to combat an inflation rate which averaged 14 per cent per month in the first quarter of 1995. From April, all refinance credit from the central bank was allocated through credit auctions, which were held on a daily basis (IMF, 1996e: 29).

In line with the IMF's advice, the CBU had also begun to tackle the fundamental problem of inherited financial norms by establishing harder credit constraints on commercial banks. Although several commercial banks continued to have trouble with making repayments on central bank loans, rather than increase the rate of credit growth, new refinancing credit from the CBU declined in the first quarter of 1995 by 37 per cent in real terms. Following staff advice, the CBU also took disciplinary action against commercial banks that failed to repay refinancing credit, including barring them from credit auctions until their debts to the central bank were repaid (IMF, 1996e: 29). With a significant decline in inflation during the second and third quarter of 1995 (see Figure 3.5), the CBU was able to lower the annual refinance rate to 125 per cent in August (IMF, 1995b: 3–4). In negotiations with Fund staff over the policy objectives of the stand-by arrangement, the authorities continued to assert their view that the country's 'political and social stability could best be maintained at a measured pace of reform'. For their part, Fund staff continued their efforts to persuade the authorities that more rapid reforms would lead to quicker benefits, but they 'accepted the political choice made by the authorities', formally acknowledging 'the right of each country to choose its own path of reform' (IMF, 1995b: 5).

With the exception of the failure to persuade the Uzbek government to speed up the pace of reforms, in general Fund staff achieved a high degree of policy cooperation with the Uzbek authorities under the systemic transformation facility loan. As a prior action for the stand-by arrangement, Fund staff required the signing of a written agreement between the Minister of Finance and the Chairman of the CBU, which explicitly stated that the government would pay interest on any funds it borrowed from the central bank at the same rate as the CBU's refinance rate (IMF, 1995e: 2). This performative act formally put the government's credit relationship with the central bank on the same footing as commercial banks. In addition, the authorities had removed their remaining restrictions on current international transactions during 1995, and Fund staff believed the government would accept Article VIII status in the IMF before the end of the year (IMF, 1995b: 13). Finally, the Uzbek parliament passed a new law governing the role of the central bank in December 1995, which Fund staff judged as conforming with international best practice and which legally established a high degree of central bank independence from the government (IMF, 1996e: 51–3).

Under the stand-by arrangement loan, the authorities agreed to undertake further policy measures to strengthen the central bank's supervision of the banking system, and to address commercial banks' non-performing loans in cooperation with IMF technical assistance missions (IMF, 1995b: 12). Fund staff thus saw the development of a stand-by arrangement with Uzbekistan as a way to build on the progress made by the authorities in the previous year under the systemic transformation facility loan and technical assistance missions, in order to steadily entrench a reduction of the state's role in the economy. While staff were not yet fully satisfied with the pace of the government's reform program, they supported the stand-by arrangement application on the basis that the authorities' plans were 'sufficiently ambitious' to warrant the IMF's support. In addition, at only 62.5 per cent of Uzbekistan's quota the commitment of the IMF's financial resources under the stand-by arrangement was relatively modest compared with loans to the Kyrgyz Republic and Kazakhstan.

The stand-by arrangement conditions therefore committed the Uzbek authorities to achieving explicit policy goals and maintaining a close working relationship with the Fund staff, but the program was largely funded by the government's own international reserves. Despite the relatively small size of the stand-by arrangement, the disbursal of IMFs would be staggered over the course of 1996. Following an initial disbursal of SDR 6.2 million when the Executive Board approved the stand-by arrangement in December 1995, the remaining purchases would be made available to Uzbekistan in five payments of SDR 23.7 million over the course of 1996 and early 1997, depending on the government's compliance with program targets (IMF, 1995b: 17, 21). Compared with the earlier stand-by arrangements with the Kyrgyz Republic and Kazakhstan, the IMF sought to keep the government of Uzbekistan on a short leash, in order to increase the material incentives for ongoing compliance with program targets and to provide frequent opportunities for normative persuasion.

Despite the improvement in the IMF's relationship with Uzbekistan throughout late 1994 and 1995, several problems quickly emerged under the stand-by arrangement loan in early 1996. When Fund staff conducted their first review of the government's progress under the stand-by arrangement in February and March, the Uzbek authorities had already been blocked from making a second purchase under the stand-by arrangement due to the failure to meet performance criteria at the end of December 1995. This included failure to meet ceilings for the expansion of credit from the CBU and for government borrowing from the banking system. While the CBU tightened monetary policy in early 1996, this was not sufficient to achieve the CBU's credit ceiling target for the end of March. The government also broke its commitment not to introduce new current account restrictions, with measures introduced in April to control access to the foreign exchange auction based on whether the terms and conditions of import transactions were deemed 'optimal' by officials. These changes indicated reluctance on the part of Uzbek policymakers to reduce discretionary bureaucratic power in favor of establishing an arm's-length relationship between the state and economic actors that sought access to foreign exchange. Fund staff subsequently made the termination of this requirement an essential prior action in order for the first review of the stand-by arrangement to be successfully completed (IMF, 1996f: 1–2, 6, 11, 15, 51). While the government had originally committed to fully eliminating the surrender requirement on foreign exchange earnings by exporters by mid-1996 as a structural benchmark for the stand-by arrangement, this target was also changed to a gradual reduction in the second half of the year with full elimination rescheduled for the beginning of 1997.

The IMF's evaluation of Uzbekistan's early performance under the stand-by arrangement focused on the need for the authorities to ensure 'strict implementation' of future policy targets. For Fund staff, it was considered 'critical that the Central Bank of Uzbekistan maintains the control over monetary expansion which it has recently achieved' (IMF, 1996f: 20, 22, 25). In light of the efforts by the CBU to tighten credit growth, Fund staff recommended granting waivers for the missed performance criteria and re-phasing the stand-by arrangement payment timetable to have four further purchases of SDR 29.625 million scheduled for May, August, and November 1996, with the final payment in February 1997.

Unlike the cooperative policy relationships that the IMF had established with the Kyrgyz Republic and Kazakhstan, Fund staff were not able to achieve the same level of input into the domestic policymaking process in Uzbekistan, and the authorities remained much more reluctant than their neighbors to consult with the IMF before introducing changes in monetary policies. While the Executive Board subsequently approved waivers for missed targets under the first review – based largely on the corrective actions taken by the CBU in early 1996 – executive directors drew attention to this point, and strongly urged the authorities to involve staff more closely in future policy decisions that might affect performance criteria under the loan program (IMF, 1996g: 1–2).

After Uzbekistan made another purchase under the stand-by arrangement in June 1996, the IMF's second review of the country's progress took place in July. Although the authorities had maintained a tight credit policy and inflation was relatively low, Fund staff were concerned about the government's exchange rate policies, which suggested that the authorities were only selectively complying with the new formal rules. In the first review in March, staff had voiced concerns over the 20 per cent spread between the official auction-determined exchange rate and the cash exchange rate charged by commercial banks that had emerged at the start of the year. Fund staff were unable to verify the cause of this difference due to the authorities' reluctance to provide further information on how the cash market functioned, which led them to assume that it had been caused by collusion among the major banks. This gap subsequently narrowed in April following action by the CBU (IMF, 1996f: 11).

Prior to the second review, however, the gap had re-emerged and had increased to approximately 25 per cent in July. Despite the government's claim that the spread was caused by non-competitive behavior by commercial banks, staff increasingly believed that it was the result of informal rationing practices or other forms of financial intervention by the authorities. Anecdotal evidence gathered by Fund staff also suggested that both firms and individuals were sometimes unable to access foreign exchange. As a result, while the staff commended the government's efforts at establishing macroeconomic stability during the course of 1996 they expressed disappointment at the failure to create an efficient market for foreign exchange. Fund staff argued that the lack of an efficient market-based exchange system was 'the single most important obstacle to foreign investment and the main reason why such investments remain relatively modest in Uzbekistan' (IMF, 1996h: 8–9, 12). From the IMF's perspective, having the right institutional structures in place would help to build the country's reputation among international audiences, with potential flow-on effects for ODA and foreign investment.

Overall, however, Fund staff were broadly satisfied with the authorities' attempts to put the stand-by arrangement back on track and with their stated intentions to adhere closely to the program targets for the rest of 1996. Staff therefore agreed to the authorities' request to modify the loan performance criteria by lowering the floor for international reserves, which would increase the scope for the CBU to intervene in the foreign exchange market in order to provide greater liquidity, and recommended to the Executive Board that the review be successfully completed (IMF, 1996h: 13). With the Board's subsequent approval of the second review, Uzbekistan was able to make a third drawing under the stand-by arrangement in September. But despite the authorities' rhetorical commitments to achieve the reforms agreed with the IMF under the stand-by arrangement, including the acceptance of Article VIII status, by the end of 1996 Uzbekistan's policy settings had been reoriented in the opposite direction.

The suspension of cooperation between Uzbekistan and the IMF

Immediately following the second review of Uzbekistan's performance under the stand-by arrangement the IMF's relations with the Uzbek authorities took a turn for the worse, with the government failing to achieve a number of quantitative targets and structural benchmarks that were due at the end of September. The authorities faced severe balance of payments problems during the second half of 1996, due to a decline in export earnings as the world price of cotton decreased, at the same time as the country experienced a poor cotton harvest. The country's import costs also substantially increased after the price of wheat rose from US$153 per ton in 1995 to US$251 per ton in 1996 (Blackmon, 2005: 398). Uzbekistan's current account deficit subsequently expanded from a projected 4.6 per cent of GDP under the stand-by arrangement to 7.7 per cent in the last three months of the year, following a deficit that had reached 13.4 per cent of GDP in the third quarter (IMF, 1997a: 29, 34). At the end of the year, Uzbekistan's current account deficit of approximately US$1.1 billion was its largest since 1991. In addition, following a rapid increase in credit expansion to the agriculture sector to help clear inter-enterprise, wage, and pensions arrears, the budget deficit reached 7.3 per cent of GDP for 1996 in the last quarter of the year, compared with the government's target under the stand-by arrangement of a 3.2 per cent deficit (IMF, 1997b: 29, 45). Failure to meet quantitative targets and structural reform benchmarks under IMF loan programs does not automatically lead to a suspension of the IMF's support, as illustrated by the cases of the Kyrgyz Republic and Kazakhstan. Rather, the two key factors that matter most for the IMF are the level of consultation and cooperation with Fund staff when economic conditions deteriorate, and the nature of the policy measures governments adopt to address these problems.

In response to the worsening economic situation in Uzbekistan, the authorities broke the terms of the stand-by arrangement and intensified exchange restrictions in the last three months of the year without consulting with the IMF. These measures included reducing the number of commercial banks granted access to the exchange auction from 12 to two (the National Bank of Uzbekistan and *Promstroibank*), and the creation of a list of 'priority' importers and import transactions that were granted preferential access to foreign currency. The CBU also issued a list of 28 categories of 'non-priority' consumer goods for which importers were explicitly denied access to foreign exchange through the official auction (IMF, 1997a: 40–1). The authorities eliminated the system of foreign exchange patents, a requirement under the stand-by arrangement, but replaced this with a more strict system of conversion licenses. These changes created a large backlog of requests for access to foreign exchange, with Fund staff receiving reports of processing times taking up to several months in some cases (IMF, 1997b: 12). The abrupt switch in policy settings added credence to the earlier concerns voiced by staff of a credibility gap between the authorities' formal policy changes towards a market-based exchange rate regime and their continued interventionist approach in practice, based on a selective application of the new formal rules.

Following a decree by President Karimov, a new multiple exchange rates (MER) system was formally introduced on 1 January 1997. In response, the IMF subsequently suspended the stand-by arrangement program without conducting the scheduled third review when it became clear that the Uzbek authorities were not prepared to contemplate any changes in the new policies. Rather than gradually persuading Uzbek policymakers to accept an IMF-friendly approach to market-based economic reforms, the IMF now found itself shut out of the domestic policymaking process entirely. Moreover, Fund staff judged that the new exchange rate regime was 'now more restrictive and distorted than before the approval of the stand-by arrangement in late 1995' (IMF, 1997a: 4, 12–14).

Under the new exchange rate regime export earnings from cotton and gold were subject to a 100 per cent surrender requirement, while foreign exchange earnings from other exports were subject to a 30 per cent surrender requirement. Priority areas included basic food imports, raw materials, and capital goods, for which importers received foreign currency at a highly preferential rate of exchange termed by the government the 'auction' rate. Other favored importers were able to access foreign exchange at the 'commercial bank rate', which was also highly preferential with only a 12 per cent spread permitted between the commercial rate and the auction rate. By comparison, the black market exchange rates in early 1997, the sole alternative for importers who were denied access to either of the official markets, commonly differed from the auction rate by over 100 per cent. This system effectively transferred financial resources from exporters to a select group of importers. It also greatly benefited commercial banks, who acquired foreign exchange at the highly appreciated official 'auction' rate through the 30 per cent surrender requirement on exports, but sold it on at the commercial bank rate (IMF, 1997a: 14). In addition to the new exchange measures, the government also raised existing trade tariffs and extended the scope of tariffs across a wider range of imports.

The IMF made several attempts to get the stand-by arrangement back on track, including a high-level meeting in Tashkent in May 1997 between President Karimov and the First Deputy Managing Director of the IMF, Stanley Fischer. But despite Karimov's confirmation to Fischer that the government wished to complete the policy reforms that had been envisaged under the stand-by arrangement and to work towards a new loan arrangement with the IMF, Fund staff subsequently made little progress in this direction in their policy dialogue with the Uzbek authorities (IMF, 1997a: 1, 17–18). Rather, relations continued to deteriorate, with the Fund staff criticizing the authorities for a lack of candor in their discussions, if not outright obfuscation by withholding economic data (IMF, 1997a: 25–6). In response to the IMF's efforts to persuade the government to abandon the multiple exchange rates system, the authorities again drew on their standard argument that 'a substantial correction of the exchange rate would reignite inflation and contribute to social instability'. To alleviate the political impact of the severe exchange controls on imported consumer goods, the government channeled foreign exchange to importers of basic food goods at the preferential 'auction' exchange rate 'to help preserve social stability' (IMF, 1997b: 59).

Economic nationalism in Uzbekistan

In the four years following the introduction of Uzbekistan's multiple exchange rates system, the IMF's research on the Uzbek economy and its Article IV consultations with the Uzbek authorities emphasized the negative welfare effects of the government's policies, in an attempt to use the IMF's intellectual resources to change the authorities' belief in the benefits of the system. Yet rather than persuading the government to change track, the Uzbek government responded to the IMF's criticism by defending the multiple exchange rate regime as an assertion of its sovereignty (Pomfret, 2000: 741). Extending negative material sanctions on a 'norm renegade' – in this case the suspension of IMF loans to a state that violated a key principle of the contemporary international monetary order – can potentially have a counter-productive psychological effect on a country, in addition to the intended material effect. While the economic cost of sanctions might be expected to help undermine domestic political support for the government's policy stance, it also allows the authorities the opportunity to portray themselves as standing up for the country's independence and its right not to be dictated to by outside actors. This can be a crucial reason for why 'sticks often fail' to generate political change, and why they may have the counter-productive effect of increasing domestic support for a country's leaders, support for their policy agenda, or both (Nincic, 2006: 323–4). In the case of Uzbekistan, crying foul over IMF 'bullying tactics' chimed with President Karimov's efforts to legitimize his regime by propagating an ideology of national independence, with Karimov representing the country's independence from the Soviet Union as allowing the Uzbek people to finally become '*the true masters of the tremendous wealth of their native land*' (cited in March, 2002: 375).

A further reason for the failure of negative sanctions to lead to a change in state behavior is the potential for the penalties for 'bad behavior' to fortify the economic interests of powerful domestic actors and thus strengthen the political constituency opposed to change (Nincic, 2006: 324). This is what occurred in the case of Uzbekistan, where the multiple exchange rates system ensured that powerful economic elites benefited from state protection of their sources of wealth against the possibility of foreign competition if the government followed the IMF's advice and established current account convertibility. Despite the formal centralization of political power in the hands of the President, the evidence suggests that Karimov lacked sufficient autonomy from powerful informal social networks in Uzbekistan to successfully implement policies that cut across their interests.

The crucial difficulty for the IMF was that the informal political and economic context in Uzbekistan inhibited the potential for formal institutional changes to be sustained. The adoption of convertibility would have threatened the large rents that elite clan groups were able to extract from the banking system as well as the exchange earnings from the cotton industry (Collins, 2004: 252–3). For instance, rival elite groups struggled with each other and the government-controlled CBU for control of the National Bank of Uzbekistan (NBU), which held 80 per cent of the country's financial assets. Control of the NBU permitted opportunities for foreign exchange speculation through the NBU's links with foreign banks, as well as the ability to demand side payments from the bank's major customers in return for the approval of loans (Said, 2000). However, despite the domestic political economy benefits gained by the authorities through avoiding current account convertibility, such benefits clearly came with substantial costs. The spread between the black market exchange rate and the two 'official' rates continued to grow between 1997 and 1999 (see Figures 5.1 and 5.2), with a steadily increasing proportion of foreign exchange transactions being conducted at the black market exchange rate as importers were unable to gain sufficient foreign currency through official channels (Rosenberg and de Reeuw, 2000: 9).

Under the multiple exchange rates system, the Uzbek authorities gradually succeeded in achieving a positive current account balance in

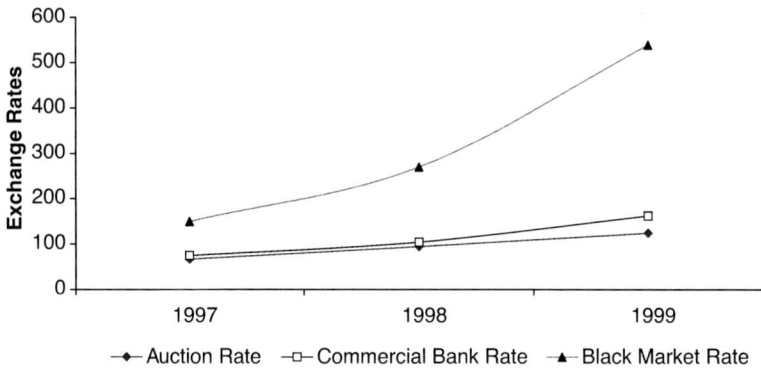

Figure 5.1   Average Exchange Rates in Uzbekistan, 1997–99 (Uzbek Sum per US$)

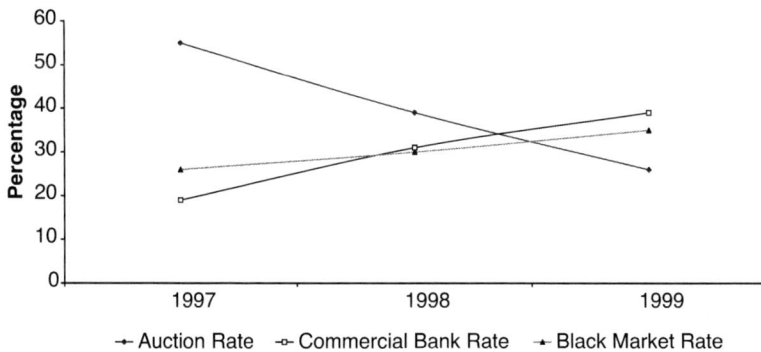

Figure 5.2   Estimated Exchange Rate Market Shares in Uzbekistan, 1997–99

Figure 5.3   Selected Balance of Payments Figures for Uzbekistan, 1994–2000

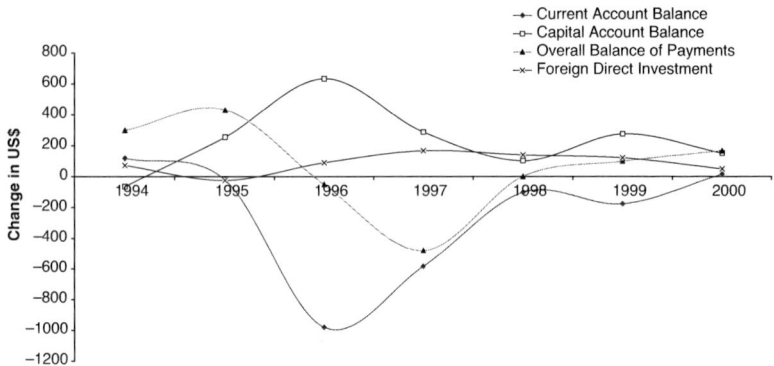

Source: IMF, 2001b: 53.
Figures should be taken as indicative only.
Figures for 2000 only include the first three quarters.

2000 for the first time since 1994 (see Figure 5.3). Yet this was achieved through the further tightening of exchange and trade restrictions to depress imports in response to continued low world market prices for cotton (IMF, 2001b: 11–12), while the foreign exchange surrender requirement for exports apart from cotton and gold was increased from 30 per cent to 50 per cent in January 1999. In 2000, the IMF estimated the net transfer of financial resources from exporters to importers through the government's trade and exchange restrictions constituted up to 16 per cent of the country's GDP (Rosenberg and de Reeuw, 2000: 4, 18). In addition to the high level of implicit taxation, importers also faced high administrative hurdles, with the CBU requiring the submission of seven separate documents before officials would consider granting approval for import transactions (Spechler, 2003: 53). In these circumstances, relations between the IMF and the Uzbek authorities failed to improve and in some respects further deteriorated throughout the late 1990s. Fund staff responsible for Article IV discussions with Uzbekistan reported that the authorities even attempted to negotiate with staff over the figures that the IMF would record for Uzbekistan's economic growth and inflation rates.

The limits of the IMF's influence

Despite the lack of any tangible progress, the IMF continued to maintain its local office in Tashkent and appointed a new resident representative,

Christoph Rosenberg, to take up the post in January 1998. Rosenberg made numerous attempts to persuade the Uzbek authorities to repeal the multiple exchange rates system and move towards the establishment of current account convertibility. These efforts included conducting research on the welfare costs of the system of trade and exchange restrictions compared with transferring the same benefits to importers through the tax system (Rosenberg and de Reeuw, 2000).

In February 2001, the IMF's resident representative put up a detailed page on the IMF's Uzbekistan website, based on his personal views, to establish the validity and the misconceptions of the 15 most common arguments against current account convertibility he encountered from Uzbek officials in defense of the multiple exchange rate system. This added an element of 'public shaming' to support the IMF's earlier attempts at persuasion. Besides inaccurate comparisons with other countries' experiences of current account convertibility, these 15 arguments included the contention that 'The IMF pushes Uzbekistan to introduce convertibility because this benefits the West'. Instead, Rosenberg (2001) argued that Uzbekistan would be the principal beneficiary from convertibility. Fund staff continued to have disagreements with officials over how they should calculate the rate of inflation, and experienced ongoing difficulties with gaining access to accurate economic information. In response, the IMF's resident representative began regularly collecting information to construct his own informal inflation index based on the prices of a basket of goods assessed each week in different cities. Such methods earned the IMF some harsh words from the Uzbek leadership, but in the short term had little impact on the authorities' policy stance.

Following a series of broken promises by President Karimov that he would undertake an imminent move towards the reintroduction of current account convertibility, the IMF eventually decided not to appoint a new resident representative to its Tashkent office when Rosenberg's term expired. When it was publicly announced, the news was widely perceived as a signal that the IMF could 'no longer do business with the government' (BBC, 2001). The IMF's office was not actually closed, but in the future would only be maintained by local staff. In their surveillance of Uzbekistan's economic policies for the 2000 Article IV consultation, Fund staff again encouraged the authorities to adopt a rapid program of reforms, but noted that they were 'willing to accept the authorities' goal of gradual progress toward the implementation of reform' in the design of a new IMF-supported program. The key condition here was that the government took tangible measures toward the introduction of current account convertibility. In addition, Fund staff were concerned by political interference in the production and use of official statistics, with the government seeking to present a favorable picture of the country's economic conditions (IMF, 2001c: 27–9). The authorities had become increasingly concerned with the image that they wanted to portray, both to the outside world and domestically, and their actions led the staff to believe that they were deliberately withholding information in order to 'blind' the IMF to their economic practices.

Relations between Uzbekistan and the IMF only began to thaw after the withdrawal of its resident representative in early 2001. Later that year the Uzbek authorities consulted with staff on the possibility of developing a new reform program with the IMF, and agreed to establish a staff-monitored program to run from January to June 2002. Staff-monitored programs are not supported by a loan from the IMF and are not subject to approval by the Executive Board. Yet they still include performance criteria and are used to establish closer policy dialogue in countries that have a poor record of implementing policy changes agreed with the IMF. A staff-monitored program therefore enables decisionmakers to build up a favorable track record of policy implementation that can allow them to apply for a loan arrangement in the future. Under this arrangement, the Uzbek authorities finally agreed to remove all current account restrictions and to unify the exchange rate by June 2002 (IMF, 2002a). This time the government followed through on its rhetorical commitments with concrete actions and implemented most of the agreed performance criteria and structural benchmarks for the staff-monitored program, including lifting official restrictions on current account transactions (IMF, 2002b). Following further consultations with Fund staff, the Uzbek authorities finally accepted Article VIII status in the IMF in October 2003 (IMF, 2003b). Nevertheless, it was widely believed that this was driven by the authorities' desire to portray a symbol of economic reform to the international financial community rather than by a substantive change in the government's policy preferences.

Despite achieving a key IMF-friendly reform landmark by finally establishing current account convertibility Uzbekistan has not yet entered a new loan arrangement with the IMF, and Fund staff remain dissatisfied with the government's conduct of economic policy. Monetary policy has simply shifted from formal exchange restrictions to reliance on informal measures and the exercise of moral suasion over commercial banks, while the government has sought to achieve many of the same goals that it did through the multiple exchange rates system by increasing trade restrictions. The IMF believes that the Central Bank of Uzbekistan continues to have little autonomy in practice, and that key decisions over monetary policy are centralized in the hands of the President and Deputy Prime Minister.

Despite the government's acceptance of Article VIII obligations, some firms have also continued to encounter difficulties in accessing foreign exchange (Ruziev et al., 2007: 15). Reports from local and foreign businesses, private bankers, and foreign diplomats suggest that the CBU operates informal monthly limits on the sale of foreign exchange to finance consumer imports, which are usually exhausted after only a few days. Unfulfilled applications for foreign exchange are then held over until the following month. Despite numerous reports of Article VIII violations, the CBU has continued to deny that any restrictions on convertibility still exist (Gemayal and Grigorian, 2006: 242). The authorities have maintained the 100 per cent surrender requirement on foreign exchange earnings from cotton and gold exports as well as the 50 per cent surrender requirement on most other exports. Furthermore, extensive restrictions remain in place that prevent banks from effectively intermediating savings from the population, while the economy continues to experience severe cash shortages, which constrains the ability of individuals to access enough *sum* to buy foreign exchange in the first place (Gemayal and Grigorian, 2006: 244–5). In addition, it is common for banks to interrogate depositors seeking to withdraw their funds over what the money will be used for, leading individuals as well as firms to seek to avoid the formal banking system altogether.

Conclusion

One of the principal lessons that can be learned from the IMF's experience with promoting market-based monetary reforms in Central Asia is that the organization's capacity to succeed in iterated games over policy efficacy rests heavily on how national policymakers interpret the circumstances that they face. When Central Asian policymakers' strategies to cope with the challenges of the postcommunist transition intersected with a need to engage and cooperate with the IMF, the organization was able to shape the process of monetary reform over time through setting prior conditions for loan programs, loan performance criteria, technical assistance advice, and involvement in the everyday policymaking process. In the former Soviet Union, the IMF's capacity to influence economic reform as an intellectual actor was driven by the informal context of institutional change. This suggests that the IMF's ideas can only be persuasive for policymakers in an uncertain environment when the authorities are persuaded that their interests lie in maintaining cooperation with the IMF.

The 'scope conditions' that an international organization such as the IMF must operate within are of enormous consequence for the organization's ability to persuade policymakers to enact politically difficult reforms (cf. Zürn and Checkel, 2005: 1055–6). This is not to suggest that a desire on the part of national policymakers to acquire the IMF's 'seal of approval' for their economic policies is a sufficient condition to persuade them to adopt its preferences for institutional change and to sustain IMF-friendly reforms over time. The IMF must engage in ongoing bargaining and negotiation with member states over the scope and direction of policy changes, and must be able to achieve compliance with formal changes that help to reconstruct how actors conceive their interests in order to embed an IMF-friendly institutional framework. When cooperation with the IMF is a secondary concern for a country's political leaders, the IMF can find itself quickly shut out of the policymaking process and left with few levers of influence.

As the IMF's experience with the Central Asian economies illustrates, inheriting common systems of political and economic governance and shared historical experiences is no guarantee that policymakers in newly independent countries will approach economic reform in a similar fashion. When the ruble zone finally collapsed during 1993, the Kyrgyz Republic moved rapidly to establish a new national currency and quickly adopted full currency convertibility in line with the advice of the IMF. Throughout the next three years Fund staff were able to achieve a high degree of input into the domestic policymaking process, and on several occasions they successfully dissuaded the Kyrgyz authorities from implementing policy measures in response to political pressure that were seen as backward steps. Moreover, a shift away from the government's early commitment to full currency convertibility was never openly countenanced. Despite the country's poor economic outlook after independence, the high level of cooperation that the authorities maintained with Fund staff enabled the Kyrgyz Republic to be the first Central Asian state to access financial support through systemic transformation facility and stand-by arrangement loans with the IMF in 1993. In addition, the Kyrgyz Republic became the first Central Asian state to accept Article VIII status in the IMF in 1995.

Kazakhstan also achieved a relatively high degree of policy cooperation with the IMF during the first half of the 1990s despite an uneven start, although the government moved slower than the Kyrgyz Republic in its approach to market-based monetary reforms. Compared with the Kyrgyz Republic, where policymakers initially proved more receptive to the IMF's advice and to the development of an IMF-friendly reform program, the Kazakh authorities were initially more concerned with maintaining their close economic relationship with Russia than establishing good relations with the IMF. When this proved to be politically impossible, the government began to make greater progress in implementing the IMF's advice on monetary reforms. Kazakh policymakers subsequently began an intensive process of engagement with the IMF through technical assistance missions and back-to-back loan arrangements after they made a final break with the ruble zone and introduced a new national currency at the end of 1993. Despite instances where the government applied pressure on the central bank to ease the burden of adjustment on domestic firms by providing cheap credit, under IMF loan arrangements the authorities implemented many of the IMF's preferences for the construction of a market-based monetary system. From the IMF's perspective, the inability to take tougher measures to change the financial behavior of firms partly undermined the authorities' progress with building a new institutional framework for the conduct of monetary policy. However, on crucial issues such as unification of the exchange rate, current account convertibility, formal central bank independence, and the use of competitive auctions to distribute financial resources, the IMF was successful within the space of only a few years in persuading Kazakh policymakers to share a common framework for analysis with regard to monetary challenges.

In stark contrast with both the Kyrgyz Republic and Kazakhstan, Uzbekistan's relations with the IMF from 1992 to when the government finally accepted Article VIII status in 2003 remained poor. A brief improvement occurred from the end of 1993 to the completion of the country's systemic transformation facility loan at the end of 1995, when relations between the Uzbek authorities and the IMF substantially improved and Fund staff believed that they were making real progress in gradually shifting the government's policy stance in a market-oriented direction. Although some important formal changes were introduced during this period, the IMF's relations with Uzbekistan soured again towards the end of 1996 and the beginning of 1997 when the government broke one of the IMF's golden rules by introducing a strict system of multiple exchange rates.

Despite some early warning signs that the Uzbek authorities were adopting formal policy changes that Fund staff wanted and then subverting them through informal means in practice, it took a long time for the government to realize that the IMF was serious about economic reform, and for the IMF to realize that Uzbekistan was not. The government's actions at the end of 1996, as well as the failure to heed the IMF's advice to take corrective actions during 1997, can be seen as a measure of the IMF's lack of success in persuading Uzbek policymakers to adopt a common intellectual framework. Unlike their neighbors in Kazakhstan and the Kyrgyz Republic, the government failed to consult with the IMF before directly violating the terms of its stand-by arrangement. Faced with a major economic challenge, the government turned to Soviet-style practices for a familiar remedy that would be less likely to jeopardize the regime's stability – or at least its ability to control economic activity and to allocate rents – rather than taking the IMF's advice to adopt current account convertibility. In contrast to three years in the Kyrgyz Republic and four years in Kazakhstan, it took 11 years for the IMF to persuade Uzbekistan to formally accept Article VIII status after the country became a member of the organization, while recent evidence suggests that the government has simply shifted to a more informal system of currency controls.

Conclusion

This book has shown how the International Monetary Fund utilizes its intellectual *and* material resources to shape institutional change in national economies during conditions of extreme economic uncertainty. The IMF's financial resources and loan policy conditionality provide an arsenal of material incentives that can create openings for normative persuasion through iterated games over policy efficacy with national policymakers – long-term political contests where the IMF does not always prevail. Especially in cases where the IMF must persuade policymakers to adopt its ideas in an environment of acute uncertainty, the informal context in which formal institutional change takes place can thwart the organization's efforts to sustain an IMF-friendly policy orientation over time. In such circumstances, institutional change is not a matter of the IMF simply diffusing formal policy changes that are internalized at the national level and automatically direct actors' behaviour. Rather, at every step of the reform process, the IMF must persuade actors to adopt – and to sustain – its long-term policy preferences, which is an ongoing struggle because of the range of political variables and unexpected events that intervene. The IMF's persuasive influence thus depends upon how policymakers interpret the political and economic circumstances they face, and whether this leads them to see the IMF as a useful means to achieve other political and economic objectives. Fund staff are at the vanguard of this process, and seek to foster persuasive environments through policy reform corridors that operate bilaterally, such as Article IV consultations and loan negotiations, or multilaterally through the Joint Vienna Institute. The IMF's intellectual influence on the scope of institutional change is further boosted through the organization's role as a reputational intermediary, which helps to create persuasive environments at the national level that encourage policymakers to sustain IMF-friendly reforms over time.

The IMF as an intellectual actor

As an intellectual actor, the IMF is not a homogenous policy enforcer. The organization has a clear preference for governments to open markets in order to increase competition, and to allocate resources through price incentives rather than administrative discretion. Above all, the IMF believes that states will benefit from policies that aim to achieve 'sound money' and 'sound public finances', which can improve their credit reputation among international audiences. But rather than blindly promoting one-size-fits-all policies (Stiglitz, 2002), the IMF recognizes the need for different policy reform mixes in different cases. In this respect the IMF constructs templates for institutional change, based on similar characteristics among like-economies (see Broome and Seabrooke, 2007), especially when the IMF perceives that states confront common economic challenges in a crisis. 'Seeing like the IMF' helps to reveal that the organization's actions cannot simply be explained by a crude principal-agent model in which staff are kept on a tight leash by the interests of major shareholders on the Executive Board. Fund staff instead have significant sources of autonomy in generating country knowledge for the design, monitoring, and evaluation of the IMF's advice for institutional change. They are the main conduit for the IMF's relations with policymakers in its member states. As such, Fund staff play a crucial role in evaluating the policy intentions of state actors and attempting to reconstruct their preferences over time.

Chapters 1 and 2 in this book help to show the dynamic relations between different aspects of the IMF's global role, and demonstrate that while the IMF has a strict hierarchical process for producing country knowledge and policy advice, this is shaped at different levels before the IMF achieves a 'single corporate line' on preferred reforms that staff seek to persuade policymakers to adopt. We should therefore be skeptical of claims that the IMF uniformly promotes the same policies, and should pay closer attention to studying the sources of *variation* in the IMF's policy advice in different countries over time. IMF persuasion is not simply about supporting the strategic interests of powerful creditor states, nor is it about enforcing one-size-fits-all universal templates for policy change. The value of 'seeing like the IMF' through its own documents is to provide an analytical cut into seeing how an international organization tries to change techniques of economic governance in its member states through persuasion over time.

As an agent of persuasion, a core component of the IMF's role is to provide the function of a reputational intermediary that attempts to help states improve their creditworthiness by communicating essential information to private actors and providing a symbolic assurance about a government's policy intentions to bilateral and multilateral donors. This provides a pragmatic motivation for the IMF to promote policies that aim to achieve low inflation and low public debt in borrowing member states. In doing so, the IMF counsels states on how to improve their ability to attract external financing within the structural constraints imposed by the contemporary international economic order, while the organization is also cognizant of its own resource constraints in an era of globalized capital markets. But this does not mean that the IMF's role as a reputational intermediary will lead to positive outcomes. As the case of the Kyrgyz Republic indicates, improving the capacity of states to access additional sources of external financing might simply lead to an unsustainable debt cycle, prompting states to turn to the IMF to access debt relief through the Paris Club process. Again, the IMF's role as a reputational intermediary comes to the fore here, with states relying on the IMF's conservative reputation for a credibility-enhancing mechanism to secure concessions from private and official creditors.

IMF-friendly institutional change

In its dealings with the Kyrgyz Republic, Kazakhstan and Uzbekistan the IMF relied primarily on the use of persuasion to achieve domestic policy change, backed up with its ability to approve or to deny loan arrangements and the associated financial and symbolic benefits that an IMF agreement can deliver. The responsibility of Fund staff to evaluate policymakers' reform intentions before a state can apply to the Executive Board for a loan agreement – as well as the IMF's capacity to approve, deny, or suspend loans – can provide scope for the IMF to exert a persuasive influence over policymakers' economic policy choices. In this regard, the application of 'prior actions' and loan conditionality are an important part of the IMF's toolkit. They are not simply incentive mechanisms that the IMF employs to 'buy' compliance with its preferences during the life cycle of a loan program. If this was the case, there would be little left to explain the maintenance of an IMF-friendly orientation towards monetary policy after a loan program has ended except for a crude 'path dependence' argument, especially if a program does not result in improved economic performance. Rather, we should see the IMF's conditionality tools, both prior to and during loan programs, as affording repeated opportunities for Fund staff to *persuade* policymakers to change the way they think about the economy. The scope for persuasion is even greater when states are likely to request back-to-back loan agreements. This reinforces the importance of the staff's role in assessing past compliance and future intentions, and can help to establish a policy reform corridor through which IMF-friendly policy changes escalate over time.

The three cases examined in this book suggest that the IMF's ability to use financial incentives and intellectual arguments to encourage Central Asian governments to adopt IMF-friendly monetary reforms depended heavily on whether policymakers could be persuaded that they had good reasons for intensifying cooperation with the IMF. The strategies that Central Asian leaders developed after independence, which flowed from how elites interpreted their political and economic constraints in each country, informed whether actors saw good relations with the IMF as a means to an end to shore up support for the new regime, or as a potential threat to social stability and regime survival. This might seem to suggest that the IMF had little independent influence at all, and what mattered was simply whether good relations with the IMF fit in with policymakers' own political and economic goals. But these scope conditions only set the stage from which the IMF draws on its intellectual resources to shape the design, process, and implementation of institutional change.

For an external actor such as the IMF, material incentives provide openings for normative persuasion. The ability to offer 'positive inducements' to states in return for policy compliance might produce two different effects on state behavior. First, by offering rewards for improved conduct, positive inducements might help to tip the balance in favor of compliance, without changing the underlying agenda and incentive structure of the regime. Here, 'the best that can be expected is to bribe finite political concessions from a basically bad regime' (Nincic, 2006: 325). In this respect, a government may adopt a posture of apparent compliance with the IMF in order to access a loan arrangement and the opportunities for greater support from the international financial community that good relations with the IMF imply. However, a government's commitment to maintaining a good policy relationship with the IMF in these circumstances will be weak, with compliance likely to be short-lived, as it was in the case in Uzbekistan.

The second potential effect that positive inducements can have on a state's behavior is to contribute to a more fundamental realignment of its policy agenda. In this situation, 'the regime's incentive structure is reconfigured, decreasing the need for bribes' (Nincic, 2006: 325). Where fundamental change occurs, this suggests that the IMF has successfully persuaded national elites into a shared way of thinking about the economy and the appropriate limits of the state's role in regulating economic activity. In addition, it may suggest that elites have taken into account the future material benefits that can be gained through cooperating with the IMF, such as the potential for greater external financing from either private or public sources. However, given the considerable political investment in institutional change and policy learning that is necessary to demonstrate substantive compliance with the IMF's policy preferences over time, both processes are likely to play important symbiotic roles in shaping political outcomes. These two effects comprise the difference between a straightforward change in policies, which governments might quickly abandon as the case of Uzbekistan demonstrates, and a substantive change in a regime's *policy orientation*. We can expect the latter to be more durable, as evidenced by the IMF-friendly policy actions that were taken by the Kyrgyz Republic, and to a lesser extent Kazakhstan, when governments encountered domestic resistance towards top-down changes in IMF-friendly monetary practices.

The IMF's record in Central Asia

The Kyrgyz Republic exhibited a strong desire from the start to work cooperatively with the IMF, in order to gain access to additional sources of official aid. However, the maintenance of IMF-friendly policy reforms despite considerable resistance from commercial banks and state-owned firms – which policymakers believed would have a major negative impact on budget revenues – also suggests that the IMF had a relatively high degree of success in persuading national officials into a common way of thinking about economic policy options. Backed up by the use of material incentives, the IMF was able to cultivate a new intellectual framework for understanding economic problems among Kyrgyz officials. Policymakers subsequently chose to apply IMF-friendly policy solutions in response to the severe monetary problems that emerged at the end of 1993, in contrast to their continued reliance on Soviet practices in similar circumstances at the start of the year.

Compared to its neighbors, Kazakhstan was an intermediate case for the IMF. Kazakh policymakers were not as open to the IMF's ideas for monetary reform as the Kyrgyz Republic, nor were they as resistant to the IMF's advice as Uzbekistan. Like the Kyrgyz Republic, the IMF attempted to persuade Kazakh policymakers to set new institutional parameters that could help to change actors' preferences in favor of a market-based monetary system, and which would circumscribe the potential for political interference in the distribution of financial resources. Fund staff notched up some notable successes in Kazakhstan during 1993 and 1994, such as persuading the authorities to increase their reliance on credit auctions to allocate central bank credit, although the IMF was not initially able to persuade Kazakh policymakers to resist political pressure for further credit bailouts of indebted firms. Kazakhstan's policymakers invested much time and energy in implementing key IMF-friendly policy changes and reaching compromises with the Fund staff in other areas where reforms required greater adjustment in order to be translated into the difficult informal environment. After the IMF approved the Kazakh authorities' application for a systemic transformation facility loan in July 1993, the country remained under back-to-back loan programs with the IMF until 2002. Despite the uneven progress during the early period of Kazakhstan's membership in the IMF towards establishing an IMF-friendly monetary policy orientation, the country subsequently fared much better than the Kyrgyz Republic in terms of its economic outcomes, largely due its greater natural resources.

Compared with both the Kyrgyz Republic and Kazakhstan, Uzbekistan has remained a troublesome case for the IMF. From the IMF's perspective, the government of Uzbekistan has become a renegade that has refused to be persuaded to implement international monetary norms in domestic policy except at its own protracted pace, despite a concern among Uzbek leaders to maintain the *appearance* of cooperation with the IMF. A brief period of intensive cooperation between Uzbek policymakers and Fund staff occurred during 1994 and 1995, when the IMF was able to achieve a tightening of monetary policy, increased use of credit auctions for allocating financial resources, and tougher budget constraints on commercial banks and major firms. This led to a significant decline in inflation under the country's systemic transformation facility loan in 1995, new legislation stipulating *de jure* independence for the central bank, and the removal of exchange restrictions and measures to expand auctions for foreign exchange. However, cooperation broke down again during 1996, due to Uzbek policymakers' response to a balance of payments crisis caused by declining foreign exchange earnings for cotton exports. By breaking the terms of their stand-by arrangement loan without first discussing possible changes with Fund staff, the actions of Uzbek policymakers prompted the IMF to suspend the agreement to pressure the authorities to rescind new measures that intensified foreign exchange restrictions. Studying 'outlier' cases like Uzbekistan, where the IMF is able to make a credible threat to suspend financing without undue political interference from the Executive Board, helps to show the limits of the IMF's influence. While it is often reported that the IMF uses its loan programs to 'impose' policy changes on unwilling governments, the Uzbek case illustrates that sovereign governments can still exercise the right to break the terms of such agreements when the domestic costs of compliance become too high. However, like Uzbekistan, they risk a high reputational cost among international audiences in doing so.

Lessons from the frontier

For the field of International Political Economy, the principal lessons from this study of the IMF's experience with institutional change in the frontier economies of Central Asia are threefold. First, while a systemic crisis might open up a window of opportunity enabling the IMF to persuade policymakers to enact formal institutional changes, in conditions of extreme uncertainty formal changes can quickly be frustrated by informal practices. Second, a crucial driver of the relationship between policymakers and the IMF is how Fund staff interpret the policy intentions of their interlocutors. This informs how staff assess compliance with 'prior conditions' before submitting loan applications to the Board, and how staff judge a country's track record under a loan program. Perhaps most important is the fact that staff assessments of a government's policy intentions and compliance under a loan program are not simply a matter of quantifying formal changes. Rather, staff must interpret whether instances of 'policy slippage' and missed targets constitute evidence of *deliberate non-compliance*, or whether local circumstances mitigated the potential for loan conditions to be fulfilled. These judgments matter when the Executive Board is considering whether to grant waivers for unfulfilled loan performance criteria, such as in the cases of the Kyrgyz Republic and Kazakhstan during 1993–6, or whether to suspend a loan program in conditions of deliberate non-compliance, as in the case of Uzbekistan in 1996.

The third main lesson from the IMF's experience with Central Asian economies is that the organization's influence often leads to unexpected outcomes. In the Kyrgyz Republic, the IMF's star pupil in Central Asia, the IMF's role as a reputational intermediary enabled the government to contract an unsustainable level of sovereign debt during the 1990s, which undermined the potential for reforms to lead to improved economic performance. In Kazakhstan, the creation of an investment-friendly climate through IMF-friendly monetary reforms enabled policymakers to build up a patronage system based on resource rents. Using state power to exploit rent-seeking opportunities does not necessarily prevent economic growth and increased economic efficiency (see MacIntyre, 2000: 270; Lim and Stern, 2002). However, in Kazakhstan the creation of a 'rentier economy' stymied the implementation of reforms in other areas of the economy (Pomfret, 2006: 11; Gleason, 2001: 172–3), leading to recent calls by the IMF for intensified structural reforms to enhance corporate transparency and governance (IMF, 2007a: 17). Finally, although Uzbekistan's track record with the IMF suggests that it was largely non-cooperative during the 1990s, the IMF's iterated games over policy efficacy with the authorities led to important reforms in some areas. In this respect, Uzbekistan is a case of slow monetary reforms, rather than simply a case of no reform. This suggests that even in non-cooperative cases, the IMF's advice can inform domestic institutional change by providing policymakers with a package of reform ideas, from which they might select those they consider least likely to threaten their political and economic interests. These three principal lessons from Central Asia have broader relevance for the IMF's relations with other frontier economies as well as emerging market economies, and warrant further comparative research.

Implications for future research

The argument and findings in this book have important implications for recent debates over the IMF's role in the contemporary world economy – especially for debates over the sources of the IMF's influence on institutional change in borrowing states – and for the study of international organizations more broadly. In particular, seeing the IMF as an intellectual actor can help to improve recent principal-agent approaches to understanding international organizations, by orienting the focus of analysis from member state control of international organizations to the sources of their autonomy as intellectual actors, and how this dynamic varies across cases and over time. 'Seeing like an international organization' in the case of other international organizations like the World Bank, the Bank for International Settlements, the Organization for Economic Cooperation and Development, and the World Trade Organization can shed light on how these organizations try to change techniques of economic governance in their member states by exploring how they see particular policy areas that are of concern.

Understanding the importance of the informal context in which reform takes place can also contribute to the wider literature on institutional change, by helping to improve our understanding of how institutions are reformed without seeing outcomes as resulting from path dependent formal rules. More important than the path dependence of inherited institutions when states are confronted with a systemic crisis is how political leaders interpret the options that are available to them – especially if these same leaders remain in power over an extended period of time, as they did in each of the cases examined here. Based on these interpretive acts, political leaders make choices that might lead them to seek good relations with the IMF as a means to achieve other political and economic ends, or they may choose to maintain a greater distance. How reforms are translated into a local context will depend in large part on *informal* processes and practices. The emerging literature on informal institutions has already made significant strides in opening up the 'black box' of institutional change (for an overview, see Helmke and Levitsky, 2004; see also Hobson and Seabrooke, 2007). This book suggests that a great deal more can be gained from linking the study of the everyday sources of institutional change with the study of international organizations and externally-sponsored economic reforms.

Another future research avenue is to explore in greater detail the IMF's role as a reputational intermediary for its member states, especially in emerging market and frontier economies that rely on external financing to fund economic development. Again, there is potential in studying how other international organizations act as reputational intermediaries, such as the United Nations Development Program, which has recently cooperated with the US State Department to finance credit ratings for African economies with the aim of improving access to international capital markets (see Sagasti et al., 2005: 62). In the case of the IMF, most of the existing research in this area has come from economists, many from the IMF itself, who have sought to establish through quantitative analysis whether, when, and why the IMF might have a catalytic effect on additional sources of finance (Bird and Rowlands, 2002; Edwards, 2005; Marchesi and Thomas, 1999; Mody and Saravia, 2002; Rowlands, 2001). To tackle this issue from another direction, future research might draw on the recent International Relations scholarship on the importance of reputation (Sharman, 2006, 2007) to explore how the IMF's reputation provides it with an important institutional resource as well as a constraint. By further unpacking the IMF's role as a reputational intermediary, we might increase our understanding of what explains change within the IMF by orienting the focus of analysis beyond the 'usual suspects'. In particular, this could help to improve principal-agent approaches to the study of international organizations by expanding the type of 'principals' that are studied.

A final avenue for future research suggested by this study is to revisit the question of what factors most determine a state's ability to access external credit through the IMF. Existing literature in this area has shown that US influence shapes the scope of IMF conditions in countries of strategic importance (Stone, 2008). In Central Asia, however, the most important determinant of the ability of states to access the IMF's financial resources – and the conditions under which they were able to do so – was the quality of the working relationship between Fund staff and national policymakers. When the relationship between Fund staff and national policymakers was poor or suffered from a lack of trust, states faced longer delays in accessing IMF loans as they slowly built up a track record of implementing market-based reforms. When they did receive loans, these were disbursed more slowly, and with a low tolerance for failure to achieve quantitative targets and structural reform benchmarks. When national policymakers engaged in a high degree of cooperation with Fund staff this helped to foster a greater degree of trust on the IMF's part with respect to policymakers' future intentions. In return, the IMF granted relatively easier access to IMF loans with a higher tolerance for 'policy slippage' and missed reform targets. Consequently, the political economy of access to credit from the IMF related less to a country's potential capacity to repay loans in the future than to the authorities' willingness to cooperate with Fund staff to implement IMF-friendly institutional change. In the case of the Kyrgyz Republic, for example, this enabled national policymakers to enter into a quasi-permanent relationship with the IMF where the country gained successive loan arrangements in the absence of a capacity to make full repayments, illustrated by its current HIPC status.

The independence of the IMF

In the frontier economies of post-Soviet Central Asia, the common result of the IMF's influence was hybrid reform outcomes – where institutions emerged that exhibited a mix of central planning and liberal market principles and practices. Hybrid outcomes were not simply pathologies that resulted from a lack of political will or from checks on reform imposed by domestic veto players, but derived from actions that made sense to the actors involved with executing institutional change in each country as they sought to translate the IMF's ideas into local contexts. In this uncertain environment, the IMF was not strictly opposed to the construction of 'hybrid' institutions, at least where it perceived these to be a step in the right direction (as in the Kyrgyz Republic and Kazakhstan) rather than a continuation of state intervention by other means (as in Uzbekistan). Although each state achieved hybrid institutional outcomes, how policymakers interpreted the different transitional contexts they confronted in the Kyrgyz Republic, Kazakhstan, and Uzbekistan shaped the degree to which the IMF was able to mould institutional change over time.

This book has advanced a straightforward argument: the International Monetary Fund is not simply a neoliberal policy enforcer that is tightly controlled by its major shareholders. Rather, it is an intellectual actor that has important sources of independence, chief among which is its ability to use financial resources to create openings for normative persuasion in borrowing states over time. To persuade national policymakers to adopt a common intellectual framework for understanding new institutional challenges the IMF employs a range of formal mechanisms to ensure compliance in the case of borrowing states. But the IMF is not a monolithic actor. Understanding the IMF as simply expressing the interests of its major shareholder principals, with little else going on in-between, is of limited utility in understanding how the IMF produces the policy advice that it seeks to persuade member states to implement. Especially in cases where the IMF's major shareholders are less likely to intervene, Fund staff are the driving force behind the IMF's efforts to change national policymakers' intersubjective ideas and behavior. Above all else, how staff interpret actors' policy intentions is crucial for a state's ability to access IMF loans, while the organization's capacity for independent action is dynamic across different cases. We should therefore understand the IMF as a semi-autonomous actor, rather than simply reading the interests of its member state principals in IMF loan decisions.

References

Abbott, Kenneth W. and Duncan Snidal. 2000. Hard and Soft Law in International Governance. *International Organization* 54(3): 421–56.

Abdelal, Rawi. 2001. *National Purpose in the World Economy: Post-Soviet States in Comparative Perspective*. Ithaca: Cornell University Press.

Abdelal, Rawi. 2003a. Contested Currency: Russia's Rouble in Domestic and International Politics. *Journal of Communist Studies and Transition Politics* 19(2): 55–76.

Abdelal, Rawi. 2003b. Purpose and Privation: Nation and Economy in Post-Habsburg Eastern Europe and Post-Soviet Eurasia. *East European Politics and Societies* 16(3): 898–933.

Abdelal, Rawi. 2007. *Capital Rules: The Construction of Global Finance*. Cambridge: Harvard University Press.

Adler, Emanuel. 1997. Seizing the Middle Ground: Constructivism in World Politics. *European Journal of International Relations* 3(3): 319–63.

Agénor, Pierre-Richard. 1993. Credible Disinflation Programs. PPAA/93/9. IMF Policy Paper on Analysis and Assessment. Washington DC: IMF.

Agzamov, Akhad, Alisher Anzarov, and Kahramon Shakirov. 1995. Economic Reform and Investment Priorities in the Republic of Uzbekistan. *Comparative Economic Studies* 37(3): 27–38.

Akiner, Shirin. 2004. Political Processes in Post-Soviet Central Asia. In *Central Eurasia in Global Politics: Conflict, Security, and Development*, edited by Mehdi Parvizi Amineh and Henk Houweling. Leiden: Brill, 117–44.

Alexeev, Michael V. and Clifford G. Gaddy. 1993. Income Distribution in the U.S.S.R. in the 1980s. *Review of Income and Wealth* 39(1): 23–36.

Anderson, John. 1999. *Kyrgyzstan: Central Asia's Island of Democracy?* London: Routledge.

Appel, Hilary. 2000. The Ideological Determinants of Liberal Economic Reform: The Case of Privatization. *World Politics* 52(4): 520–49.

Appel, Hilary. 2004. Western Financial Institutions, Local Actors, and the Privatization Paradigm. *Problems of Post-Communism* 51(5): 3–10.

Åslund, Anders. 1995. *How Russia Became a Market Economy*. Washington DC: The Brookings Institution.

Asselain, J.C. 1991. Convertibility and Economic Transformation. *European Economy*, Special Edition No. 2: 217–41.

Assetto, Valerie J. 1988. *The Soviet Bloc in the IMF and the IBRD*. Boulder, Colorado: Westview Press.

Auty, Richard M. 1999. The IMF Model and Resource-Abundant Transition Economies: Kazakhstan and Uzbekistan. UNU World Institute for Development Economics Research Working Papers No. 169. Helsinki: UNU/WIDER. <www.wider.unu.edu/publications/wp169.pdf> (accessed 20/06/06).

Auty, Richard M. 2003. Natural Resources and 'Gradual' Reform in Uzbekistan and Turkmenistan. *Natural Resources Forum* 27(4): 255–66.

Babb, Sarah. 2003. The IMF in Sociological Perspective: A Tale of Organizational Slippage. *Studies in Comparative International Development* 38(2): 3–27.

Barnett, Michael and Martha Finnemore. 1999. The Politics, Power, and Pathologies of International Organizations. *International Organization* 53(4): 699–732.

Barnett, Michael and Martha Finnemore. 2004. *Rules for the World: International Organizations in Global Politics*. Ithaca: Cornell University Press.

Bayulgen, Oksan. 2005. Foreign Capital in Central Asia: Curse or Blessing? *Communist and Post-Communist Studies* 38(1): 49–69.

BBC. 2001. Uzbekistan Rapped by IMF. *BBC News Online*. <http://news.bbc.co.uk/2/hi/asia-pacific/1246538.stm> (accessed 10/01/07).

Beeson, Mark and André Broome. 2008. Watching from the Sidelines? The Decline of the IMF's Crisis Management Role. *Contemporary Politics* 14(4): 393–409.

Ben-Ner, Avner and Louis Putterman. 1999. Values and Institutions in Economic Analysis. In *Economics, Values, and Organization*, edited by Avner Ben-Ner and Louis Putterman. Cambridge: Cambridge University Press, 3–69.

Bernhard, William, Lawrence J. Broz, and William Roberts Clark. 2002. The Political Economy of Monetary Institutions. *International Organization* 56(4): 693–723.

Best, Jacqueline. 2003. From the Top-Down: The New Financial Architecture and the Re-embedding of Global Finance. *Review of International Political Economy* 8(3): 363–84.

Best, Jacqueline. 2005. *The Limits of Transparency: Ambiguity and the History of International Finance*. Ithaca: Cornell University Press.

Best, Jacqueline. 2007. Legitimacy Dilemmas: The IMF's Pursuit of Country Ownership. *Third World Quarterly* 28(3): 469–88.

Bibow, Jörg. 2004. Reflections on the Current Fashion for Central Bank Independence. *Cambridge Journal of Economics* 28(4): 549–76.

Bienen, Henry. 1990. The Politics of Trade Liberalization in Africa. *Economic Development and Cultural Change* 38(4): 713–32.

Bienen, Henry and Mark Gersovitz. 1985. Economic Stabilization, Conditionality, and Political Stability. *International Organization* 39(4): 729–54.

Bigman, David and Sérgio Pereira Leite. 1993. Enterprise Arrears in Russia: Causes and Policy Options. IMF Working Paper WP/93/61. Washington DC: IMF.

Bird, Graham. 1996. The International Monetary Fund and Developing Countries: A Review of the Evidence and Policy Options. *International Organization* 50(3): 477–511.

Bird, Graham. 2002a. The Completion Rate of IMF Programmes: What We Know, Don't Know and Need to Know. *The World Economy* 25(6): 833–47.

Bird, Graham. 2002b. The Credibility and Signalling Effect of IMF Programmes. *Journal of Policy Modeling* 24(9): 799–811.

Bird, Graham. 2003. Restructuring the IMF's Lending Facilities. *The World Economy* 26(2): 229–45.

Bird, Graham and Dane Rowlands. 2002. The Catalyzing Role of Policy-Based Lending by the IMF and the World Bank: Fact or Fiction? *Journal of International Development* 12: 951–73.

Bird, Graham and Thomas D. Willett. 2004. IMF Conditionality, Implementation and the New Political Economy of Ownership. *Comparative Economic Studies* 46(3): 423–50.

Blackmon, Pamela. 2005. Back to the USSR: Why the Past Does Matter in Explaining Differences in the Economic Reform Processes of Kazakhstan and Uzbekistan. *Central Asian Survey* 24(4): 391–404.

Blyth, Mark. 2003. Structures Do Not Come with an Instruction Sheet. *Perspectives on Politics* 1(4): 695–706.

Bofinger, Peter. 1991. Options for the Payments and Exchange-Rate Systems in Eastern Europe. *European Economy*, Special Edition No. 2: 243–61.

Bomhoff, Eduard J. 1992. Monetary Reform in Eastern Europe. *European Economic Review* 36(2/3): 454–8.

Boone, Catherine and Clement Henry. 2004. Neoliberalism in the Middle East and Africa: Divergent Banking Reform Trajectories, 1980s to 2000. *Commonwealth and Comparative Politics* 42(3): 356–92.

Boughton, James M. 2001. *Silent Revolution: The International Monetary Fund 1979–1989*. Washington DC: IMF.

Brooker, David C. 2004. Founding Presidents of the Soviet Successor States: A Comparative Study. *Demokratizatsiya* 12(1): 133–45.

Broome, André. 2006. Civilizing Labor Markets: The World Bank in Central Asia. In *Global Standards of Market Civilization*, edited by Brett Bowden and Leonard Seabrooke. London: Routledge/RIPE Studies in Global Political Economy, 119–33.

Broome, André. 2008. The Importance of Being Earnest: The IMF as a Reputational Intermediary. *New Political Economy* 13(2): 125–51.

Broome, André. 2009. Money for Nothing: Everyday Actors and Monetary Crises. *Journal of International Relations and Development* 12(1): 3–30.

Broome, André. 2010a. The IMF, Crisis Management, and the Credit Crunch. *Australian Journal of International Affairs* 64(1), forthcoming.

Broome, André. 2010b. Global Monitor: The Joint Vienna Institute. *New Political Economy* 15(3), forthcoming.

Broome, André and Leonard Seabrooke. 2007. Seeing Like the IMF: Institutional Change in Small Open Economies. *Review of International Political Economy* 14(4): 576–601.

Bunce, Valerie. 1999. The Political Economy of Postsocialism. *Slavic Review* 58(4): 756–93.

Burn, Gary. 1999. The State, the City and the Euromarkets. *Review of International Political Economy* 6(2): 225–61.

Calvert, Randall L. 1995. Rational Actors, Equilibrium, and Social Institutions. In *Explaining Social Institutions*, edited by Jack Knight and Itai Sened. Ann Arbor: The University of Michigan Press, 57–93.

Campbell, John L. 1997. Recent Trends in Institutional Political Economy. *International Journal of Sociology and Social Policy* 17(7/8): 15–56.

Campbell, John L. 2004. *Institutional Change and Globalization*. Princeton: Princeton University Press.

Campbell, John L. and Ove K. Pedersen (eds). 1996. *Legacies of Change: Transformations of Postcommunist European Economies*. New York: Aldine de Gruyter.

Carlin, Wendy, Steven Fries, Mark Schaffer, and Paul Seabright. 2000. Barter and Non-Monetary Transactions in Transition Economies: Evidence from a Cross-Country Survey. In *The Vanishing Ruble: Barter Networks and Non-Monetary Transactions in Post-Soviet Societies*, edited by Paul Seabright. Cambridge: Cambridge University Press, 236–56.

Chavin, James. 1994. Independent Central Asia: A Primer. *Current History* 93(582): 160–3.

Chwieroth, Jeffrey M. 2007a. Testing and Measuring the Role of Ideas: The Case of Neoliberalism in the International Monetary Fund. *International Studies Quarterly* 51(1): 5–30.

Chwieroth, Jeffrey M. 2007b. Neoliberal Economists and Capital Account Liberalization in Emerging Markets. *International Organization* 61(2): 443–63.

Clark, Ian D. 1996. Inside the IMF: Comparisons with Policy-making Organizations in Canadian Governments. *Canadian Public Administration* 39(2): 157–91.

Clarke, Simon. 2000. The Household in a Non-Monetary Market Economy. In *The Vanishing Ruble: Barter Networks and Non-Monetary Transactions in Post-Soviet Societies*, edited by Paul Seabright. Cambridge: Cambridge University Press, 176–206.

Cohen, Benjamin J. 1998. *The Geography of Money*. Ithaca: Cornell University Press.

Collins, Kathleen. 2004. The Logic of Clan Politics: Evidence from the Central Asian Trajectories. *World Politics* 56(1): 224–61.

Collins, Kathleen. 2006. *Clan Politics and Regime Transition in Central Asia*. Cambridge: Cambridge University Press.

Conway, Patrick. 1994. Kazakhstan: Land of Opportunity. *Current History* 93: 164–8.

Conway, Patrick. 1995. Currency Proliferation: The Monetary Legacy of the Soviet Union. *Essays in International Finance*, No. 197. Princeton, NJ: Princeton University Press.

Conway, Patrick. 1997. Ruble Overhang and Ruble Shortage: Were They the Same Thing? *Journal of Comparative Economics* 24(1): 1–24.

Cooley, Alexander. 2000. International Aid to the Former Soviet States: Agent of Change or Guardian of the Status Quo. *Problems of Post-Communism* 47(4): 34–44.

Cooley, Alexander. 2003. Western Conditions and Domestic Choices: The Influence of External Actors on the Post-Communist Transition. In *Nations in Transit 2003: Democratization in East Central Europe and Eurasia*. New York: Freedom House.

Cooper, Richard N. 1999. Should Capital Controls be Banished? *Brookings Papers on Economic Activity* 1999(1): 89–141.

Cortell, Andrew P. and Susan Peterson. 1999. Altered States: Explaining Domestic Institutional Change. *British Journal of Political Science* 29(1): 277–303.

Cottarelli, Carlo. 2005. Efficiency and Legitimacy: Trade-Offs in IMF Governance. WP/05/107. IMF Working Paper. Washington DC: International Monetary Fund. <www.imf.org/external/pubs/ft/wp/2005/wp05107.pdf> (accessed 30/06/06).

Cottarelli, Carlo and Curzio Giannini. 1998. Inflation, Credibility, and the Role of the International Monetary Fund. PPAA/98/12. IMF Paper on Policy Analysis and Assessment, September 1998. Washington DC: IMF.

Coudouel, Aline, Alastair McAuley, and John Micklewright. 1997. Transfers and Exchange between Households in Uzbekistan. In *Household Welfare in Central Asia*, edited by Jane Falkingham, Jeni Klugman, Sheila Marnie, and John Micklewright. New York: St Martin's Press, 202–20.

Crouch, Colin. 2007. Neoinstitutionalism: Still No Intellectual Hegemony? *Regulation and Governance* 1(3): 261–70.

Cukierman, Alex, Geoffrey P. Miller, and Bilin Neyapti. 2002. Central Bank Reform, Liberalization and Inflation in Transition Economies – an International Perspective. *Journal of Monetary Economics* 49(2): 237–64.

Daviddi, Renzo and Efisio Espa. 1995. Regional Trade and Foreign Currency Regimes Among the Former Soviet Republics. *Economics of Planning* 28: 29–57.

Dhonte, Pierre. 1997. Conditionality as an Instrument of Borrower Credibility. PPAA/97/2. Paper on Policy Analysis and Assessment of the IMF. February, 1997. <www.imf.org/external/pubs/ft/ppaa/ppaa9702.pdf> (accessed 06/10/06).

Dijkstra, A. Geske. 2002. The Effectiveness of Policy Conditionality: Eight Country Experiences. *Development and Change* 33(2): 307–34.

Dinello, Natalia. 1999. The Russian F-Connection: Finance, Firms, Friends, Families, and Favorites. *Problems of Post-Communism* 46(1): 24–33.

Dodd, Nigel. 1994. *The Sociology of Money: Economics, Reason and Contemporary Society*. Cambridge: Polity Press.

Dolowitz, David P. and David Marsh. 2000. Learning from Abroad: The Role of Policy Transfer in Contemporary Decision-Making. *Governance: An International Journal of Policy and Administration* 13(1): 5–24.

Easterly, William and Paulo Vieira da Cunha. 1994. Financing the Storm: Macroeconomic Crisis in Russia, 1992–93. World Bank Policy Research Working Paper 1240, January 1994. Washington DC: World Bank.

Edwards, Martin S. 2005. Investor Responses to IMF Program Suspensions: Is Non-Compliance Costly? *Social Science Quarterly* 86(4): 857–73.

Eichengreen, Barry. 1996. *Globalizing Capital: A History of the International Monetary System*. Princeton, NJ: Princeton University Press.

Eijffinger, Sylvester C.W. and Jakob De Haan. 1996. The Political Economy of Central Bank Independence. *Special Papers in International Economics* No. 19. Princeton: International Finance Section, Princeton University.

Ellman, Michael. 1991. Convertibility of the Rouble. *Cambridge Journal of Economics* 15(4): 481–97.

Erlanger, Steven. 1994. 2 Western Economists Quit Russia Posts. *The New York Times*, 22 January 1994, 4.

Esanov, Akram, Martin Raiser, and Willem Buiter. 2001. Nature's Blessing or Nature's Curse: The Political Economy of Transition in Resource-Based Economies. EBRD Working Paper 66. London: EBRD. <www.ebrd.com/pubs/econo/wp0066.pdf> (accessed 10/12/06).

Fearon, James D. 1997. Signaling Foreign Policy Interests: Tying Hands Versus Sinking Costs. *The Journal of Conflict Resolution* 41(1): 68–90.

Feldmann, Magnus. 2001. The Fast Track from the Soviet Union to the World Economy: External Liberalization in Estonia and Latvia. *Government and Opposition* 36(4): 537–58.

Fernandez, Raquel and Dani Rodrik. 1991. Resistance to Reform: Status Quo Bias in the Presence of Individual-Specific Uncertainty. *The American Economic Review* 81(5): 1146–55.

Finnemore, Martha and Kathryn Sikkink. 1998. International Norm Dynamics and Political Change. *International Organization* 52(4): 887–917.

Forder, James. 2000. Central Bank Independence and Credibility: Is There a Shred of Evidence? *International Finance* 3(1): 167–85.

Galbis, Vicente. 1996. Currency Convertibility and the Fund: Review and Prognosis. IMF Working Paper WP/96/39. Washington DC: IMF.

Ganev, Venelin. I. 2005. Post-communism as an Episode of State Building: A Reversed Tillyan Perspective. *Communist and Post-Communist Studies* 38(4): 425–45.

Garuda, Gopal. 2000. The Distributional Effects of IMF Programs: A Cross-Country Analysis. *World Development* 28(6): 1031–51.

Gemayel, Edward R. and David A. Grigorian. 2006. How Tight is Too Tight? A Look at Welfare Implications of Distortionary Policies in Uzbekistan. *The European Journal of Comparative Economics* 3(2): 239–61.

Gleason, Gregory. 1997. *The Central Asian States: Discovering Independence*. Boulder: Westview.

Gleason, Gregory. 2001. Foreign Policy and Domestic Reform in Central Asia. *Central Asian Survey* 20(2): 167–82.

Gleason, Gregory. 2004. Reform Strategies in Central Asia: Early Starters, Late Starters, and Non-Starters. In *In the Tracks of Tamerlane*, edited by Daniel Burghardt. Washington DC: National Defense University Press, 41–63.

Gold, Joseph. 1983. Strengthening the Soft International Law of Exchange Arrangements. *The American Journal of International Law* 77(3): 443–89.

Gold, Joseph. 1984. Legal Models for the International Regulation of Exchange Rates. *Michigan Law Review* 82(5/6): 1533–54.

Goldberg, Linda S., Barry W. Ickes, and Randi Ryterman. 1994. Departures from the Ruble Zone: The Implications of Adopting Independent Currencies. *The World Economy* 17(3): 293–322.

Goldstein, Judith and Robert O. Keohane. 1993. Ideas and Foreign Policy: An Analytical Framework. In *Ideas and Foreign Policy: Beliefs, Institutions, and Political Change*, edited by Judith Goldstein and Robert O. Keohane. Ithaca: Cornell University Press, 3–30.

Gould, Erica R. 2003. Money Talks: Supplementary Financiers and International Monetary Fund Conditionality. *International Organization* 57(3): 551–86.

Grabel, Ilene. 2000. The Political Economy of 'Policy Credibility': The New-Classical Macroeconomics and the Remaking of Emerging Economies. *Cambridge Journal of Economics* 24(1): 1–19.

Grafstein, Robert. 1988. The Problem of Institutional Constraint. *The Journal of Politics* 50(3): 577–99.

Grubel, Herbert G. 1970. The Theory of Optimum Currency Areas. *Canadian Journal of Economics* 3(2): 318–24.

Guitián, Manuel. 1996. Concepts and Degrees of Currency Convertibility. In *Currency Convertibility in the Middle East and North Africa*, edited by Manuel Guitián and Saleh M. Nsouli. Washington DC: IMF, 21–33.

Haas, Peter M. and Ernst B. Haas. 1995. Learning to Learn: Improving International Governance. *Global Governance: A Review of Multilateralism and International Organizations* 1(3): 255–84.

Hall, Rodney Bruce. 2003. The Discursive Demolition of the Asian Development Model. *International Studies Quarterly* 47(1): 71–99.

Hall, Rodney Bruce. 2008. *Central Banking as Global Governance: Constructing Financial Credibility*. Cambridge: Cambridge University Press.

Harper, Richard H.R. 1998. *Inside the IMF: An Ethnography of Documents, Technology and Organisational Action*. San Diego: Academic Press.

Hawkins, Darren G., David A. Lake, Daniel L. Nielson, and Michael J. Tierney. 2006. Delegation Under Anarchy: States, International Organizations, and

Principal-Agent Theory. In *Delegation and Agency in International Organizations*, edited by Darren G. Hawkins, David A. Lake, Daniel L. Nielson, and Michael J. Tierney. Cambridge: Cambridge University Press, 3–38.

Hedlund, Stefan and Niclas Sundstrom. 1996. The Russian Economy after Systemic Change. *Europe-Asia Studies* 48(6): 887–914.

Helleiner, Eric. 1994. *States and the Reemergence of Global Finance: From Bretton Woods to the 1990s*. Ithaca: Cornell University Press.

Helmke, Gretchen and Steven Levitsky. 2004. Informal Institutions and Comparative Politics: A Research Agenda. *Perspectives on Politics* 2(4): 725–40.

Hilbers, Paul. 1993. Monetary Instruments and Their Use During the Transition from a Centrally Planned to a Market Economy. WP/93/87. IMF Working Paper. Washington DC: IMF.

Hobson, John M. and Leonard Seabrooke. 2007. Everyday IPE: Revealing Everyday Forms of Change in the World Economy. *Everyday Politics of the World Economy*, edited by John M. Hobson and Leonard Seabrooke. Cambridge: Cambridge University Press, 1–23.

Hoffman, Lutz. 2001. Introduction: The Project Response to Real Needs. In *Kazakhstan 1993–2000: Independent Advisors and the IMF*, edited by Lutz Hoffman, Peter Bofinger, Heiner Flassbeck, and Alfred Steinher. New York: Physica-Verlag, 1–3.

Hopf, Ted. 1998. The Promise of Constructivism in International Relations Theory. *International Security* 23(1): 171–200.

Howell, Jude. 1996. Coping with Transition: Insights from Kyrgyzstan. *Third World Quarterly* 17(1): 53–68.

IEO (Independent Evaluation Office). 2005. *Evaluation of the Technical Assistance Provided by the International Monetary Fund*. Washington DC: IMF. <www.imf.org/external/np/ieo/2005/ta/eng/pdf/013105a.pdf> (accessed 08/10/06).

Iida, Keisuke. 1993. Analytic Uncertainty and International Cooperation: Theory and Application to International Economic Policy Coordination. *International Studies Quarterly* 37(4): 431–57.

IMF. 1965. Multilateralism in Trade and Currency Convertibility Under the Soviet Bloc Economic Systems. DM/65/60. Prepared by Marcin R. Wyczalkowski, European Department. October 21, 1965. Washington DC: IMF.

IMF. 1966. The Economy of Hungary. DM/66/42. Prepared by the Central and Eastern European Division, European Department. July 27, 1966. Washington DC: IMF.

IMF. 1988. Report by Staff – Soviet Visit. EBM/88/171. Executive Board Meeting Minutes. November 23, 1988. Washington DC: IMF.

IMF. 1990a. Currency Convertibility and the Transformation of Centrally Planned Economies. SM/90/214. Prepared by the Research Department. November 6, 1990. Washington DC: IMF.

IMF. 1990b. Currency Convertibility and the Transformation of Centrally Planned Economies. EBM/90/175. Executive Board Meeting Minutes. December 17, 1990. Washington DC: IMF.

IMF. 1990c. Currency Convertibility and the Transformation of Centrally Planned Economies. EBM/90/176. Executive Board Meeting Minutes. December 17, 1990. Washington DC: IMF.

IMF. 1991a. U.S.S.R. – Related Work – Report by Managing Director. EBM/91/147. Executive Board Meeting Minutes. November 6, 1991. Washington DC: IMF.

IMF. 1991b. U.S.S.R. – Recent Developments and Fund Activities. EBM/91/157. Executive Board Meeting Minutes. November 22, 1991. Washington DC: IMF.

IMF. 1991c. U.S.S.R. – Recent Developments and Fund Activities. EBM/91/167. Executive Board Meeting Minutes. December 11, 1991. Washington DC: IMF.

IMF. 1992a. Former U.S.S.R. Republics – Recent Developments, Fund Activities, and Related Matters. EBM/92/3. Executive Board Meeting Minutes. January 10, 1992. Washington DC: IMF.

IMF. 1992b. Reform Strategy in the Former Soviet Union. SM/92/146. Prepared by the European II Department. July 27, 1992. Washington DC: IMF.

IMF. 1992c. Former U.S.S.R. Republics – Recent Developments, Fund Activities, and Related Matters. EBM/92/14. Executive Board Meeting Minutes. February 5, 1992. Washington DC: IMF.

IMF. 1992d. Russian Federation – Pre-Membership Economic Review. EBM/92/39. Executive Board Meeting Minutes. March 30, 1992. Washington DC: IMF.

IMF. 1992e. Report by Managing Director. EBM/92/66. Executive Board Meeting Minutes. May 27, 1992. Washington DC: IMF.

IMF. 1992g. States of the Former U.S.S.R. Other Than Russian Federation. EBM/92/94. Executive Board Meeting Minutes. July 24, 1992. Washington DC: IMF.

IMF. 1992h. Interstate Monetary and Payments Arrangements in the Former Soviet Union. EBS/95/205. Prepared by the European II Department and the Monetary and Exchange Affairs Department. December 7, 1992. Washington DC: IMF.

IMF. 1992i. Kyrghyzstan – Pre-Membership Economic Review. SM/92/64. Prepared by the European II Department. March 17, 1992. Washington DC: IMF.

IMF. 1992j. Kyrgyzstan – Pre-Membership Economic Review. EBM/92/52. Executive Board Meeting Minutes. April 10, 1992. Washington DC: IMF.

IMF. 1992k. Uzbekistan – Pre-Membership Economic Review. SM/92/80. Prepared by the European II Department. April 2, 1992. Washington DC: IMF.

IMF. 1992l. Kazakhstan – Pre-Membership Economic Review. SM/92/41, Supplement 1. Prepared by the European II Department. March 6, 1992. Washington DC: IMF.

IMF. 1992m. Kazakhstan – Pre-Membership Economic Review. SM/92/41. Prepared by the European II Department. February 28, 1992. Washington DC: IMF.

IMF. 1993a. Russian Federation – 1993 Article IV Consultation. EBM/93/59. Executive Board Meeting Minutes. April 21, 1993. Washington DC: IMF.

IMF. 1993b. A Facility to Help Members Respond to Systemic Disruptions in Economies in Transition. EBS/93/56. Aide Memoire. April 1, 1993. Washington DC: IMF.

IMF. 1993c. A Fund Facility to Help Members Respond to Systemic Disruptions in Their Trade and Payments Arrangements. EBS/93/58. Prepared by the Policy Development and Review Department. April 9, 1993. Washington DC: IMF.

IMF. 1993d. Proposed Facility to Assist Economies in Transition. EBM/93/44. Executive Board Meeting Minutes. April 1, 1993. Washington DC: IMF.

IMF. 1993e. Systemic Transformation Facility. EBM/93/61. Executive Board Meeting Minutes. April 23, 1993. Washington DC: IMF.

IMF. 1993f. Statement by the Managing Director on the Currency Conversion in the Russian Federation. BUFF/93/41. Executive Board Meeting Minutes. July 28, 1993. Washington DC: IMF.

IMF. 1993g. Russian Federation – Review of Developments Under Stand-By Arrangement. EBM/93/5. Executive Board Meeting Minutes. January 11, 1993. Washington DC: IMF.

IMF. 1993h. Russian Federation – 1993 Article IV Consultation. EBM/93/59. Executive Board Meeting Minutes. April 21, 1993. Washington DC: IMF.

IMF. 1993i. Russian Federation – Staff Report for the 1993 Article IV Consultation. SM/93/66. Prepared by the Staff Representatives for the 1993 Consultation with the Russian Federation. April 1, 1993. Washington DC: IMF.

IMF. 1993j. Financial Relations Among Countries of the Former Soviet Union. EBS/93/158. Prepared by the European II Department in collaboration with the Monetary and Exchange Affairs and Policy Development and Review Departments. September 22, 1993. Washington DC: IMF.

IMF. 1993k. Camdessus Says IMF Supports Introduction of New Currencies in the Former Soviet Union. PR/93/16. IMF News Brief. November 15, 1993. Washington DC: IMF.

IMF. 1993l. Kazakhstan – Background Paper and Statistical Appendix. SM/93/73. Prepared by a Staff Team. April 7, 1993. Washington DC: IMF.

IMF. 1993m. Kyrgyzstan – Request for Stand-By Arrangement. EBS/93/54, Supplement 1. Prepared by the European II and Policy Development and Review Departments. April 15, 1993. Washington DC: IMF.

IMF. 1993n. Kyrgyzstan – Request for Stand-By Arrangement – Letter of Intent. EBS/93/54. March 31, 1993. Washington DC: IMF.

IMF. 1993o. The Kyrgyz Republic – Recent Economic Developments. SM/93/205. Prepared by a Staff Mission. September 2, 1993. Washington DC: IMF.

IMF. 1993p. Republic of Kyrgyzstan – Stand-By Arrangement; and Purchase Transaction – System Transformation Facility. EBM/93/68. Executive Board Meeting Minutes. May 12, 1993. Washington DC: IMF.

IMF. 1993q. Republic of Kyrgyzstan – Request for Stand-By Arrangement, and Request for Purchase Under the Systemic Transformation Facility. EBM/93/69. Executive Board Meeting Minutes. May 12, 1993. Washington DC: IMF.

IMF. 1993r. Kyrgyz Republic – Staff Report for the 1993 Article IV Consultation, First Review Under the Stand-By Arrangement, and Request for Second Purchase Under the Systemic Transformation Facility. EBS/93/146. Prepared by the Staff Representatives for the 1993 Article IV Consultation with the Kyrgyz Republic, August 26, 1993. Washington DC: IMF.

IMF. 1993s. Kyrgyz Republic – 1993 Article IV Consultation; Review Under Stand-By Arrangement; and Purchase Transaction – Systemic Transformation Facility. EBM/93/138. Executive Board Meeting Minutes, September 20, 1993.

IMF. 1993t. Kazakhstan – Report for the 1993 Article IV Consultation. SM/93/60. Prepared by the Staff Representatives for the 1993 Consultation with Kazakhstan. March 19, 1993. Washington DC: IMF.

IMF. 1993u. Kazakhstan – Use of Fund Resources – Request for Purchase Under the Systemic Transformation Facility (STF). EBS/93/113. Prepared by the European II Department. July 9, 1993. Washington DC: IMF.

IMF. 1993v. Republic of Kazakhstan – Purchase Transaction – Systemic Transformation Facility. EBM/93/103. Executive Board Meeting Minutes. July 23, 1993. Washington DC: IMF.

IMF. 1993w. Republic of Uzbekistan – Staff Report for the 1993 Article IV Consultation. SM/93/259. Prepared by the Staff Representatives for the 1993 Consultation with Uzbekistan. Washington DC: IMF.

IMF, 1994a. The Adoption of Indirect Instruments of Monetary Policy. SM/94/270. Prepared by the Monetary and Exchange Affairs Department. November 7, 1994. Washington DC: IMF.

IMF. 1994b. Republic of Kazakhstan – Request for Stand-By Arrangement and Purchase Under the Systemic Transformation Facility. EBS/93/204, Supplement 1. Prepared by European II Department. January 7, 1994. Washington DC: IMF.

IMF. 1994c. Republic of Kazakhstan – Stand-By Arrangement; and Purchase Transaction – Systemic Transformation Facility. EBM/94/6. Executive Board Meeting Minutes. January 26, 1994. Washington DC: IMF.

IMF. 1994d. Republic of Uzbekistan – Background Paper and Statistical Appendix. SM/94/8. Prepared by a Staff Team. January 7, 1994. Washington DC: IMF.

IMF. 1994e. Republic of Uzbekistan – Staff Report for the 1993 Article IV Consultation – Supplementary Information. SM/93/259, Supplement 1. Prepared by the European II Department. January 13, 1994. Washington DC: IMF.

IMF. 1994f. Republic of Uzbekistan – 1993 Article IV Consultation. EBM/94/4. Executive Board Meeting Minutes. January 21, 1994. Washington DC: IMF.

IMF. 1994g. Republic of Uzbekistan – Staff Report for the 1994 Article IV Consultation and Request for a Purchase Under the Systemic Transformation Facility. EBS/94/248. Prepared by the European II Department. December 22, 1994. Washington DC: IMF.

IMF. 1994h. Kyrgyz Republic – Request for Arrangement Under the Enhanced Structural Adjustment Facility – Letter of Intent. EBS/94/127. June 20, 1994. Washington DC: IMF.

IMF. 1994i. Kyrgyz Republic – Staff Report for the Request for Three-Year ESAF Arrangement and First Annual ESAF Arrangement. EBS/94/127, Supplement 1. Prepared by the European II and Policy Development and Review Departments, June 24, 1994. Washington DC: IMF.

IMF. 1994j. Kyrgyz Republic – Enhanced Structural Adjustment Arrangement. EBM/94/66. Executive Board Meeting Minutes, July 20, 1994. Washington DC: IMF.

IMF. 1994k. Kyrgyz Republic – Staff Report for the 1995 Article IV Consultation and Mid-term Review Under the First Annual ESAF Arrangement. EBS/95/39. Prepared by the European II and Policy Development and Review Departments, March 16, 1995. Washington DC: IMF.

IMF. 1994l. Kyrgyz Republic – Request for the Second Annual Arrangement Under the Enhanced Structural Adjustment Facility. EBS/95/194. Prepared by the European II and Policy Development and Review Departments, November 22, 1995. Washington DC: IMF.

IMF. 1994m. Republic of Kazakhstan – Request for Stand-By Arrangement and Purchase Under the Systemic Transformation Facility. EBS/93/204, Supplement 2. Prepared by European II Department. January 24, 1994. Washington DC: IMF.

IMF. 1994n. Republic of Kazakhstan – Use of Fund Resources – Review and Modification of the Stand-By Arrangement. EBS/94/154. Prepared by the European II Department. August 5, 1994. Washington DC: IMF.

IMF. 1994o. Republic of Kazakhstan – Staff Report for the 1994 Article IV Consultation and Second Review Under Stand-By Arrangement. EBS/94/220. Prepared by the European II Department. November 16, 1994. Washington DC: IMF.

IMF. 1995a. Review of Operations and Experience Under the Systemic Transformation Facility (STF). SM/95/49. Prepared by the Policy Development and Review Department. March 8. 1995. Washington DC: IMF.

IMF. 1995b. Republic of Uzbekistan – Request for Stand-By Arrangement and for a Second Purchase Under the Systemic Transformation Facility. EBS/95/191. Prepared by the European II Department. November 27, 1995. Washington DC: IMF.

IMF. 1995c. The Acting Chairman's Summing Up at the Conclusion of the 1994 Article IV Consultation with the Republic of Uzbekistan. SUR/94/12. January 25, 1995. Washington DC: IMF.

IMF. 1995d. Republic of Kazakhstan – Request for Stand-By Arrangement. EBS/95/78. Prepared by the European II Department. May 23, 1995. Washington DC: IMF.

IMF. 1995e. Republic of Uzbekistan – Requests for a Stand-By Arrangement and for a Second Purchase Under the Systemic Transformation Facility. EBS/95/191, Supplement 2. Prepared by the European II Department. December 15, 1995. Washington DC: IMF.

IMF. 1996a. Prior Actions – Fund Policy and Practice. EBS/96/164. Prepared by the Policy Development and Review and Legal Departments. October 21, 1996. Washington DC: IMF.

IMF. 1996b. Republic of Kazakhstan – Request for Waiver of Performance Criterion Under the Stand-By Arrangement. EBS/96/77. Prepared by the European II Department. May 17, 1996. Washington DC: IMF.

IMF. 1996c. Republic of Kazakhstan – First Review Under the Extended Arrangement and Request for Waiver and Modification of Performance Criteria. EBS/96/199, Supplement 1. Prepared by the European II Department. December 26, 1996. Washington DC: IMF.

IMF. 1996d. Kazakhstan Accepts Article VIII Obligations. Press Release No. 96/41. July 23, 1996. Washington DC: IMF. <http://www.imf.org/external/np/sec/pr/1996/pr9641.htm> (accessed 20/01/07).

IMF. 1996e. Republic of Uzbekistan – Selected Issues and Statistical Appendix. SM/96/134. Prepared by a Staff Team. June 10, 1996. Washington DC: IMF.

IMF. 1996f. Republic of Uzbekistan – Staff Report for the 1996 Article IV Consultation and First Review Under the Stand-By Arrangement. EBS/96/88. Prepared by the European II Department. June 4, 1996. Washington DC: IMF.

IMF. 1996g. The Acting Chairman's Summing Up at the Conclusion of the 1996 Article IV Consultation with Uzbekistan. SUR/96/63. July 1, 1996. Washington DC: IMF.

IMF. 1996h. Republic of Uzbekistan – Second Review Under the Stand-By Arrangement. EBS/96/139. Prepared by the European II Department. September 5, 1996. Washington DC: IMF.

IMF. 1997a. Republic of Uzbekistan – Staff Report for the 1997 Article IV Consultation. SM/97/157. Prepared by the Staff Representatives for the 1997 Consultation with the Republic of Uzbekistan. June 19, 1997. Washington DC: IMF.

IMF. 1997b. Republic of Uzbekistan – Recent Economic Developments. SM/97/171. Prepared by a Staff Team. June 17, 1997. Washington DC: IMF.

IMF. 2000. Kazakhstan Repays the IMF Ahead of Schedule. News Brief No. 00/35. June 1, 2000. <http://www.imf.org/external/np/sec/nb/2000/nb0035.htm> (accessed 20/01/07).

IMF. 2001a. Strengthening Country Ownership of Fund-Supported Programs. Prepared by the Policy Development and Review Department. Washington DC: IMF. <www.imf.org/external/np/pdr/cond/2001/eng/strength/120501.pdf> (accessed 22/08/06).

IMF. 2001b. Republic of Uzbekistan – Recent Economic Developments. SM/01/19. Prepared by a Staff Team. January 19, 2001. Washington DC: IMF.

IMF. 2001c. Republic of Uzbekistan – Staff Report for the 2000 Article IV Consultation. SM/01/18. Prepared by Staff Representatives for the 2000 Consultation with the Republic of Uzbekistan. January 19, 2001. Washington DC: IMF.

IMF. 2002a. Uzbekistan – Letter of Intent, Memorandum of Economic and Financial Policies, and Technical Memorandum of Understanding. January 31, 2002. Washington DC: IMF. <www.imf.org/external/np/loi/2002/uzb/01/ index.htm> (accessed 20/07/06).

IMF. 2002b. Republic of Uzbekistan – Letter of Intent. July 29, 2002. Washington DC: IMF. <www.imf.org/external/np/loi/2002/uzb/02/index.htm> (accessed 20/07/06).

IMF. 2003a. IMF Technical Assistance: Transferring Knowledge and Best Practice. Washington DC: IMF. <www.imf.org/external/pubs/ft/exrp/techass/techass.htm> (accessed 03/11/05).

IMF. 2003b. The Republic of Uzbekistan Accepts Article VIII Obligations. Press Release No. 03/188. November 11, 2003. Washington DC: IMF. <www.imf.org/ external/np/sec/pr/2003/pr03188.htm> (accessed 15/01/07).

IMF. 2005. Policy Support and Signaling in Low-Income Countries. Prepared by the Policy Development and Review Department. June 10, 2005. <www.imf.org/ external/ np/pp/eng/2005/061005.pdf> (accessed 19/02/07).

IMF. 2006. IMF Executive Board Deems Kyrgyz Republic Eligible for Assistance Under the HIPC Initiative. Press Release No. 06/221. October 18, 2006. Washington DC: IMF. <http://www.imf.org/external/np/sec/pr/2006/pr06221. htm> (accessed 20/02/07).

IMF. 2007a. Republic of Kazakhstan: 2007 Article IV Consultation – Staff Report; and Public Information Notice on the Executive Board Discussion. IMF Country Report No. 07/235. June 1, 2007. Washington DC: IMF. <www.imf.org/external/ pubs/ft/scr/2007/cr07235.pdf> (accessed 10/08/07).

IMF. 2007b. *Annual Report of the Executive Board for the Financial Year Ended 30 April, 2007* (Washington DC: IMF). Available online at: <www.imf.org/external/ pubs/ft/ar/2007/eng/pdf/file7.pdf> (accessed 10/11/08).

IMF. 2009. *Articles of Agreement of the International Monetary Fund.* Washington DC: IMF. <www.imf.org/external/pubs/ft/aa/index.htm> (accessed 10/07/09).

IMF, The World Bank, The Organisation for Economic Cooperation and Development, The European Bank for Reconstruction and Development. 1990. *The Economy of the U.S.S.R.: Summary and Recommendations.* Washington DC: The World Bank.

Jacoby, Wade. 2001. Tutors and Pupils: International Organizations, Central European Elites, and Western Models. *Governance: An International Journal of Policy and Administration* 14(2): 169–200.

James, Harold. 1996. *International Monetary Cooperation Since Bretton Woods.* Washington DC: IMF and Oxford University Press.

Johnson, Juliet. 2000. *A Fistful of Rubles: The Rise and Fall of the Russian Banking System.* Ithaca: Cornell University Press.

Joyce, Joseph P. 2006. Promises Made, Promise Broken: A Model of IMF Program Implementation. *Economics and Politics* 18(3): 339–65.

Junisbai, Barbara and Azamat Junisbai. 2005. The Democratic Choice of Kazakhstan: A Case Study in Economic Liberalization, Intraelite Cleavage, and Political Opposition. *Demokratizatsiya* 13(3): 373–92.

Kang, Seonjou. 2007. Agree to Reform? The Political Economy of Conditionality Variation in International Monetary Fund Lending, 1983–1997. *European Journal of Political Research*, 46(5): 685–720.

Kangas, Roger D. 1994. Uzbekistan: Evolving Authoritarianism. *Current History* 93(582): 178–82.

Katz, Mark N. 2006. Revolutionary Change in Central Asia. *World Affairs* 168(4): 157–71.

Kazemi, Leila. 2003. Domestic Sources of Uzbekistan's Foreign Policy, 1991 to the Present. *Journal of International Affairs* 56(2): 205–16.

Keeler, John T.S. 1993. Opening the Window for Reform: Mandates, Crises, and Extraordinary Policy-Making. *Comparative Political Studies* 25(4): 433–86.

Keeley, James F. 1990. Towards a Foucauldian Analysis of International Regimes. *International Organization* 44(1): 83–105.

Killick, Tony. 1997. Principals, Agents and the Failings of Conditionality. *Journal of International Development* 9(4): 483–95.

Kirshner, Jonathan. 2003. Money is Politics. *Review of International Political Economy* 10(4): 645–60.

Knight, Jack. 1995. Models, Interpretations, and Theories: Constructing Explanations of Institutional Emergence and Change. In *Explaining Social Institutions*, edited by Jack Knight and Itai Sened. Ann Arbor: The University of Michigan Press, 94–119.

Krasner, Stephen D. 1984. Approaches to the State: Alternative Conceptions and Historical Dynamics. *Comparative Politics* 16(2): 223–46.

Kuehnast, Kathleen and Nora Dudwick. 2004. Better a Hundred Friends than a Hundred Rubles? World Bank Working Paper No. 39. Washington DC: World Bank.

Kyriazis, Nicholas C. and Michael S. Zouboulakis. 2005. Modeling Institutional Change in Transition Economies. *Communist and Post-Communist Studies* 38(1): 109–20.

Laffey, Mark and Jutta Weldes. 1997. Beyond Belief: Ideas and Symbolic Technologies in the Study of International Relations. *European Journal of International Relations* 3(2): 193–237.

Leiteritz, Ralf. 2005. Explaining Organizational Outcomes: The International Monetary Fund and Capital Account Liberalization. *Journal of International Relations and Development* 8(1): 1–26.

Libman, Alexander. 2006. Government-Business Relations and Catching Up Reforms in the CIS. *The European Journal of Comparative Economics* 3(2): 263–88.

Lim, Linda Y.C. and Aaron Stern. 2002. State Power and Private Profit: The Political Economy of Corruption in Southeast Asia. *Asia-Pacific Economic Literature* 16(2): 18–52.

Litwack, John M. 1991. Legality and Market Reform in Soviet-type Economies. *Journal of Economic Perspectives* 5(4): 77–89.

Lloyd, John. 1993. IMF Watches as Kyrgyzstan Fights the Battle of the Som. *Financial Times*. 21 May 1993, 5.

Lohmann, Susanne. 2003. Why Do Institutions Matter? An Audience-Cost Theory of Institutional Commitment. *Governance: An International Journal of Policy, Administration, and Institutions* 16(1): 95–110.

Lombardi, Domenico and Ngaire Woods. 2008. The Politics of Influence: An Analysis of IMF Surveillance. *Review of International Political Economy* 15(5): 711–39.

Lubin, Nancy. 1989. Uzbekistan: The Challenges Ahead. *Middle East Journal* 43(4): 619–34.

Luong, Pauline Jones. 2002. *Institutional Change and Political Continuity in Post-Soviet Central Asia: Power, Perceptions, and Pacts.* Cambridge: Cambridge University Press.

Luong, Pauline Jones and Erika Weinthal. 2001. Prelude to the Resource Curse: Explaining Oil and Gas Development Strategies in the Soviet Successor States and Beyond. *Comparative Political Studies* 34(4): 367–99.

Macdonald, Laura and Arne Ruckert (eds). 2009. *Post-Neoliberalism in the Americas.* Basingstoke: Palgrave Macmillan.

MacIntyre, Andrew. 2000. Funny Money: Fiscal Policy, Rent-Seeking and Economic Performance in Indonesia. In *Rents, Rent-Seeking and Economic Development: Theory and Evidence*, edited by Mushtaq H. Khan and Kwame Sundaram Jomo. Cambridge: Cambridge University Press, 248–73.

March, Andrew F. 2002. The Use and Abuse of History: 'National Ideology' as Transcendental Object in Islam Karimov's 'Ideology of National Independence'. *Central Asian Survey* 21(4): 371–84.

March, James G. and Johan P. Olsen. 1989. *Rediscovering Institutions: The Organizational Basis of Politics.* New York: The Free Press.

Marchesi, Silvia and Jonathan P. Thomas. 1999. IMF Conditionality as a Screening Device. *The Economic Journal* 109(454): 111–25.

Marcussen, Martin. 2005. Central Banks on the Move. *Journal of European Public Policy* 12(5): 903–23.

Martin, Lisa L. 2006. Distribution, Information, and Delegation to International Organizations: The Case of IMF Conditionality. In *Delegation and Agency in International Organizations*, edited by Darren G. Hawkins, David A. Lake, Daniel L. Nielson, and Michael J. Tierney. Cambridge: Cambridge University Press, 140–64.

Mas, Ignacio. 1995. Central Bank Independence: A Critical View from a Developing Country Perspective. *World Development* 23(10): 1639–52.

Matveeva, Anna. 1999. Democratization, Legitimacy and Political Change in Central Asia. *International Affairs* 71(1): 23–44.

Maxfield, Sylvia. 1994. Financial Incentives and Central Bank Authority in Industrializing Nations. *World Politics* 46: 556–88.

McKinnon, Ronald I. 1963. Optimum Currency Areas. *American Economic Review* 53(4): 717–25.

McKinnon, Ronald I. 1991. Financial Control in the Transition. *Journal of Economic Perspectives* 5(4): 107–22.

McKinnon, Ronald I. 1993. *The Order of Economic Liberalization: Financial Control in the Transition to a Market Economy*, Second Edition. Baltimore: The Johns Hopkins University Press.

McNamara, Kathleen R. 2002. Rational Fictions: Central Bank Independence and the Social Logic of Delegation. *West European Politics* 25(1): 47–76.

Melliss, C.L. and M. Cornelius. 1994. New Currencies in the Former Soviet Union: A Recipe for Hyperinflation or the Path to Price Stability? *Bank of England Working Paper Series* No. 26, September 1994. London: Bank of England.

Meyer, Klaus E. and Christina Pind. 1999. The Slow Growth of Foreign Direct Investment in the Soviet Union Successor States. *Economics of Transition* 7(1): 201–14.

Mody, Ashoka and Diego Saravia. 2002. Catalyzing Capital Flows: Do IMF Programs Work as Commitment Devices? IMF Working Paper WP/02. Washington DC: IMF. <http://www.imf.org/external/pubs/ft/wp/2003/ wp03100.pdf> (accessed 30/01/07).

Momani, Bessma. 2004. American Politicization of the International Monetary Fund. *Review of International Political Economy* 11(5): 880–904.

Momani, Bessma. 2005a. Limits on Streamlining Fund Conditionality: The International Monetary Fund's Organizational Culture. *Journal of International Relations and Development* 8(2): 142–63.

Momani, Bessma. 2005b. Recruiting and Diversifying IMF Technocrats. *Global Society* 19(2): 167–87.

Momani, Bessma. 2006. Assessing the Utility of, and Measuring Learning from, Canada's IMF Article IV Consultations. *Canadian Journal of Political Science* 39(2): 249–69.

Momani, Bessma. 2007. IMF Staff: Missing Link in Fund Reform Proposals. *Review of International Organizations* 2: 39–57.

Moschella, Manuela. 2009. When Ideas Fail to Influence Policy Outcomes: Orderly Liberalization and the International Monetary Fund. *Review of International Political Economy*, forthcoming.

Mosley, Layna. 2001. Room to Move: International Financial Markets and National Welfare States. *International Organization* 54(4): 737–73.

Mundell, Robert A. 1961. A Theory of Optimum Currency Areas. *American Economic Review* 51(4): 657–65.

Nazpary, Joma. 2002. *Post-Soviet Chaos: Violence and Dispossession in Kazakhstan.* London: Pluto Press.

Nelson, Joan M. 1984. The Political Economy of Stabilization: Commitment, Capacity, and Public Response. *World Development* 12(10): 983–1006.

Nielson, Daniel L., Michael J. Tierney, and Catherine E. Weaver. 2006. Bridging the Rationalist–Constructivist Divide: Re-engineering the Culture of the World Bank. *Journal of International Relations and Development* 9(2): 107–39.

Nincic, Miroslav. 2006. The Logic of Positive Engagement: Dealing with Renegade Regimes. *International Studies Perspectives* 7: 321–41.

Noguera, José and Susan J. Linz. 2006. Barter, Credit and Welfare: A Theoretical Inquiry into the Barter Phenomenon in Russia. *Economics of Transition* 14(4): 719–45.

North, Douglass C. 1990. *Institutions, Institutional Change, and Economic Performance.* New York: Cambridge University Press.

North, Douglass C. 1999. Where Have we Been and Where are we Going? In *Economics, Values, and Organization*, edited by Avner Ben-Ner and Louis Putterman. Cambridge: Cambridge University Press, 491–508.

Oatley, Thomas and Jason Yackee. 2004. American Interests and IMF Lending. *International Politics* 41(3): 415–29.

Odling-Smee, John. 1992. Personal View – To Russia with Resolve. *Financial Times*. 10 December, 1992, 18.

Odling-Smee, John and Gonzalo Pastor. 2001. The IMF and the Ruble Area, 1991–93. WP/01/101. IMF Working Paper, August 2001. Washington DC: IMF. <http://www.imf.org/external/pubs/ft/wp/2001/wp01101.pdf> (accessed 15/09/04).

Orlowski, Lucjan T. 1993. Indirect Transfers in Trade among Former Soviet Union Republics: Sources, Patterns and Policy Responses in the Post-Soviet Period. *Europe-Asia Studies* 45(6): 1001–24.

Orlowski, Lucjan T. 1995. Direct Transfers Between the Former Soviet Union Central Budget and the Republics: Past Evidence and Current Implications. *Economics of Planning* 28(1): 59–73.

Panitch, Leo and Martin Konings (eds). 2008. *American Empire and the Political Economy of Global Finance*. Basingstoke: Palgrave Macmillan.

Pauly, Louis W. 1997. *Who Elected the Bankers? Surveillance and Control in the World Economy*. Ithaca: Cornell University Press.

Pauly, Louis W. 1999. Good Governance and Bad Policy: The Perils of International Organizational Overextension. *Review of International Political Economy* 6(4): 401–24.

Pazarbaşioğlu, Ceyla and Jan Willem van der Vossen. 1997. Main Issues and Challenges in Designing Bank-Restructuring Strategies. In *Central Bank Reform in the Transition Economies*, edited by V. Sundararajan, Arne B. Petersen, and Gabriel Sensenbrenner. Washington DC: IMF, 27–61.

Perotti, E.C. 1998. Inertial Credit and Opportunistic Arrears in Transition. *European Economic Review* 42(9): 1703–25.

Polak, Jacques J. 1991. Convertibility: An Indispensable Element in the Transition Process in Eastern Europe. In *Currency Convertibility in Eastern Europe*, edited by John Williamson. Washington DC: Institute for International Economics, 21–30.

Pomfret, Richard. 2000. The Uzbek Model of Development, 1991–99. *Economics of Transition* 8(3): 733–48.

Pomfret, Richard. 2002. *Constructing a Market Economy: Diverse Paths from Central Planning in Asia and Europe*. Cheltenham: Edward Elgar.

Pomfret, Richard. 2003a. Trade and Exchange Rate Policies in Formerly Centrally Planned Economies. *The World Economy* 26(4): 585–612.

Pomfret, Richard. 2003b. Economic Performance in Central Asia Since 1991: Macro and Micro Evidence. *Comparative Economic Studies* 45: 442–65.

Pomfret, Richard. 2006. *The Central Asian Economies Since Independence*. Princeton: Princeton University Press.

Pop-Eleches, Grigore. 2009. *From Economic Crisis to Reform: IMF Programs in Latin America and Eastern Europe*. Princeton: Princeton University Press.

Poser, Jan Amrit. 1998. Monetary Disruptions and the Emergence of Barter in FSU Economies. *Communist Economies and Economic Transformation* 10(2): 157–77.

Ricci, Luca A. 1997. A Model of an Optimum Currency Area. WP/97/76. IMF Working Paper. Washington DC: IMF.

Roeder, Philip G. 1994. Varieties of Post-Soviet Authoritarian Regimes. *Post-Soviet Affairs* 10(1): 61–101.

Rose, Richard. 1993. Contradictions Between Micro- and Macro-Economic Goals in Post-Communist Societies. *Europe-Asia Studies* 45(3): 419–44.

Rosenberg, Christoph and Maarten de Zeeuw. 2000. Welfare Effects of Uzbekistan's Foreign Exchange Regime. WP/00/61. IMF Working Paper. Washington DC: IMF. <www.imf.org/external/pubs/ft/wp/2000/wp0061.pdf> (accessed 25/03/06).

Rosenberg, Christoph. 2001. 15 Arguments About Currency Convertibility Frequently Heard in Uzbekistan. <www.imf.uz/arguments.htm> (accessed 15/12/05).

Rowlands, Dane. 2001. The Response of Other Lenders to the IMF. *Review of International Economics* 9(3): 531–46.

Ruggie, John Gerrard. 1982. International Regimes, Transactions, and Change: Embedded Liberalism in the Postwar Economic Order. *International Organization* 36(2): 379–415.

Ruggie, John Gerrard. 1998. What Makes the World Hang Together? Neo-utilitarianism and the Social Constructivist Challenge. *International Organization* 52(4): 855–85.

Rutland, Peter. 1999. Mission Impossible? The IMF and the Failure of the Market Transition in Russia. *Review of International Studies* 25(5): 183–200.

Ruziev, Kobil, Dipak Ghosh, and Sheila C. Dow. 2007. The Uzbek Puzzle Revisited: An Analysis of Economic Performance in Uzbekistan Since 1991. *Central Asian Survey* 26(1): 7–30.

Sagasti, Francisco, Keith Bezanson, and Fernando Prada. 2005. *The Future of Development Financing: Challenges, Scenarios and Strategic Choices*. Sussex: Institute of Development Studies/Ministry for Foreign Affairs, Government of Sweden.

Said, Farangis. 2000. Machinations Mar Uzbekistan's Banking System. *Central Asia-Cauasus Analyst* November 8, 2000. <www.cacianalyst.org/view_article.php?articleid=308> (accessed 10/05/06).

Scharpf, Fritz W. 2000. Institutions in Comparative Policy Research. *Comparative Political Studies* 33(6–7): 762–90.

Schoors, Koen. 2003a. The Effect of Soviet Monetary Disintegration on the Collapse of Trade Between Members of the Commonwealth of Independent States. *Economic Systems* 27: 1–26.

Schoors, Koen. 2003b. The Fate of Russia's Former Banks: Chronicle of a Restructuring Postponed and a Crisis Foretold. *Europe-Asia Studies* 55(1): 75–100.

Scott, James C. 1998. *Seeing Like a State: How Certain Schemes to Improve the Human Condition Have Failed*. New Haven: Yale University Press.

Seabright, Paul (ed.). 2000a. *The Vanishing Ruble: Barter Networks and Non-Monetary Transactions in Post-Soviet Societies*, edited by Paul Seabright. Cambridge: Cambridge University Press.

Seabright, Paul. 2000b. Introduction: Barter Networks and 'Information Islands'. In *The Vanishing Ruble: Barter Networks and Non-Monetary Transactions in Post-Soviet Societies*, edited by Paul Seabright. Cambridge: Cambridge University Press, 1–11.

Seabrooke, Leonard. 2006. *The Social Sources of Financial Power*. Ithaca: Cornell University Press.

Seabrooke, Leonard. 2007a. Why Political Economy Needs Historical Sociology. *International Politics* 44(4), 390–413.

Seabrooke, Leonard. 2007b. Legitimacy Gaps in the World Economy: Explaining the Sources of the IMF's Legitimacy Crisis. *International Politics* 44(2/3): 250–68.

Seleny, Anna. 1999. Old Political Rationalities and New Democracies: Compromise and Confrontation in Hungary and Poland. *World Politics* 51(4): 484–519.

Sharman, J.C. 2006. *Havens in a Storm: The Struggle for Global Tax Regulation.* Ithaca: Cornell University Press.

Sharman, J.C. 2007. Rationalist and Constructivist Perspectives on Reputation. *Political Studies* 55(1): 20–37.

Silverman, Bertram and Murray Yanowitch. 1997. *New Rich, New Poor, New Russia: Winners and Losers on the Russian Road to Capitalism.* Armonk, NY: M.E. Sharpe.

Simmons, Beth A. 1996. Rulers of the Game: Central Bank Independence During the Interwar Years. *International Organization* 50(3): 407–43.

Simmons, Beth A. 2000. The Legalization of International Monetary Affairs. *International Organization* 54(3): 573–602.

Sinclair, Timothy J. 2005. *The New Masters of Capital: American Bond Rating Agencies and the Politics of Creditworthiness.* Ithaca: Cornell University Press.

Snoek, Harry and Ron van Rooden. 1999. Monetary Policy and Progress with Stabilization. In *Economic Reforms in Kazkhastan, Kyrgyz Republic, Tajikistan, Turmenistan, and Uzbekistan,* edited by Emine Gürgen. IMF Occasional Paper 183. Washington DC: IMF, 23–34.

Soulsby, Anna and Ed Clark. 1996. Economic Restructuring and Institutional Change: Post-Communist Management in the Czech Republic. *Journal of Socio-Economics* 25(4): 473–96.

Spechler, Martin C. 2003. Returning to Convertibility in Uzbekistan? *Journal of Economic Policy Reform* 6(1): 51–6.

Stern, Nicholas, with Ferreira, Francisco. 1997. The World Bank as 'Intellectual Actor'. In *The World Bank: Its First Half Century, Volume Two: Perspectives,* edited by Devesh Kapur, John P. Lewis, and Richard Webb. Washington, D.C.: The Brookings Institution Press, 523–609.

Stiglitz, Joseph E. 2002. *Globalization and Its Discontents.* London: Allen Lane.

Stolze, Frank. 1997. The Central and East European Currency Phenomenon Reconsidered. *Europe-Asia Studies* 49(1): 23–41.

Stone, Randall W. 2002. *Lending Credibility: The International Monetary Fund and the Post-Communist Transition.* Princeton: Princeton University Press.

Stone, Randall W. 2004. The Political Economy of IMF Lending to Africa. *American Political Science Review* 98(4): 577–91.

Stone, Randall W. 2008. The Scope of IMF Conditionality. *International Organization* 62(4): 589–620.

Thacker, Strom. 1999. The High Politics of IMF Lending. *World Politics* 52(1): 38–74.

The Economist. 1992. The Rouble Zone: Behind the Facade. 19 September, 1992, 96.

Thomas, Alun and Uma Ramakrishnan. 2006. The Incidence and Effectiveness of Prior Actions in IMF-Supported Programs. IMF Working Paper WP/06/213. Washington DC: IMF. <www.imf.org/external/pubs/ft/wp/2006/wp06213.pdf> (accessed 20/03/07).

Thompson, Alexander. 2006. Screening Power: International Organizations as Informative Agents. In *Delegation and Agency in International Organizations,* edited by Darren G. Hawkins, David A. Lake, Daniel L. Nielson, and Michael J. Tierney. Cambridge: Cambridge University Press, 229–54.

Tompson, William. 1997. Old Habits Die Hard: Fiscal Imperatives, State Regulation and the Role of Russia's Banks. *Europe-Asia Studies* 49(7): 1159–85.

Treisman, Daniel. 1995. The Politics of Soft Credit in Russia. *Europe-Asia Studies* 47(6): 949–76.

Treisman, Daniel. 1998. Fighting Inflation in a Transitional Regime: Russia's Anomalous Stabilization. *World Politics* 50(2): 235–65.

Tsai, Kellee S. 2006. Adaptive Informal Institutions and Endogenous Institutional Change in China. *World Politics* 59(1): 116–41.

Van Selm, Gijsbertus and Hans-Jürgen Wagener. 1995. The CIS Payments Union: A Post-Mortem. *Moct-Most* 5: 25–36.

Van Zon, Hans. 2001. Neo-Patrimonialism as an Impediment to Economic Development: The Case of Ukraine. *Journal of Communist Studies and Transition Politics* 17(3): 71–95.

Vetterlein, Antje. 2006. Change in International Organizations: Innovation or Adaptation? A Comparison of the World Bank and the International Monetary Fund. In *The World Bank and Governance: A Decade of Reform and Reaction*, edited by Diane Stone and Christopher Wright. London: Routledge, 125–44.

Volkov, Vadim. 2000. Between Economy and State: Private Security and Rule Enforcement in Russia. *Politics and Society* 28(4): 483–501.

Vreeland, James Raymond. 2002. The Effect of IMF Programs on Labor. *World Development* 30(1): 121–39.

Vreeland, James Raymond. 2003a. *The IMF and Economic Development*. Cambridge: Cambridge University Press.

Vreeland, James Raymond. 2003b. Why Do Governments and the IMF Enter into Agreements? Statistically Selected Cases. *International Political Science Review* 24(3): 321–43.

Vreeland, James Raymond. 2006. IMF Program Compliance: Aggregate Index *versus* Policy Specific Research Strategies. *Review of International Organizations* 1(4): 359–78.

Way, Lucan A. 2002. The Dilemmas of Reform in Weak States: The Case of Post-Soviet Fiscal Decentralization. *Politics and Society* 30(4): 579–98.

Wedel, Janine R. 2003. Clans, Cliques and Captured States: Rethinking 'Transition' in Central and Eastern Europe and the Former Soviet Union. *Journal of International Development* 15(4): 427–40.

Widmaier, Wesley W. 2004. The Social Construction of the 'Impossible Trinity': The Intersubjective Bases on Monetary Cooperation. *International Studies Quarterly* 48(2): 433–53.

Willett, Thomas D. 1998. Credibility and Discipline Effects of Exchange Rates as Nominal Anchors: The Need to Distinguish Temporary from Permanent Pegs. *The World Economy* 21(6): 803–26.

Willett, Thomas D. 2001. Understanding the IMF Debate. *The Independent Review* 5(4): 593–610.

Williamson, John (ed.). 1991. *Currency Convertibility in Eastern Europe*. Washington DC: Institute for International Economics.

Winiecki, Jan. 1995. The Applicability of Standard Reform Packages to Eastern Europe. *Journal of Comparative Economics* 20: 347–67.

Woodruff, David M. 2000. Rules for Followers: Institutional Theory and the New Politics of Economic Backwardness in Russia. *Politics and Society* 28(4): 437–82.

Woods, Ngaire. 2006. *The Globalizers: The IMF, the World Bank and their Borrowers*. Ithaca: Cornell University Press.

World Bank. 1993. Kazakhstan: The Transition to a Market Economy. World Bank Country Study. Washington DC: World Bank.

Xu, Yi-chong. 2005. Models, Templates and Currents: The World Bank and Electricity Reform. *Review of International Political Economy* 12(4): 647–73.

Young, Oran R. 1991. Political Leadership and Regime Formation: On the Development of Institutions in International Society. *International Organization* 45(3): 281–308.

Zecchini, Salvatore. 1995. The Role of International Financial Institutions in the Transition Process. *Journal of Comparative Economic* 20: 116–38.

Zürn, Michael and Jeffrey T. Checkel. 2005. Getting Socialized to Build Bridges: Constructivism and Rationalism, Europe and the Nation-State. *International Organization* 59(4): 1045–79.

Zweynert, Joachim. 2006. Economic Ideas and Institutional Change: Evidence from Soviet Economic Debates: 1987–1991. *Europe-Asia Studies* 58(2): 169–92.

Index